THE METHUEN EEC SERIES
General Editor: R. A. Butlin

**The Common Fisheries Policy
of the European Community**

To my parents

In the same series:

The Common Agricultural Policy – Past, Present and Future
Brian E. Hill

Competition and Industrial Policy in the European Community
Dennis Swann

Forthcoming:

A Rural Policy for the EEC?
Hugh Clout

Energy in Europe – Issues and Policies
T. G. Weyman-Jones

The Common Fisheries Policy of the European Community

MARK WISE

METHUEN
LONDON AND NEW YORK

First published in 1984 by
Methuen & Co. Ltd
11 New Fetter Lane, London EC4P 4EE

Published in the USA by
Methuen & Co.
in association with Methuen, Inc.
733 Third Avenue, New York, NY 10017

Typeset by Graphicraft Typesetters Ltd, Hong Kong
Printed in Great Britain at the
University Press, Cambridge

British Library Cataloguing in Publication Data
Wise, Mark
  The common fisheries policy of the European
  Community. — (The Methuen EEC series)
  1. Fisheries — European Community countries
  2. Common Fisheries Policy
  I. Title
  338.3' 727' 094   SH253

  ISBN 0-416-32390-1
  ISBN 0-416-32400-2

Library of Congress Cataloging in Publication Data
Wise, Mark, 1944–
  The common fisheries policy of the European Community.

  (Methuen EEC series)
  Bibliography: p.
  Includes index.
  1. Fishery policy — European Economic Community
countries. 2. Territorial waters — European Economic
Community countries. I. Title. II. Series.
  HD9465.E82W57 1984   338.3' 727094   84-573
  ISBN 0-416-32390-1
  ISBN 0-416-32400-2 (pbk.)

Contents

Abbreviations viii
Figures, Maps and Tables x
General editor's preface xiv
Author's preface xvi
Acknowledgements xviii

1 **Introduction** 1
Some basic elements of fishery management 2
The institutions of the European Community 7

2 **The fishing industries of western Europe** 17
The spatial pattern of fishing 20
The relative importance of fishing industries 21
The major flows of fish trade within Europe 28
Fishing industries in the original EEC states 28
Fishing industries in the newer member states 41
Fishing industries in the old and new applicant states 51
The problem of overfishing 58

3 **The control of European fisheries before the CFP** 68
The development of national fishing limits 68
Britain's call for a new 'European' settlement 73
The development of European fishery conservation regimes 78
The problem of herring conservation 82
Conclusion 83

4 **The original CFP in the Community of Six** 85
French fishing interests and demands 86
The interests of France's EEC partners 88
Proposals for a comprehensive CFP 88
Reaction in the European Parliament and ECOSOC 93
Conflicting objectives 93

Compromises   98
A finely balanced agreement   102
Conservation: 'A final problem'   105
Conclusions   107

5   **Enlargement negotiations of 1970–2**   108
Norwegian interests   108
British interests   112
Irish interests   115
Danish interests   117
Interests of the 'Six'   118
Negotiations between the 'Six' and the 'Four'   119
Final agreement among all except Norway   129
Agreement between the 'Six' and Norway   136
Norway refuses to join the Community   139
The conservation problem?   140
Conclusion   140

6   **The advent of 200-mile fishing zones:**
    the need for a new CFP   142
The development of 200-mile/median line EEZs   142
The consequences of EEZs for the Community   143
The Commission's proposals for a revised CFP   149
The 'Hague Resolutions' of 1976   157
Community action in external fisheries policy   159
Member states adopt 200-mile/median line fishing zones   159

7   **Equality of access or exclusive national fishing zones?**   162
The problem of allocation   164
The case for equality of access   164
The case for exclusive national fishing zones   169
A conflict of great complexity   176

8   **Persistent deadlock in the search for a new CFP**   180
The 1977 standstill agreement   180
The Irish autonomous measures of 1977   181
The UK autonomous measures of 1977   182
The UK demand for 'dominant preference'   185
The Commission's proposals for 1978   187
The Irish government acceptance   198
British rejection   199
Persistent stalemate   200

National elections hinder negotiations   201
A CFP settlement through majority voting?   202

9 Step-by-step towards a revised CFP   204
Decisions in the European Court of Justice   204
The 'Norway Pout Box' issue   205
Community agreement on conservation measures   209
Reform of the CFP's market system   211
Towards a new structural policy   214
A fisheries settlement as part of a larger package-deal?   220

10 Agreement on access and quotas in a new CFP   223
Towards solution of the access problem   223
New proposals on quotas   231
Agreement among all member states except Denmark   237
Factors facilitating final agreement   244
The prospect of Spanish entry into the Community   247

11 Conclusion   250
A comprehensive policy   250
Future challenges   254

Appendix 1   258
Appendix 2   262
References   298
Select bibliography   308
Index   311

Abbreviations

CAP	Common Agricultural Policy
CCT	Common Customs Tariff
CFP	Common Fisheries Policy
COREPER	Committee of Permanent Representatives
EAGGF	European Agricultural Guidance and Guarantee Fund
EC	European Community (ies)*
ECOSOC	Economic and Social Committee of the European Communities
ECSC	European Coal and Steel Community
ECU	European Currency Unit used in European Monetary System (same value as EUA)
EEC	European Economic Community
EEZ	Exclusive Economic Zone
EFTA	European Free Trade Association
EP	European Parliament
EUA	EEC Unit of Account (approx. 1 US dollar)
GATT	General Agreement on Tariffs and Trade
GNP	Gross National Product
GRT	Gross Registered Tonnage
ICES	International Council for Exploration of the Sea
ICNAF	International Commission for the North West Atlantic Fisheries
MEP	Member of the European Parliament
MEY	Maximum Economic Yield

* Strictly speaking, one should refer to the European Communities in that, although there is now a single set of institutions running the three Communities, there are still three separate founding Treaties (Chapter 1). However, in this book the more commonly used singular form is employed.

MSY	Maximum Sustainable Yield
NEAFC	North East Atlantic Fisheries Commission
OECD	Organization for Economic Co-operation and Development
POs	Producers' Organizations
TAC	Total Allowable Catch
UNCLOS	United Nations Conference on the Law of the Sea
USD	US Dollar

Figures, Maps and Tables

Figures

1.1	Simple model of relationship between sustainable yield and fishing effort	3
1.2	Simple model of relationships between various sustainable yield levels, total cost and fishing effort	3
1.3	Links between European Community institutions and member states	9
2.1	Community share of total catches in major fishing zones in 1970 and 1980	20
2.2	Nominal catches in North East Atlantic fishing zones, 1970	22
2.3	Nominal catches in North East Atlantic fishing zones, 1980	23
2.4	Total nominal catches of fish, crustaceans, molluscs, etc., made in 1960, 1970 and 1980 by West European states	24
2.5	Proportions of the total catch from the North East Atlantic fishing zone taken by different states in 1970 and 1980	25
2.6	GRT of fishing fleets in West European countries, 1958–81	26
2.7	Numbers of fishermen (full- and part-time) in West European countries, 1958–81	27
2.8	Imports and exports of fishery products, by value, 1980	29
2.9	Imports and exports of fishery products, by volume, 1960–80	30
2.10	Numbers of regularly employed fishermen in UK distant-water ports, 1970–80	50
2.11	North Sea herring landings, 1950–78	61

2.12   Mackerel catches by the EEC 'Nine', 1968–80   63
8.1   Summary flow chart of Commission's quota
       allocation procedure   192

Maps

2.1   Major Atlantic fishing zones   18
2.2   Fishing zones in the North East Atlantic   19
2.3   Percentage of total Belgian catch taken in different
       fishing zones in 1965, 1970, 1975 and 1980   31
2.4   Percentage of total French catch taken in different
       fishing zones in 1965, 1970, 1975 and 1980   34
2.5   Percentage of total West German catch taken in
       different fishing zones in 1965, 1970, 1975 and 1980 36
2.6   Percentage of total Dutch catch taken in different
       fishing zones in 1965, 1970, 1975 and 1980   39
2.7   Percentage of total Danish catch taken in different
       fishing zones in 1965, 1970, 1975 and 1980   43
2.8   Percentage of total Faroese catch taken in different
       fishing zones in 1965, 1970, 1975 and 1980   46
2.9   Percentage of total Irish catch taken in different
       fishing zones in 1965, 1970, 1975 and 1980   48
2.10   Percentage of total English and Welsh catch taken in
       different fishing zones in 1965, 1970, 1975 and 1980 52
2.11   Percentage of total Scottish catch taken in different
       fishing zones in 1965, 1970, 1975 and 1980   53
2.12   Percentage of total Norwegian catch taken in
       different fishing zones in 1965, 1970, 1975 and 1980 55
2.13   Herring in the North Sea and Irish Sea   59
2.14   Fishing and spawning areas for cod   64
2.15   Distribution, nursery and spawning areas for North
       Sea plaice   65
2.16   Fishing and spawning areas for haddock   67
5.1   The 12-mile special exception fishing zones permitted
       until 1982 by the EEC Treaty of Accession 1972   133
7.1   200-mile/median line fishing limits in the North
       Atlantic   171
9.1   The Norway Pout Box   206
10.1   Fishing zones exploited by Breton trawlers around
       the British Isles   225

10.2   Proposed and agreed protected fishing zones around
          the UK   227
Appendix Map 1.1   Fishing rights within British coastal
                   zone following European Convention of
                   1964   259
Appendix Map 1.2   Fishing rights in 6–12-mile zone
                   around UK, 1972–82, following Treaty
                   of Accession   260
Appendix Map 1.3   Fishing rights within British coastal
                   zone after 1 January 1983   261

Tables

2.1   Employment of French fishermen in different sectors,
       1976–81   32
2.2   Geographical distribution of French fishermen by
       fishing type, 1968   33
2.3   Geographical distribution of Italian fishermen by
       fishing type, 1968   41
2.4   Geographical distribution of Danish fishing for
       human and industrial consumption, 1981   42
2.5   Composition of the Danish industrial catch, 1981   42
4.1   Simplified matrix of objectives among the 'Six'   100
4.2   Simplified matrix of elements in agreement among
       the 'Six'   101
5.1   Simplified matrix of objectives among the 'Ten'   120
5.2   Simplified matrix of elements in agreement among
       the 'Ten'   121
6.1   EEC member-state catches ('000 tonnes) in different
       zones, 1973   144
6.2   Some estimated potential gains and losses for the
       EEC under a 200-mile fishing limit regime (based on
       1973 figures)   146
6.3   Estimated potential losses for EEC member states
       under a 200-mile fishing limit regime (based on 1973
       figures for species listed in Table 6.2)   147
7.1   Potential catches within the UK 200-mile/median
       line zone   166
7.2   Comparison of member states' proposed 1978 quota
       shares (in weight) with their share of the

	200-mile/median line zones of the Community in the Atlantic and North Sea	173
8.1	Community fishing vessels operating in waters around Ireland	182
8.2	Check-list of steps taken by Commission in deciding allocation of quotas	191
8.3	The Commission's calculation of national losses in third-country waters, 1978	195
8.4	The Commission's national quota proposals for 1978	197
9.1	Various fishing-effort options in the Norway Pout Box	209
10.1	Proposed quota allocation in tonnes of cod equivalent produced by applying criteria of May 1980 Declaration to six major species (cod, haddock, saithe, whiting, plaice, redfish)	233
10.2	Proposed quota allocation in tonnes of cod equivalent using seven major species (mackerel added)	234
10.3	The Commission's July 1981 quota proposals in cod equivalents by categories	236
10.4	Allocations of seven major species (cod, haddock, saithe, whiting, redfish, plaice, mackerel) compared to 1973–8 reference period (in tonnes of cod equivalent)	238
10.5	Community funds to adjust capacity and improve productivity in the fisheries sector 1983–6, provided for in the CFP agreement of January 1983	245
10.6	Community funds (EAGGF) for construction and modernization of vessels, 1973–82	245

General editor's preface

The European Economic Community came into existence on 1 January 1958, having formally been established by the signature of the Treaty of Rome on 25 March 1957 and by its subsequent ratification by the governments of the original six member states. The Rome Treaty also established the European Atomic Energy Community (Euratom), and the European Coal and Steel Industry had been created in 1952 by the Treaty of Paris. These bodies, united since 1967 under a common Council and with a common Commission and generally known as the EEC or the European Communities, are a powerful and complex force, affecting the lives of the citizens of all member states and the economies and policies of many non-member states.

Since 1958 many of the main policy objectives of the Rome (and the Paris) Treaty have been realized. There remain, however, policy areas where progress has been very slow and difficult, and on the whole it is these problems that draw attention and criticism. There is no doubt that the member states and sectoral interest groups of the enlarged and enlarging Community are still experiencing considerable difficulty in reaching an acceptable balance between national and Community interest, a situation that is not greatly assisted by the low level of general interest in the populace at large of the character, aims and procedures of the Community and its institutions.

The more widespread dissemination of information and opinion about the Community deserves higher priority than has hitherto been given. This series of books, in consequence, is designed to cater for the needs of both those with more specialist interests and those with a more general desire for ready access to fact and informed opinion. Each book is written by an expert on the particular subject, yet with a style and structure that will make it accessible to the non-specialist. The series is designed to facilitate the crossing of disciplinary boundaries and hence to encourage discussion and debate in a multi-disciplinary context (in the field of European Studies, for example) of one of the most powerful and dynamic communities in the world.

R. A. Butlin
Loughborough University of Technology

Author's preface

This book developed over several years, following the fits and starts of the Common Fisheries Policy's tortuous evolution from the early days of the EEC to the beginning of 1983. My interest in the CFP was first stimulated at the start of the 1970s when Britain was negotiating to enter the European Community. After all the major problems in these negotiations had been resolved (or temporarily fudged) final agreement was left pending as politicians, from Prime Ministers downwards, were engaged in somewhat desperate discussion about what one commentator contemptuously dismissed as 'a few tiddlers'. How could the major political issue of Community enlargement appear to be dependent on satisfactory resolution of a conflict over fishing rights? For someone keen to learn more of international relations and, in particular, the workings of the European Community, the CFP offered itself as a most attractive case study.

The original analysis stemming from this interest was incorporated in a doctoral thesis. Later, the desire to present its findings to a wider audience led to the idea of this book. However, by the mid-1970s it was clear that reform of the CFP was inevitable; it thus seemed sensible to delay publication until after these anticipated changes had occurred. However, despite the recurrent setting of year-end deadlines, the recasting of the policy was a long time in coming. Consequently, the book kept growing, year after year, chapter after chapter as the quest for agreement dragged on throughout the 1970s and into the 1980s. Eventually, in January 1983, the adoption of a new CFP gave me the long-awaited chance to decide that the book stops here!

The main aim of this book is to explain why fishery conflicts have arisen and proved so difficult to resolve within the European Community. In pursuit of this objective I have doubtless been influenced by my background as a geographer interested in politics. However, I have tried not to restrain myself within any particular academic straitjacket and trust that people within a variety of spheres will find this effort useful. Furthermore, I hope that readers will not find my analysis distorted in favour of particular national viewpoints or sectional interests. Keenly aware of how the mass-media in EEC member states often convey, consciously or not, nationally biased versions of Community affairs to peoples enclosed in different linguistic laagers, I have attempted to present all the major arguments as dispassionately as possible.

By aiming at a general audience I have run the risk of attracting criticisms from specialists who will feel that particular aspects have been neglected or inadequately examined within some or other analytical framework. Like most authors, no doubt, I am well aware of certain shortcomings as well as the inevitable limitations imposed by time and space. However, I hope that critics and others will, at the very least, find this book useful as a base from which to launch their further investigations into the supranational workings of the much-maligned, but persistent reality of the European Community.

Mark Wise
Plymouth Polytechnic

Acknowledgements

Various people over many years have helped in the preparation of this book, although I obviously take full responsibility for its contents. First, I wish to acknowledge the great help I have received from people within the European Commission and the Council of Ministers over the years; these 'Eurocrats' have always been very responsive to my requests for information. Certain officials in the UK's Ministry of Agriculture, Fisheries and Food have also provided willing assistance from time to time. A special word of thanks is also due to Howard Smith and others involved in the publication of Agra Europe's well-informed *Eurofish Report*. Also, I extend my thanks to colleagues in Plymouth Polytechnic's Department of Geographical Sciences, in particular to Sarah Webber who drew the bulk of the maps and diagrams. John Abraham and Christine Harris will also recognize some of their mapwork in these pages, while Seana Doyle may recall some of the many words she has typed for me and Dick Hartley will note some of the numerous references he channels in my direction. At Methuen, Mary Ann Kernan and Mary Cusack have proved very patient and sympathetic in dealing with the trials of someone producing his first book. Similarly, I am very grateful to Robin Butlin for the opportunity he has provided and the encouragement he has given. Finally, I recognize the real debt I owe my wife Martine, as well as our children, Luc, Sophie and Louis. I now know that authors expressing gratitude to their families are making much more than a generous gesture: they are acknowledging that those around them have to tolerate a great deal when authors become enclosed in the egocentric process of producing a book.

1 Introduction

Her Majesty's Government made clear their interest in the settlement
of common fishery problems on a European basis. (Mr Edward Heath,
Commons 1963-4)

This book analyses the development of the European Community's
Common Fisheries Policy (CFP). It traces its antecedents in
international fishery policies before examining its evolution from
obscure origins in the early 1960s to much publicized reform in the
early 1980s. Despite its relatively modest socio-economic importance
within most member states, fishing has frequently been a source of
serious political contention within the Community. At one time, for
example, the momentous decision of whether or not Britain should
enter the common market seemed inordinately influenced by conflict
over fishing rights, and Norway's rejection of Community membership owed not a little to the attitudes of its fishermen. Disputes over
who should fish what and where seem to stir national emotions far
more than dour problems associated with, for example, the production
of cars or steel, despite the greater economic importance of the latter.
The image of brave, individualistic fishermen hunting for food in an
often hostile environment seems to attract more sympathy than those
conjured up by the mass-production of metal or motor vehicles.
Moreover, complex fishery disputes can be easily, if erroneously,
reduced to the simplistic, emotive issue of a national struggle against
'foreign invaders' of 'our' sea space. Faced with the confusing
uncertainties of exploiting a diverse, mobile resource in a vast, often
ill-understood, underwater wilderness, what mental relief it must be to
make straightforward demands for a 12- or 50- or 200-mile national
fishing limit! It does not matter that such arbitrarily defined zones
rarely correlate with the geography of migratory fish stocks; they
represent basic claims for 'territory' that win broad national support in
a way that more sophisticated schemes of international fishery resource
allocation do not.

This study covers all aspects of the CFP, but the prime focus is on its
provisions dealing with fishing rights and conservation. This focal

theme stems from both the author's political–geographical interests and the fact that disputes over the spatial allocation of catch opportunities and overfishing have always been at the centre of conflict about Community fishery policy. However, examination of these central management issues inevitably leads to consideration of all other aspects of the CFP relating to market organization, external trade, structural reform, and so on. For example, arguments over access to fishing grounds are invariably linked to questions of access to fish markets, and calls to reduce catches of overfished stocks lead logically on to the issue of restructuring fleets.

It is beyond the scope of this book to review the substantial bodies of literature on both European policy-making and fishery management. However, to allow the uninitiated reader to make sense of the following analysis, brief introductions to these subjects are included in this opening chapter.

Some basic elements of fishery management

Those concerned with the making of fishery policy have a substantial volume of theory and empirical research findings emanating from fishery scientists and economists at their disposal. A very rudimentary survey of this literature will help the uninitiated reader follow some of the arguments involved in the making of the CFP.

Optimum concepts of fishing exploitation – notably that of maximum sustainable yield (MSY) – have long been defined and formed the intellectual base of attempts to manage fisheries. Fish stocks form potentially renewable resources that can be exploited at various sustainable yield levels. A sustainable yield can be harvested year after year without significantly affecting the size of the stock; in other words, the sustainable yield for any given fish population is equal to its rate of growth for that size. Figure 1.1 is an extremely simple model demonstrating the basic relationship between levels of sustainable yield and levels of fishing effort. At first, increases in effort produce sustainable increases in yield. Eventually, however, the point of MSY will be reached, forming a biologically optimum level of production. Beyond this point increases in fishing effort lead to decreases in the level of sustainable yields, and overfishing begins. From now on, the more fishing effort grows, the more the stock contracts and develops an unbalanced population structure dominated by the youngest age groups or 'year-classes'. This greater dependence

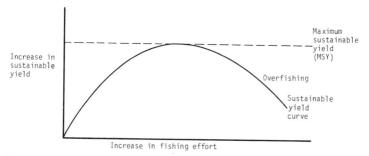

Figure 1.1 Simple model of relationship between sustainable yield and fishing effort
Source: Coull (1972).

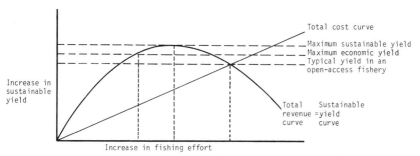

Figure 1.2 Simple model of relationships between various sustainable yield levels, total cost and fishing effort
Source: Christy and Scott (1965).

on the younger year-classes produces a diminution in the average size of fish caught and increases the likelihood of large fluctuations in stock size owing to natural factors. Large year-classes and small year-classes can no longer balance each other as they can in fish populations with a wide-ranging age structure. Levels of fishing effort can, and sometimes do, build up to a point where a stock becomes virtually extinct as a viable commercial resource.

Figure 1.2 is based on Figure 1.1 but translates the simple biological model into economic terms. By making the crude assumption of a constant price for fish, the sustainable yield curve is converted into the total revenue curve and juxtaposed with a total cost curve. In fact, this latter curve is a straight line based on the simplistic assumption that total costs increase in direct proportion to increases in fishing effort. This model introduces the distinctive optimum notion of maximum economic yield (MEY) which does not conform with that of the MSY. MEY occurs where the gap between the cost and revenue curves is greatest; theoretically this point is reached before MSY.

Figure 1.2 indicates that, in an open-access fishery, effort increases well beyond the MEY and MSY optimums and is checked only when costs outstrip revenues. Effort increases beyond these optimum levels to create overfishing largely because, until recently, sea fisheries were essentially an international open-access common-property resource, unexpropriated by an individual or state. Even when a state extends its jurisdiction over the seas, its fishermen do not individually own the stocks in the exclusive national fishing zone and continue to compete with their fellow countrymen in the hunt for fish. In such open-access situations there are few of the legal and economic constraints that control the exploitation of private or publicly owned resources. One consequence of this is that new producers will find it 'rational', and feasible, to enter a fishery as long as they perceive the possibility of a profit. As fishing builds up in this uncontrolled way, the point of MSY is passed and the catch per unit effort of individual fishermen begins to decline. Eventually, fishermen find that, despite increasing prices for scarcer fish, their catches no longer earn them enough to cover their total costs. At this point they must either leave the fishery or increase their catches to compensate for falling revenue. Very frequently the latter course of action is adopted, stepping up fishing effort once again and, ultimately, exacerbating the overfishing of the stock. Individual fishermen acting in isolation only gradually become aware of this vicious circle where lower catches per unit effort lead to increased effort (often by investment in more efficient equipment) to boost catches, which in turn lead to even lower catches per unit effort. When and if fishermen do become aware of this inexorable process they, as individuals, are understandably reluctant to withdraw from the fishery for the good of the whole; few are prepared to abandon a traditional livelihood unless there is the concrete prospect of something much more attractive. Thus, in an open-access fishery there is little chance of the MSY being achieved by any self-regulatory process and every chance of overfishing developing as individual fishermen strive to maximize their share of the available resources.

The vicious circle of overfishing described above has obviously been a major factor pulling states ever further into the field of fisheries control. In their attempts to manage fish stocks they have the MSY objective to aim at. However, this target is difficult to achieve for many reasons in addition to those already described. The problems of obtaining accurate and undisputed scientific evidence on the precise state of fish stocks remain substantial, despite the progress made in fishery research. Consequently, honest conflict over the MSY for a particular stock remains common. Such problems are made all the more acute when, as is frequently the case, mixed stocks are involved; fish do not stay neatly separated like, for example, Friesian cows in a field. As a result mixed catches and by-catches are commonplace. A by-catch results when a fisherman seeking, say, Norway pout, picks up a proportion of haddock in his nets. If Norway pout is an underexploited species and haddock is overfished, what management controls should be imposed on that fisherman and similarly placed colleagues? There are no simple answers, particularly as it is virtually impossible to judge the exact motivations of the fishermen concerned. Do they deliberately seek the by-catch or is it the inevitable consequence of their quest for other species?

Beyond these formidable problems of formulating management objectives based on clear scientific evidence, there are others to daunt the fishery policy-maker, notably those concerned with employment. The achievement of the MSY for an overfished stock requires a reduction in fishing effort. This invariably raises the spectre of unemployment or underemployment in fishing communities. Policy-makers might judge it more 'efficient' or 'rational' to maintain employment in an overexploited fishery if the cost of providing alternative forms of employment is greater than any benefit that might accrue from the attainment of MSY or MEY. Moreover, the electoral costs of making fishermen redundant in the pursuit of some biological or economic optimum might well be considered too high.

In effect, politicians have to be concerned with the distributional aspects of fishery policy as well as those aimed at the maximization of biomass production or whatever. Even assuming that agreement among different states and producers could be achieved on what constitutes the MSY for a particular stock, the problem of sharing out that MSY remains. What generally acceptable criteria can be devised to decide which fishermen get what share of that maximum sustainable total? Confronted with such formidable allocational issues, fishery managers have long been attracted by minimum-mesh-size regulations. By increasing the minimum permitted mesh size, the younger year-classes in a given stock are protected, total fishing mortality (losses by all causes) is reduced, and a movement back to some defined MSY is achieved without placing any other restrictions on the activities of those exploiting that stock. In other words, odious allocational choices about who should fish and who should not are avoided.

Unfortunately for politicians, minimum-mesh-size regulations eventually proved insufficient in the fight against overfishing. One reason for this is that from 1946 onwards – at least around western Europe – the increase in fishing effort was so great that total fishing mortality on virtually all stocks grew rapidly, outstripping the ability of policy-makers to introduce appropriately enlarged mesh sizes. Further, mesh-size regulations could not cope adequately with the problem that the size of spawning stocks varies from year to year, influencing the amount of subsequent recruitment to particular fisheries. The need to limit fishing effort in addition to imposing net regulations became apparent. Political decisions about who should fish what, where and when became inevitable if overfishing was to be contained.

In the debate over criteria upon which such allocational choices should be based, the notion that preference should be given to those countries or regions which are particularly 'dependent' on fishing has been prominent. But objective means of measuring such dependence are lacking. A high contribution of the fishing industry to the Gross National Product (GNP), or an alleged lack of employment alternatives in fishing regions, are frequently cited by those trying to establish their especial reliance on fisheries. However, a country in which the fishing industry is small in relation to other sectors of the economy might argue that its dependence is just as great in that its fishermen make a vital contribution to the national food supply and balance of payments. Besides, all fishermen are dependent on fishing, regardless of whether they are a small or large group in comparison with their country's population. Hence the political struggles over fishing rights cannot be settled by reference to some neat set of management criteria.

This lack of generally acceptable allocational norms is one reason behind the spread of exclusive national fishing limits over the last two decades. Such a crude partitioning of the seas has a simple appeal when more sophisticated attempts at international control become bogged down in interminable debate leading to little or no effective action to curb overfishing. At least, goes the argument, national fishing zones settle some of the distributional issues and extend a jurisdictional framework within which conservation measures can be enforced. But conflict over what exactly these measures should be continues among national fishermen. Should there be a limit on the number of boats allowed to fish? Should a total allowable catch be established and then divided among fishermen? If so, how should it be divided? Further, it is often an illusion to think that national fishing zones seal off a piece of sea space within which a state can sort out its management problems free from international entanglements. Fish are migratory and do not respect national boundaries. Consequently, management of fish stocks still frequently requires international co-operation.

Another major problem confronting fishery policy-makers, national and international, is that of enforcement. It is certainly a great achievement when conservation measures are agreed among conflicting parties, but the problem of making sure they are obeyed remains. The possibilities of vessels evading regulations on the vast sea areas where they operate are considerable. To police such an environment with rigorous efficiency can easily become prohibitively costly. Similarly, the administrative expense of checking landings at the multitude of ports in many fishing regions can threaten to exceed any benefit that might accrue from reducing illegal fishing. Proposals that fish should be landed only at specified ports in order to verify that catch limits are not being exceeded invariably get a hostile reception from fishermen wary of losing their traditional liberty.

All the fishery management problems sketched out above, and others, confronted those concerned with the development of the CFP and do much to explain why it has been a source of conflict in European Community politics for so long and is likely to be again in the future. The following section describes the supranational institutions within which this conflict had to be resolved.

The institutions of the European Community

Strictly speaking there are three European Communities: the European Coal and Steel Community (ECSC), established in 1952; the European Atomic Energy Community (Euratom), set up in 1958; and the European Economic Community, which also started to function in 1958. Until 1967 these Communities had separate executive Commissions (known as the High Authority in the case of the ECSC) and Councils of Ministers, although the European Parliament and Court of Justice had been shared by all three since 1958. After 1967 a single Commission and a single Council assumed all the powers and responsibilities vested in the original institutions by the three founding

Community Treaties. Although a single Treaty has yet to replace the Paris Treaty (ECSC) and Rome Treaties (EEC and Euratom), the singular term 'European Community' is now widely used and thus employed in this text. The following description of institutions and decision-making procedures is based on the provisions of the EEC Treaty, for fishery policy falls under its jurisdiction.

The supranational institutions of the Community are unique. Unlike more simple inter-governmental organizations, for example, the Community produces binding legislation and finances its activities from its 'own resources'. However, it does not conform to conventional definitions of federalism where state parliaments and governments are subordinate to separate, central federal institutions for certain functions, or vice versa. Figure 1.3 describes the major linkages in this complex and evolving 'Community system' where national and supranational institutions are inextricably enmeshed. At its heart lie the Council of Ministers and the Commission. Put at its simplest, Community legislation emerges mainly out of the interaction between these two bodies: the Commission proposes, the Council disposes.

THE EUROPEAN COMMISSION

In broad terms the duties of the Commission are: to be guardian of the Community Treaties; to be the executive arm of the Communities; and, most important, to be the initiator of Community policy and the defender of 'the Community interest' in dialogue with the member-state representatives in the Council. As guardian of the Treaties and the legislation stemming from them, the Commission must investigate alleged infringements of Community rules. If it concludes that there is a breach of such legislation, it requests the state in question to reply to the accusations within a specified time period (usually two months). If the Commission is unconvinced by the member state's counter-arguments and the alleged illegalities continue, then it issues a 'reasoned opinion' with which the erring country must conform by a set date. If the member state refuses to comply, the Commission may then refer the case to the European Court of Justice, whose judgement is legally binding on all concerned. As executive arm of the Communities, the Commission has powers stemming direct from the Treaties as well as those conferred on it subsequently by the Council. In simple terms, the member states in the Council make Community law, whereas the Commission has the task of implementing and

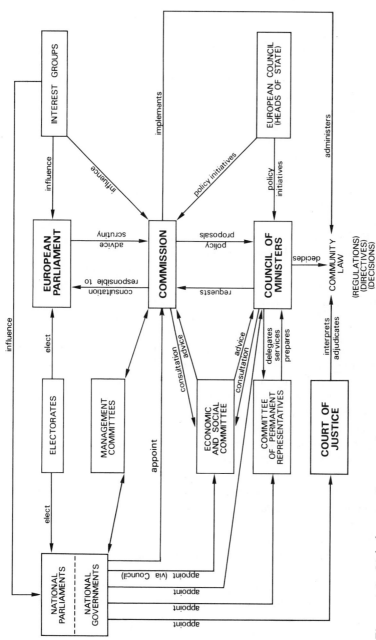

Figure 1.3 Links between European Community institutions and member states

administering it. For example, the Council established the Common Agricultural Policy (CAP) and modifies it year by year, but the Commission must enact its regulations and ensure that it functions. The Commission is also responsible for the administration of Community funds as well as the 'safeguard clauses' in the founding Treaties which allow their requirements to be waived in exceptional circumstances. In detail, these executive functions of the Commission are complex and difficult to summarize, but it must always be remembered that they stem from decisions made by member-state governments in the Council or incorporated in the original Community Treaties.

The main power of the Commission resides in its role of policy initiator. The EEC Treaty established a broad framework within which common policies could develop, and the Commission has the job of proposing them. Only in rare cases can the Council act without a proposal from the Commission. Of course, the original impetus for some action may come from outside the Commission – from the Council, from a member state, from the European Parliament, from a non-Community country or whatever. However, the formal proposal put to the Council must be formulated by the Commission. This is a major element maintaining the importance of the Commission in the Community system. In formulating these proposals the Commission is supposed to seek the elusive 'Community interest' common to all member states. In reality, this means that the Commission has the difficult task of constructing proposals that represent a compromise among widely varying national and sectional interests. Clearly, the Commission would waste its energies if it pursued concepts of 'Community interest' that had no chance of being accepted in the Council. It is often described as an 'honest broker' among the conflicting governments, seeking out commonly accepted formulas and applying what negotiating pressure it can accumulate to help forge eventual agreement on one of its proposals. It is not always successful!

The Commission, properly speaking, is composed of fourteen Commissioners appointed by agreement among the member-state governments for a fixed four-year renewable term. In practice, the larger states provide two members each, and the smaller ones all contribute a further Commissioner apiece. However, these Commissioners are not official representatives of their respective countries of origin and are expected to work as a single body in pursuit of 'the Community interest'. Each Commissioner is assigned a portfolio to deal with a particular area of policy, such as agriculture or the Community budget. A convention has developed whereby the Presidency of the Commission is rotated among nationals of different member states, although this is not a requirement. The Council cannot remove any Commissioner during his or her term of office, but the European Parliament can compel the Commission to resign as a body by passing a vote of censure. However, in this delicate attempt to balance powers, it should be remembered that member-state governments remain predominant in that they appoint the Commissioners every four years through a process of mutual agreement.

The work of detailed policy formulation and administration by the Commission is carried on within a series of departments known as Directorates-General headed by Directors-General. In practice, there is an attempt to prevent any national group from having an excessive sway in any particular area. For example, at the time of writing, there is a Greek Commissioner in charge of fishery policy, an Irish Director-General of Fisheries and a scatter of other nationalities in charge of the different aspects of fishery policy, such as resource management and market organization. Whether such delicate balancing acts always achieve the desired results is a matter of debate.

The manpower of the Commission is not great in relation to national civil services or even local governments. At the time of the first Community enlargement in 1973 there were about 5500 employees of all grades from porter to Commissioner. By 1979 the staff had grown to 8302, of whom 2145 are in administrative and executive grades, with 1214 engaged in translation and interpreting. This last statistic is a reminder of the additional, albeit essential, burden imposed upon the Commission by the existence of seven official languages. Such problems are not shared in the various ministries and departments of member-state governments, which often employ over 20,000 people each.

It would be wrong to assume that this relatively small Commission staff operates in isolation when drawing up proposals for submission to the Council. Extensive consultations with politicians, national civil servants, employers' organizations and trade unions precede any action. Through a network of committees linking Community and national institutions, detailed work is carried out by people from both Commission and national civil services together, often with representatives of interest groups as well. In carrying out its executive function of implementing policy agreed in the Council, the

Commission also makes use of 'management committees'. An implementing measure the Commission intends to enact is submitted in draft form to the appropriate committee, which is made up of representatives from the member states. The committee then gives its opinion by qualified majority, using the same weightings as those in the Council (see below). This opinion is not binding and the Commission may choose to ignore it. However, in this case, the matter would be referred to the Council, which has the power to reverse the Commission's decision. Once again we see the Commission as a unique supranational body, intricately interwoven with national institutions and organizations, with substantial powers of initiative, but ultimately held in check by member-state governments and the Council.

THE COUNCIL OF MINISTERS

Community policy and law is finally decided in the Council of Ministers after an acceptable proposal from the Commission. In the highly unlikely event of the Commission not submitting proposals, the Council would be paralysed. The Council is composed of representatives from the member-state governments. Its composition varies according to the subject under discussion; consideration of agricultural proposals would obviously group Ministers of Agriculture, for example. Especially contentious problems are often referred to Councils made up of the Foreign Ministers of member states. Since 1974, 'summit' meetings, also known as 'European Councils', are held three times a year among heads of state in order to define broad strategies and resolve particularly sharp conflicts of interest within the Community.

   Article 148 of the Treaty of Rome states that 'save as otherwise provided in this Treaty, the Council shall act by a majority of its members'. More precisely, the Council is required, in several areas, to proceed on the basis of a qualified majority. In the Community of 'Ten' voting is weighted as follows: West Germany, France, Italy and the UK have 10 votes each; Greece, Belgium and the Netherlands each have 5; Denmark and Ireland have 3 apiece and Luxembourg 2. The Treaty specifies that, in order to be adopted, Acts of the Council shall require at least 45 votes in favour when they are based on a proposal from the Commission, and 45 votes in favour, cast by at least six members, in other cases. Furthermore, it is laid down that abstentions shall not prevent the adoption by the Council of Acts that require unanimity. However, in practice, the application of the majority voting principle has not been as widespread as the Treaty envisaged. In 1965 a serious crisis developed on this issue at a moment when a major extension of the areas subject to majority decision was due. The French government could not accept that it, the elected representative of France, might be overruled by other member states against its will in the Council. Faced with opposition on this point, the French adopted an 'empty chair' policy in the Community for some seven months. This meant that no French representatives attended Community meetings and France's permanent representative in Brussels (see below) was recalled to Paris. The crisis was eventually resolved, albeit in a rather inconclusive manner, by the so-called 'Luxembourg Compromise' of 1966. In somewhat tortuous terms this agreement provided that when a member state considers one of its 'vital interests' to be at stake the Council will continue discussions until a unanimous decision can be achieved. However, the six member states noted their divergence of views on what should be done in the event of failure to reach complete agreement. In practice, if not in strict legal terms, a virtual national veto had been established by the French boycott and resultant compromise. This was accepted with varying degrees of enthusiasm; after entry into the EEC, UK governments resolutely upheld this practice as an essential element in Community decision-making. Nevertheless, majority voting in the Council remained in the basic Treaties and continued to be used in cases where 'vital' interests were not thought to be at stake. As the history of the CFP was to demonstrate, the 'Luxembourg Compromise' did not resolve this issue once and for all.

The work of the Council is assisted by the Committee of Permanent Representatives (COREPER) made up of the heads (ambassadors) of the permanent delegations of the member states in Brussels. When the Council receives a proposal from the Commission it is referred to the COREPER for detailed preparatory analysis before the matter is passed back to the Council for final discussion and decision. Although powers of decision are not formally delegated to this committee, a large proportion of uncontentious issues are settled by it and then formally accepted by the Council with little or no debate. However, more difficult problems have to be argued out by national Ministers in the Council after the COREPER has progressed as far as it can. The Commission is represented at meetings of the COREPER, underlining again how Community policy emerges out of a complex dialogue between supranational and national institutions. Beneath COREPER well over 100 subcommittees and working groups operate within the framework of the Council. They are variously composed of officials from the permanent representatives' delegations, of national civil servants seconded to deal with particular policies, or a mixture of the two. Within this network, information is gathered, interests are clarified and compromise solutions sought before negotiations pass on to full COREPER and Council meetings.

THE EUROPEAN PARLIAMENT

The European Parliament was established by the architects of the Community as an element of democratic control over the Commission and the Council. Provision was made in the Rome Treaty for direct elections to this assembly, but the first of these did not take place until June 1979. Previously it was composed of members nominated by national parliaments. It is not composed of national parties; the members belong to groupings organized on a European basis. For example, British Conservatives belong to the European Democratic Group and Labour Party members to the Socialist Group. However, member states are allocated seats more or less according to their population size; the four largest states each have 81 seats, the Netherlands 25, Greece and Belgium 24, Denmark 16, Ireland 15 and Luxembourg 6.

The Parliament has to be consulted before the Council decides on any legislation. In this consultative capacity, the Parliament examines the Commission's proposals in specialist committees. Draft resolutions prepared by them are then debated in plenary sessions of the Parliament and an opinion transmitted to the Council. In their monitoring role, parliamentary members address both written and oral questions to the Commission and the Council. Although appointed by the member states who make up the Council, the Commission is answerable to the Parliament for its activities. In fact, Parliament can dismiss the Commission, although this ability to provoke a serious crisis within the Community has never been employed. When the Council introduced the Community's self-financing system of 'own resources' in 1970, the Parliament was granted increased powers of budgetary control. It now has the final say on expenditure that is not the automatic, or near-automatic, result of Community legislation. This gives it considerable influence over administrative and operational spending (Social Fund, Regional Fund, research and energy, industrial restructuring, etc.). However, the Parliament has much less control over compulsory expenditure that basically arises out of the legal requirements of the CAP. Given that this policy has absorbed nearly three-quarters of the Community budget in recent years, the limitations of the Parliament's budgetary powers become evident. The Parliament can propose modifications to compulsory spending and, provided these do not entail increases, they are accepted unless the Council rejects them by a qualified majority. The Parliament can also reject the Community budget as a whole, as indeed it did in 1979, and require a new one to be presented. However, aware of the weakness of its institutional and electoral roots in comparison with national bodies, the Parliament has to exercise with care these powers of provoking a crisis. Consequently, the crucial dialogue within the Community remains that between the Commission and the Council, with real legislative powers still remaining beyond the Parliament's grasp.

THE ECONOMIC AND SOCIAL COMMITTEE

The Economic and Social Committee (ECOSOC) was established as a permanent means of feeding opinions from different sections of society into the Community's policy-making process. Its members, who are proposed by the member-state governments and appointed by the Council of Ministers, fall into three main groups: union officials, employers' representatives and people concerned with more general public interests such as consumer protection. It must be consulted before decisions are taken on a large range of policy matters and can also submit opinions on its own initiative. Clearly it is another means by which Community institutions are linked to national and sectional bodies. However, most of the socio-economic pressures moulding Community policy enter the system by one or more of the many other routes as well, making the ECOSOC's role somewhat peripheral.

THE COURT OF JUSTICE OF THE EUROPEAN COMMUNITIES

The Court of Justice is composed of ten Judges, assisted by several Advocates-General, who are appointed on the basis of unanimous agreement among the member states. The founding Treaties guarantee their independence in various ways; for example, 'a Judge may be deprived of his office ... only if, in the unanimous opinion of the [other] Judges and Advocates-General of the Court, he no longer fulfils the requisite conditions or meets the obligations arising from his office'. The essential function of the Court is to resolve disputes arising out of the application of Community law. This involves conflicts between Community institutions and member states as well as actions brought by, or against, individuals and private firms. For example, the Commission has often brought a case before the Court alleging that a member state has infringed the Treaties or legislation stemming from them. In turn, governments have challenged decisions of the Commission before the Court and private individuals have sought judgements in their favour. As the corpus of Community law grows, becoming ever more intricately interwoven with national law, the role of the Court in ruling on the interpretation and application of common legislation becomes more prominent, as the case of fisheries policy will demonstrate.

CONCLUSION

The process of decision-making within the Community is complex, and excessively formal descriptions of it can be misleading. It is typified by intricate negotiating at various levels. Much of this negotiating in the Council of Ministers is subjected to fairly intense, if not particularly well-informed, attention from the various national media. This often leads to derogatory reports about 'rows', 'horse-trading', or whatever, as being typical of a much-criticized Community. However, conflict and bargaining between opposed interests is an inevitable reality of all political life, and the EEC can obviously be no exception (although there sometimes seems to be a popular assumption that somehow the Community should be above these facts of life!). One way to generate 'give-and-take' among different common market governments in order to produce agreement is to deal with several contentious issues at the same time. This can give greater scope to 'trade-off' one interest against another so that a generally acceptable balance of costs and benefits can be built up in a so-called 'package .deal'. The degree to which the unique supranational institutions of the European Community have been able to permit adequate resolution of the multi-faceted conflicts arising from the exploitation of sea fisheries by its member states is clearly a theme to be pursued throughout the following chapters.

2 The fishing industries of western Europe

> Fisheries naturally vary greatly in importance in Europe, and the general tendency is for them to become less important both from north to south and from west to east. As well as differences at national level, there are also important variations at regional level, although measures of this are few, as most statistics are kept on national bases. (Coull 1972, 228)

Clearly any effort to understand the CFP requires a knowledge of the fishing industries in the countries involved in its development. To this end, this chapter first describes the basic characteristics of, and major trends within, West European fisheries. In addition to the member states of the European Community other countries that have had some influence on the evolution of the CFP are examined. This is particularly so with regard to Norway because of the significant part the country played in the modification of the original policy during the enlargement negotiations of the early 1970s. In the second part of the chapter, the importance of the overfishing problem, which increasingly influenced the development of the CFP, is described.

The fishery resources in the sea areas adjacent to western Europe – essentially those of the North East Atlantic zone – are among the richest in the world because of favourable temperature, current and continental shelf conditions (Maps 2.1 and 2.2 and Figure 2.1). During the 1970s over 80 per cent of the total catch of EEC states came from the North East Atlantic. This proportion has been steadily increasing as yields from the North West Atlantic declined and European vessels were ejected from distant grounds after the progressive extension of national fishing limits in recent decades (see Chapter 3). The retreat of European fishing effort back towards nearer waters is illustrated in Maps 2.3–2.12, particularly those referring to England and Wales, France, West Germany and the Faroes.

Italy does not share this common interest in the marine resources of the North East Atlantic. Some 80 per cent of its catch is taken from the Mediterranean, with the bulk of the remainder coming from the East

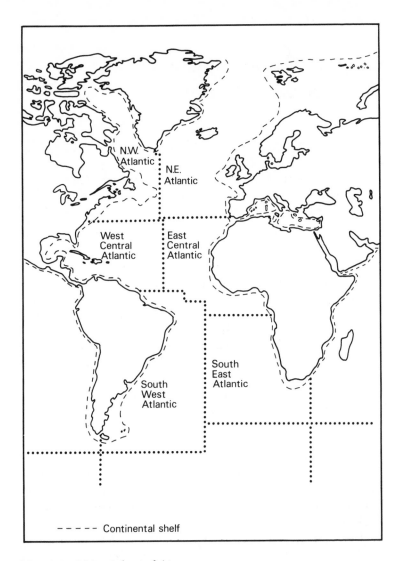

Map 2.1 Major Atlantic fishing zones
Source: FAO.

Map 2.2 Fishing zones in the North East Atlantic
Source: ICES (1965–81).

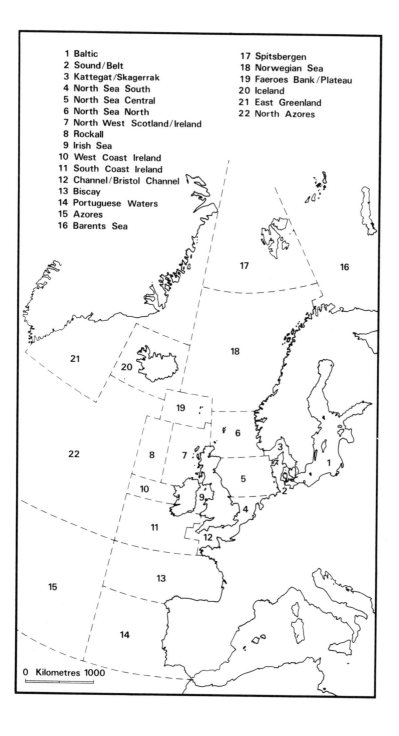

1 Baltic
2 Sound/Belt
3 Kattegat/Skagerrak
4 North Sea South
5 North Sea Central
6 North Sea North
7 North West Scotland/Ireland
8 Rockall
9 Irish Sea
10 West Coast Ireland
11 South Coast Ireland
12 Channel/Bristol Channel
13 Biscay
14 Portuguese Waters
15 Azores
16 Barents Sea

17 Spitsbergen
18 Norwegian Sea
19 Faeroes Bank/Plateau
20 Iceland
21 East Greenland
22 North Azores

0 Kilometres 1000

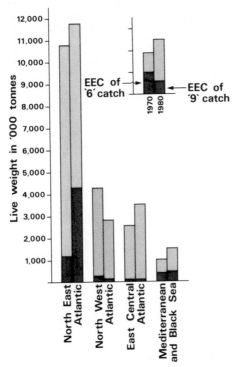

Figure 2.1   Community share of total catches in major fishing zones in 1970 and 1980
Source: FAO (1960–80).

Central Atlantic. Greece, which entered the EEC in January 1981, has a similar geographical pattern of fishing activities. France also operates within the Mediterranean but has taken a mere 5–6 per cent of its national catch from this sea in recent decades.

The spatial pattern of fishing

Not all areas of the North East Atlantic are equally well endowed with fish. In general terms, the most productive fisheries are found in waters to the north of the Channel. In these more northerly grounds there is both greater abundance and a wider variety of the major commercial species (Figures 2.2 and 2.3), largely because of the marine environment associated with the Gulf Stream and a broad continental shelf. The tapering off of the latter feature helps explain the relatively poorer fisheries south of the Western Approaches, but important catches of such species as mackerel, pilchards, sardines and anchovies are made from the Bay of Biscay to the Mediterranean.

The spatial distribution of fish resources obviously affects the movements of fishing fleets. Maps 2.3–2.12 illustrate this by showing the percentages of national catches taken in different fishing zones. It can be seen how the 'fish-rich' northern countries have usually confined the bulk of their fishing to adjacent waters, whereas the relatively 'fish-deficient' countries to the south have frequently sent vessels far north and west to distant grounds. This tendency for fishing effort to move north-westwards takes place on various scales. For example, whereas British distant-water trawlers for long sailed as far away as North America, Iceland and Norway in search of larger catches, so smaller French, Dutch, West German and Belgian boats made shorter voyages to exploit grounds around the British Isles.

This north-westerly movement of fishermen lies at the heart of much conflict over access to fishing grounds in this region. More southerly states have traditionally striven for as much access as possible to the richer fishing grounds to the north, whereas the more northerly countries have sought, with increasing success (see Chapter 3), to extend their exclusive national fishing limits. Certain intermediate states, such as the UK and Denmark, have tended to find themselves in increasingly ambivalent positions in such disputes. The dominant fishing interests in England and continental Denmark have had a long tradition of fighting to preserve the international character of sea fisheries. But fishermen from Scotland, South West England and the Danish dependencies of Greenland and the Faroes have long sought to exclude 'foreign' fishermen from the waters adjacent to them.

The relative importance of fishing industries

In general terms, fishing is most important in the more north-westerly regions of Europe. However, attempts to quantify the degree of this 'importance' must not obscure the fact that subjective judgements are inevitably involved in such a process. As will be seen in our analysis of the CFP, much is made, in international fishery disputes, of how 'dependent' a country – or region – is upon fishing. However, such notions of 'dependence' defy precise objective definition. It is, for example, commonly accepted that Iceland is more dependent upon fishing than the UK. A middle-aged, unemployed Humberside

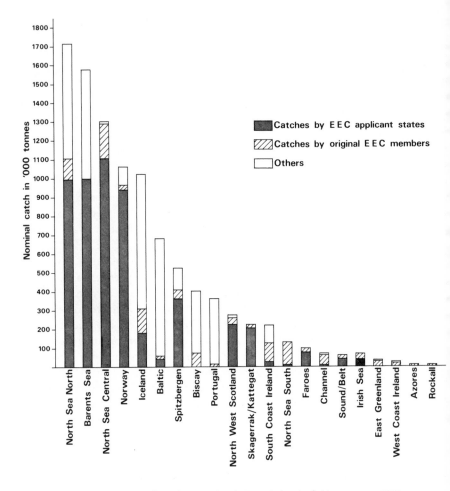

Figure 2.2 Nominal catches in North East Atlantic fishing zones, 1970
Source: ICES (1970).

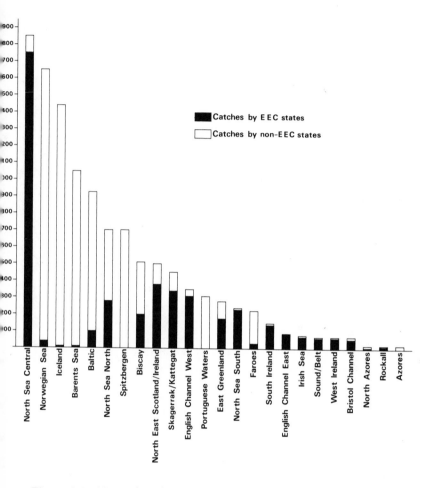

Figure 2.3 Nominal catches in North East Atlantic fishing zones, 1980
Source: ICES (1965–81).

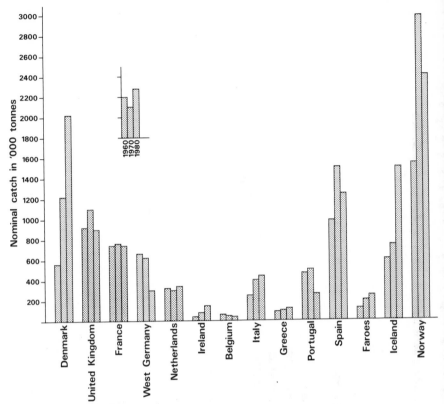

Figure 2.4 Total nominal catches of fish, crustaceans, molluscs, etc. made in 1960, 1970 and 1980 by West European states
Source: FAO (1960–80).

trawlerman might well agree in general terms, but feel that the dependence of people like him on fishing gets forgotten in such broad international comparisons. Moreover, in the process of political decision it is the 'importance' governments attach to the demands of fishing interests that is crucial, rather than some elusive measure of national or regional dependence upon fishing. These cautionary comments should be borne in mind when reading the general survey below.

The northern states of Europe are by far the largest fish producers (Figures 2.4 and 2.5). The national catches of Iceland (1970 pop. 231,000), Norway (1970 pop. 4,075,000), Denmark (1970 pop. 4,830,000) and the Faroes (1970 pop. 37,000) are particularly high in relation to their populations. The dominance of Scandinavian countries in fish production is also reflected in the fact that their fishing fleets

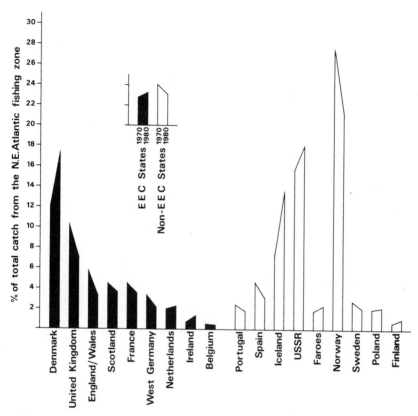

Figure 2.5 Proportions of the total catch from the North East Atlantic fishing zone taken by different states in 1970 and 1980
Source: ICES (1965–81).

have often been growing in recent decades whereas those based in more southern states have often been characterized by severe contraction (Figure 2.6). The Nordic states are also characterized by large numbers of fishermen, especially in relation to their comparatively small national populations (Figure 2.7). However, substantial fishing communities exist elsewhere in Europe, although the large totals of fishermen recorded in Mediterranean countries such as Italy and Greece include many who have only a very tenuous, part-time link with fishing.

When the contribution of fishing industries to national economies is examined, the familiar pattern of greater relative importance towards the north and west emerges again. Iceland has long been more dependent on fishing than any other European state. Although less than 10 per cent of the labour force were directly employed as

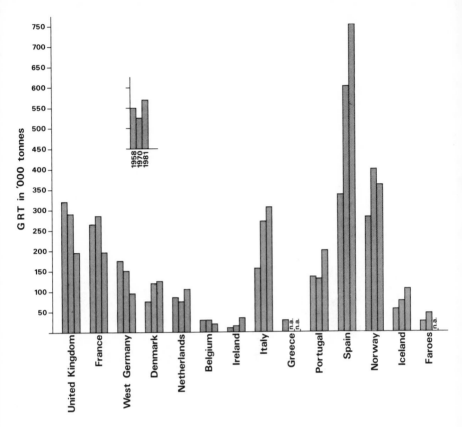

Figure 2.6 GRT of fishing fleets in West European countries, 1958–81
Source: OECD (1969–82).

fishermen by 1970, fish production and processing contributed around 25 per cent of the country's GNP during the 1960s and 1970s. At times some 90 per cent of Icelandic exports and earnings in foreign trade have been composed of fishery products. This means that many other industries in Iceland depend, more or less directly, on fishing. Only in the semi-independent Danish dependencies of the Faroes and Greenland does fishing occupy a similar position of dominance. The tiny Faroese economy depends overwhelmingly on its fishing industry, which accounts for about one-third of the GNP. In recent times about 30 per cent of the working population have been involved in catching fish, and a similar proportion have been concerned with processing and marketing it. Well over 90 per cent of its exports comprise fish products. A similar picture prevails in Greenland, where fish is seen as a resource vital to the development of the country's 50,000 people.

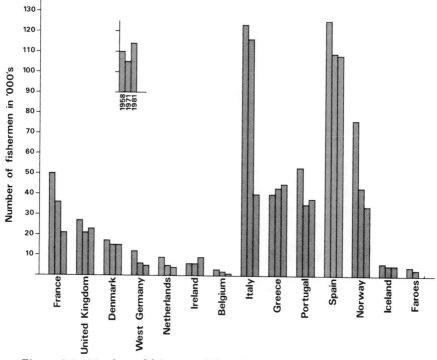

Figure 2.7 Numbers of fishermen (full- and part-time) in West European countries, 1958–81
Source: OECD (1969–82).

However, these tiny Scandinavian countries are exceptional in their dependence on fishing. In Norway the fishing industry produced some 2.5 per cent of the GNP during the 1960s, before Norwegian efforts to enter the EEC. Elsewhere in western Europe the equivalent figure is invariably a fraction of 1 per cent. For example, as Denmark and Britain approached Community membership in the early 1970s, fishing contributed 0.8 and 0.17 per cent, respectively, to their GNP. The comparable figures for France and the Netherlands were almost identical to that for Britain, whereas for West Germany it was around 0.04 per cent.

In reality, these GNP figures are of little use in assessing the economic and political importance of the fishing industry in different countries. First, they obscure the proportion of the population that is indirectly dependent on fishing in some way. For example, in the period leading up to Norway's abortive attempt to join the EEC, it was estimated that one in five Norwegians were concerned with the fishing industry in some way – as shipbuilders, fish processors, traders and providers of diverse services (Millward 1964). Secondly, national GNP figures conceal the importance of fishing in particular regions and localities. Such geographical variations inevitably have electoral consequences that influence politicians more than statistics measuring the importance of this industry to the total national economy.

The major flows of fish trade within Europe

In detail, the movements of trade in fishery products among European states are very complex, with all countries importing and exporting fish to some extent. However, some major trade flows can be discerned among the multitude of more minor exchanges. Most important, there is the export of fishery products southwards from the fish-rich countries of the north. Norway, Denmark, the Faroes, the Netherlands and Scotland are major exporters of fish to the large markets of England, West Germany, France, Belgium and Italy (Figures 2.8, 2.9). The 37,000 Faroese habitually export more than the total fish production of either Belgium or Ireland, and their fish exports per capita are, along with Iceland, the highest in the world.

Although some countries can be clearly identified as major exporters and others as large importers, virtually all are substantially involved in both sides of the trade. This reflects the great diversity of fish and fish products. In general, the internationalization of fishery commerce has increased over the last two decades (Figure 2.9) as trade barriers have fallen within such organizations as the EEC, EFTA and GATT.

Fishing industries in the original EEC states

BELGIUM

Belgium's fleet, the smallest in the Community, has been steadily declining over the last two decades (see Figure 2.6). Vessel numbers fell by 38 per cent during the 1970s to a mere 205 in 1981, and total GRT (gross registered tonnage) fell by nearly one-third over the same period. Similarly, the number of fishermen fell from 1650 in 1970 to just over 1000 in 1981. The national catch, however, fell by only 8 per cent in volume in this decade and doubled in value, reflecting both inflation and the industry's concentration on high-value species for direct human consumption.

Belgian boats have traditionally operated in the North Sea, off the

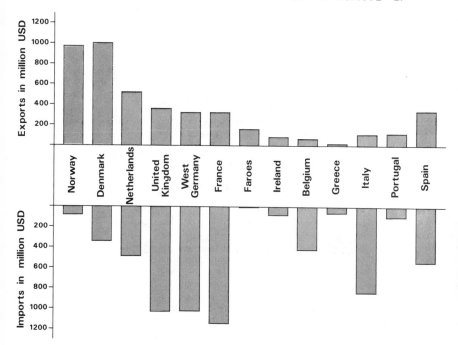

Figure 2.8 Imports and exports of fishery products, by value, 1980
Source: FAO (1960–80).

southern British Isles and around Iceland (Map 2.3). However, the
limited rights of the two remaining vessels operating in Icelandic
waters in 1980 could not be transferred to any future operators.
Belgium's interest in maintaining maximum access to grounds in the
North Sea and around the British Isles is thus obvious.

Although very small in relation to the Community as a whole, the
Belgian fishing industry is a significant element in the economy of
coastal Flanders. One estimate put fishing as the most important
source of employment in this region, directly generating around 6000
jobs (Martens 1977, 12). Zeebrugge, with over 50 per cent of the fleet,
and Ostend, with some 30 per cent, are the two dominant fishing
centres.

FRANCE

By all measures, France is a major Community fish producer (see
Figures 2.4–2.7). Like most of its partners in the EEC, it has seen its
fishing fleet shrink in size. In 1970 there were 13,430 vessels fishing

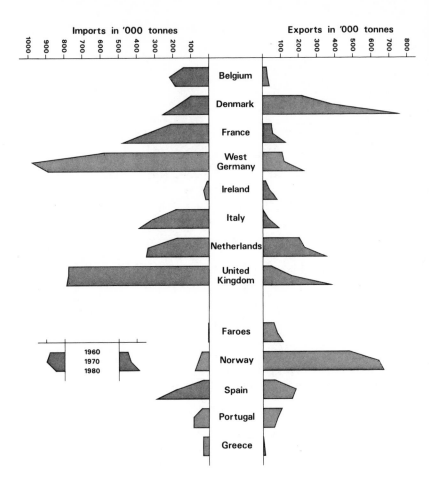

Figure 2.9 Imports and exports of fishery products, by volume, 1960–80
Source: FAO (1960–80).

Map 2.3 Percentage of total Belgian catch taken in different fishing zones in 1965, 1970, 1975 and 1980
Source: ICES (1965–81).

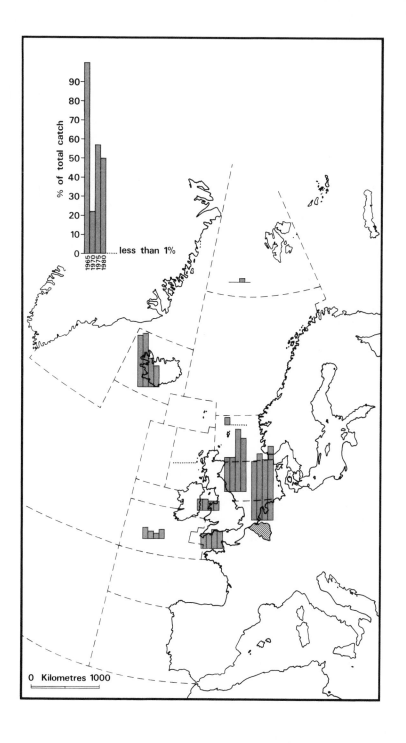

% of total catch

90
80
70
60
50
40
30
20
10
0

1965
1970
1975
1980

.... less than 1%

0 Kilometres 1000

from French ports, totalling 282,857 GRT. By 1981 the number of such boats had fallen by 20 per cent, and the decline in gross tonnage of 30 per cent was even greater, reflecting the loss of distant-water rights in the North Atlantic. However, the sector exploiting the most distant grounds – the *Grande Pêche* – showed some expansion in recent years. The drop in the numbers of fishermen has been particularly sharp during the 1970s, although France still has one of the largest national fishing populations in the EEC, totalling just over 21,000 in 1981. Table 2.1 shows how this decline was distributed among the different sectors of the French fishing industry.

Table 2.1 Employment of French fishermen in different sectors, 1976–81

	1976	1981	% change 1976-81
Distant-water fishing (Grande Pêche)	397	614	+ 35%
Deep-sea fishing (Pêche au large)	5,128	3,920	− 24%
Coastal fishing (Pêche côtière)	2,584	2,356	− 9%
Small-scale fishing (Petite Pêche)	16,287	14,143	− 13%

Source: OECD (1981).

This physical contraction of the French fleet was not matched by a similar fall in total national fish production, which remained fairly stable over the last two decades (see Figure 2.4). The average price of catches more than doubled during the inflationary 1970s, partially reflecting the fact that the overwhelming bulk of the French catch – 95 per cent or more – goes for direct human consumption. It is also significant that around 20 per cent of France's total fish production comes from the cultivation of molluscs rather than open-sea fisheries.

France has many inshore fishermen using small boats (Table 2.1). In 1981 there were 10,366 vessels below 50 GRT making up some 97 per cent of the total number in the French fleet. This large *Pêche Artisanale* sector, where skipper-ownership predominates, contributes nearly 50 per cent of the total French GRT and is politically influential in peripheral regions like Brittany where unemployment is frequently a contentious issue.

In addition to intensive exploitation of their coastal zones, French fishermen have long fished in distant grounds and the waters around the British Isles (Map 2.4). After eviction from the ever-widening national fishing zones around Scandinavian and North American states, French determination to maintain access to stocks off the UK and Ireland has stiffened. Furthermore, efforts to find new opportunities for the distant-water sector in African, South American and Indian Ocean seas took place during the 1970s, as well as attempts to develop fishery resources adjacent to French overseas territories. These efforts, often in the context of some joint venture with another country, met with some success, although distance from France kept the distant-water sector in a precarious position. The dominant emphasis on nearer North East Atlantic waters seemed certain to continue as the 1980s arrived; coastal fishing's share of total national production grew from 50 per cent in 1974 to 66 per cent in 1979.

Inshore and middle-water fishing ports are scattered around the entire French coastline, with major concentrations in Brittany, northern France and the Mediterranean (Table 2.2). The distant-water fleet is still concentrated in Saint-Malo, Fécamp and Bordeaux. Boulogne remained the leading port for fresher trawlers in the early 1980s, followed closely by Lorient, Concarneau, Etel, Douarnenez, La Rochelle, Fécamp, Grand-Fort Philippe and numerous smaller centres such as Sète on the Mediterranean coast. The tuna fleet is based mainly

Table 2.2 Geographical distribution of French fishermen by fishing type, 1968

Fishing type	Number of fishermen	Region/port
Distant-water fishing	2,098 (5.1% of total)	Brittany (Saint-Malo) 50% Normandy (Fécamp) 30% South West (Bordeaux) 20%
Middle-water fishing	13,386 (32.6% of total)	South Brittany 55% Normandy 22% La Rochelle 16% Others 7%
Inshore fishing	25,619 (62.3% of total)	South Brittany 38% North Brittany 13% Normandy 11% Mediterranean 27%

Source: Commission (1968b).

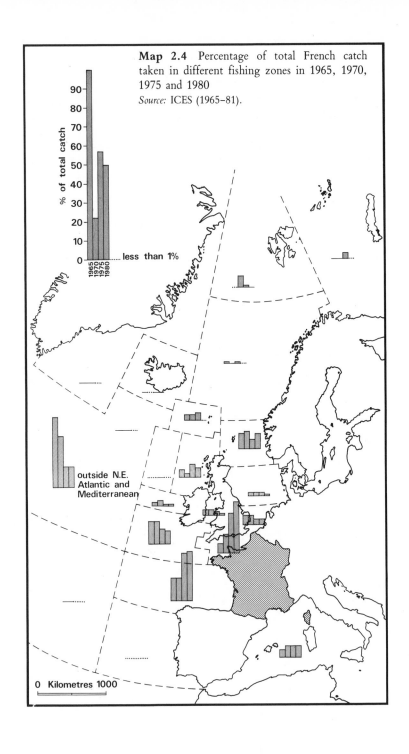

Map 2.4 Percentage of total French catch taken in different fishing zones in 1965, 1970, 1975 and 1980
Source: ICES (1965–81).

% of total catch

90
80
70
60
50
40
30
20
10
0 .... less than 1%

1965
1970
1975
1980

outside N.E. Atlantic and Mediterranean

0 Kilometres 1000

at Concarneau, but nearly half the catch from this recently expanded activity is landed in West African states adjacent to the national fishing zones exploited. Some estimate that about 100,000 French jobs depend on fisheries to one degree or another. Clearly, this industry makes an important contribution to local economies in many of France's electoral constituencies, a political–geographical fact that politicians cannot ignore.

WEST GERMANY

The West German fishing industry has contracted sharply in recent years (see Figures 2.4–2.7). With its short national coastline, West Germany has traditionally had a heavy dependence on distant-water fishing (Map 2.5). In 1970, 54 per cent of West German fishermen were employed on deep-sea trawlers, 36 per cent on middle-water vessels and 10 per cent on coastal boats. As fishing rights in far-off grounds were progressively eliminated in the last two decades, the West German fleet has shrunk. Between 1970 and 1981 the number of fishing vessels with engines fell from 1788 to a mere 690; a drop of some 61 per cent. The 37 per cent decline in total fleet GRT over the same period further underlines the drastic nature of this contraction. The distant-water sector was obviously the most affected, falling from 62 vessels in 1978 to 32 vessels at the beginning of 1982.

In contrast to the situation in several other Community countries, this physical contraction of the fleet was paralleled by a sharp drop in the total national catch as well which, between 1970 and 1980, fell from 612,000 tonnes (live weight) to 296,000 tonnes, a decline of some 52 per cent. However, average fish prices rose by 78 per cent over the same period, thus exceeding the 50 per cent rise in the general consumer price index in West Germany and suggesting that many of those elements surviving the ruthless reduction process were in a reasonable economic position.

The number of full-time fishermen fell from 9528 in 1960 to 6667 in 1970 to 3687 in 1981. This steady, steep decline was primarily due to the contraction of the deep-sea fleet. The skipper-owner element – affecting about 20 per cent of vessels in 1970 – is not strong in West Germany, where big companies dominate the industry. But there were still some 1455 part-time fishermen in the country in 1981.

Despite the cutbacks in West German fishing, this industry continues to exert considerable political influence in port regions

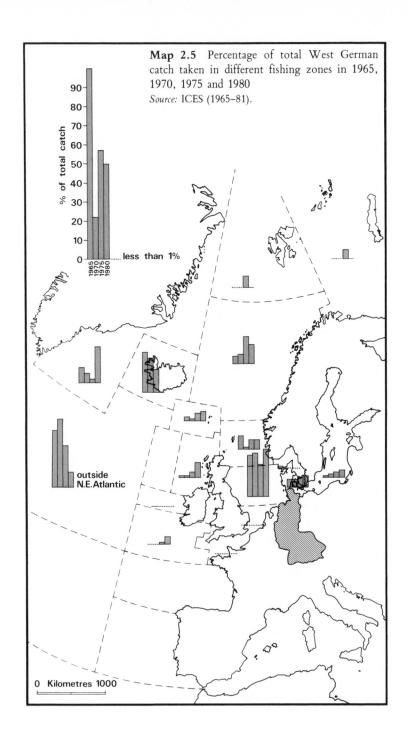

Map 2.5 Percentage of total West German catch taken in different fishing zones in 1965, 1970, 1975 and 1980
Source: ICES (1965–81).

% of total catch

90
80
70
60
50
40
30
20
10
0

1965
1970
1975
1980

.... less than 1%

outside
N.E. Atlantic

0 Kilometres 1000

where, at the beginning of the 1980s, some 11,000 were still employed in fish processing, and many others serviced this sector in one way or another. The main distant-water ports are Bremerhaven and Cuxhaven – which account for over 90 per cent of deep-sea landings – followed by Kiel and Hamburg. Over half of the essentially middle-water cutter fleet is based in Schleswig-Holstein, with its activities split between the North and Baltic Seas. The remainder is scattered throughout the ports of Lower Saxony, as well as Hamburg and Bremen. Over 90 per cent of the inshore vessels are found in Schleswig-Holstein, with the majority concentrated on the Baltic coast.

Despite West Germany's meagre share of the political partition of the seas in recent years, its fishermen and politicians show no desire to preside over the total collapse of the fishing industry. Substantial government-aided efforts to survive continued throughout the 1960s and 1970s, with West German politicians – such as former Chancellor Schmidt from Hamburg – ready to fight vigorously for their fishing constituents.

THE NETHERLANDS

The Netherlands has a substantial fishing industry with a tradition of competitive efficiency. It entered the 1980s without having suffered the severe problems of contraction endured by several of its Community partners. Certainly the number of fishing vessels dropped by 23 per cent during the period 1970–81, while that of fishermen fell by 26 per cent, so that some 2600 men were manning about 560 sea-fishing boats at the end of the decade. A further 800 or so operated the large inland freshwater fishing fleet of some 340 vessels. But the decline in the numbers of boats and fishermen was not matched by a similar fall in total fleet tonnage, which grew overall by some 18 per cent during the 1970s to reach 106,370 GRT in 1981 (see Figures 2.4–2.7). The increase in the size of vessel reflected in these trends was also linked to a 54 per cent growth in the total engine capacity of the Dutch fleet between 1972 and 1977, which contrasted sharply with an EEC average of 14 per cent for the same troubled period of diminishing fishing opportunities. So the capacity of a modernized Dutch fleet increased significantly during the 1970s, permitting the total national catch to grow from 300,800 tonnes (live weight) in 1970 to 340,400 tonnes in 1980. Again in contrast to prevailing trends throughout the Community, the increase in average catch prices during the 1970s in the Netherlands remained below that of the general national price index.

The very modern character of the Dutch fishing industry was illustrated by the fact that only 10 per cent of its fishermen owned their boats in 1970. By 1980 the dominant middle-water section of the fleet belonged to only twelve companies, but on some 90 per cent of vessels in 1981 the crew were involved in a profit-sharing partnership scheme of remuneration. This efficient middle-water fleet operates primarily in the North Sea, off Scotland and around Ireland (Map 2.6). In recent years, only about 10–15 per cent of the catch made by this sector came from the relatively small Dutch 200-mile/median marine zone. The need to maintain access to long-exploited waters around the British Isles in search of valuable whitefish, as well as herring and mackerel, is evident.

The inshore and coastal fleet is dominated by skipper-owners who operate in the southern North Sea, the Channel and the Irish Sea, often concentrating on high-value species such as sole and plaice. Even this nearer-water sector takes about 40 per cent of its catch value outside the Dutch fishing zone, underlining the Netherlands' vital interest in open international-access arrangements. A shrimping fleet of some 150 vessels takes around 70 per cent of its catch in Dutch waters, the remainder coming from the adjacent German Bight. At the end of the 1970s there were still some 800 freshwater fishermen working on the Ijsselmeer producing about 2 per cent of the total value of species sold for human consumption.

The two main Dutch fishing ports of Scheveningen and Ijmuiden absorb over half the total landings. Smaller quantities are unloaded at various centres scattered along the Dutch coast from Harlingen to Vlissingen. The Dutch Ministry of Agriculture calculated that some 14,000 persons were employed in fishing and related industries at the beginning of the 1980s. Clearly, the fishing industry of the Netherlands was dynamic in character and formed an effective group influencing government policies.

ITALY

Until the entry of Greece into the Community in 1981, Italy was very much a country apart in EEC fishing terms, with a Mediterranean rather than a North Atlantic outlook. In contrast to the trend in most

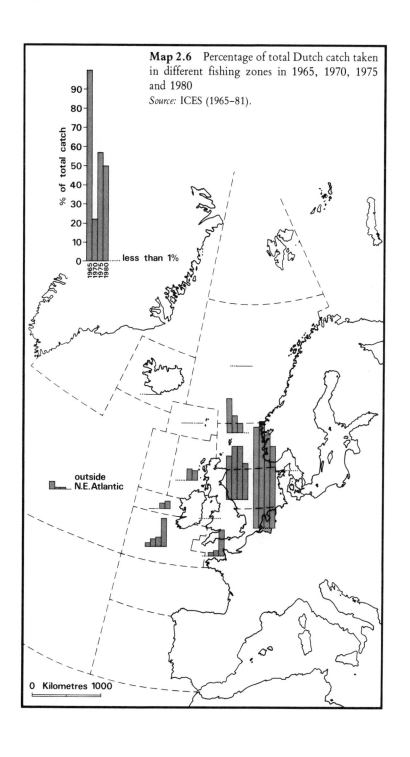

Map 2.6 Percentage of total Dutch catch taken in different fishing zones in 1965, 1970, 1975 and 1980

Source: ICES (1965–81).

% of total catch

90
80
70
60
50
40
30
20
10
0 .... less than 1%

1965
1970
1975
1980

outside
N.E. Atlantic

0 Kilometres 1000

northern member states, the Italian fishing fleet increased over the 1970–81 period; total numbers of vessels with engines grew to 22,492 – an increase for 11 per cent – while total tonnage expanded by 12 per cent to 305,855 GRT (see Figure 2.6). Engine capacity increased by about one-third over the same decade. This growth in fleet capacity was most marked – about 25 per cent – in the medium-tonnage sector designed for operation in the Mediterranean, although failure to report all vessel withdrawals probably inflates this figure. However, the ocean-going fleet, designed primarily to exploit stocks off West Africa, declined from 80 vessels (65,000 GRT) in the early 1970s to a mere 46 boats (40,500 GRT) in 1981 after the extension of exclusive national fishing zones.

Despite the loss of distant-water rights and the great pressure on Mediterranean fishing grounds, the Italian national catch in 1980 (444,500 tonnes, landed weight) was 12 per cent up on the 1970 figure. The increase in the total value of the national catch almost quadrupled over the same period. However, such catch figures should be treated with great caution in a country where there are very large numbers of traditional fishermen operating on the margins of the 'official' recorded economy in innumerable scattered locations. The overall species composition of the Italian catch is very different from that in most of its partners, with sardines, anchovies, pilchards and tuna predominant. The great bulk of production is for direct human consumption.

Statistics about employment are very suspect, with large numbers of registered fishermen no longer working or regularly active. Moreover, Italy has considerable numbers of part-time fishermen engaged in such activities as agriculture and tourism as well. Official statistics have generally reported a stable fishing population of around 62,000 throughout the 1970s, but in 1981 the OECD was estimating, more realistically, that there were some 40,000 fishermen 'on board' vessels. Many of these would be using one of the several thousand boats without engines in very small inshore operations. There was a very sharp decline in the reported numbers of such boats in the single year 1980–1, from 18,256 to 12,718. Grants to encourage withdrawal and conversion to motorized vessels help to explain this drastic drop. The fact that 95 per cent of vessels with engines were still in the 0–50 GRT category in 1981 illustrates the continuing dominance of small individual fishing activities in Italy. Table 2.3 underlines the geographically fragmented nature of an industry where fishermen

Table 2.3 Geographical distribution of Italian fishermen by fishing type, 1968

Fishing type	Number of fishermen	Regions
Distant-water fishing	2,065 (2% of total)	Tyrrhenian Sea 24% Sicily 23% Middle Adriatic Sea 33% Other regions 20%
Middle-water fishing	22,843 (20% of total)	South Tyrrhenian Sea 13% Sicily 34% Middle Adriatic Sea 17% Other regions 36%
Inshore fishing	88,328 (78% of total)	South Tyrrhenian Sea 17% Sicily 29% South Adriatic Sea 15% North Adriatic Sea 13% Other regions 26%

Source: Commission (1968b).

operate out of ports large and small around the entire Italian coastline. Thus, although fishing is not thought of as a major Italian 'national interest', it does involve many thousands of voters in many regions. Politicians in search of their support obviously press for national or Community funds to protect or modernize this industry, not least in the Mezzogiorno where the quest for regional development aids is a fundamental fact of political life.

Fishing industries in the newer member states

DENMARK

Denmark catches more fish – some 2,026,800 tonnes (live weight) in 1980 – than any other EEC country. An exceptionally high proportion of this national catch – around 80 per cent – is reduced to fish meal and oil. Consequently the bulk of Danish landings are made up of low-value species like Norway pout, sandeel, sprat, herring, blue whiting and mackerel. Contrary to trends common among many of its partners, there were considerable increases in both the volume and value of Denmark's catches during the 1970s. Between 1970 and 1980 the total national catch rose by 65 per cent in volume (see Figures 2.4 and 2.5). The so-called 'industrial' catch (i.e. for reduction purposes) rose by some 63 per cent in volume over the same period, while the equivalent figure for direct human consumption landings was 77 per cent. This increased effort continued to be concentrated in the North Sea (Map 2.7), putting even greater pressure on stocks where overfishing was a problem and bringing Danes into ever sharper conflict with Community partners fishing mainly for direct human consumption. The geographical distribution of the Danish catches for human and industrial consumption is shown in Table 2.4. Table 2.5 shows the species composition of the large Danish industrial catch.

Table 2.4 Geographical distribution of Danish fishing for human and industrial consumption, 1981

	% industrial catch	% human consumption catch
North Sea	83%	32%
Kattegat/Skagerrak	10%	26%
Baltic Sea	6%	39%
Others	1%	3%
Total	100%	100%

Source: OECD (1969–82).

Table 2.5 Composition of the Danish industrial catch, 1981

	Tonnes	%
Sandeel	521,109	39.2%
Sprat	396,642	29.9%
Norway pout	237,466	17.9%
Gadus species	91,146	6.9%
Others	80,274	6.1%
Total	1,326,637	100.0%

Source: OECD (1969–82).

Increasing Danish catches during the 1960s and 1970s were made possible by a growing fleet capacity. Between 1970 and 1976 the total tonnage rose by 24 per cent to 149,149 GRT, while overall fleet engine power increased by nearly half over the same period and was

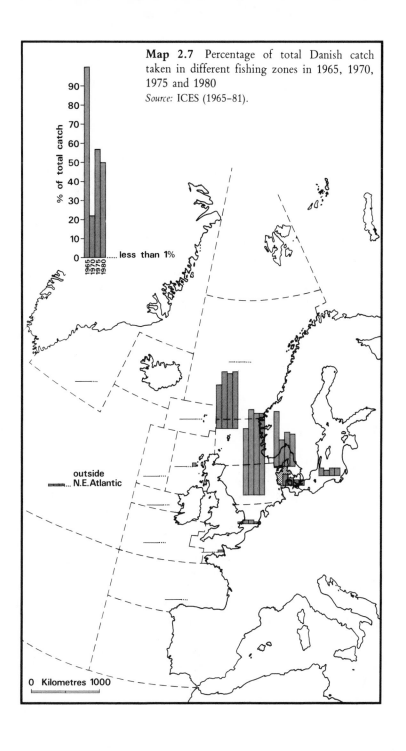

Map 2.7 Percentage of total Danish catch taken in different fishing zones in 1965, 1970, 1975 and 1980
Source: ICES (1965–81).

particularly marked in the medium-tonnage and deep-sea categories (see Figure 2.6). However, this picture of persistent growth must be modified by the knowledge that the majority of vessels were very old; in 1977 some 70 per cent of the fleet had been in operation for more than thirty years. Total fleet tonnage peaked in 1976, to be followed by a decline of 16 per cent to 125,105 GRT in 1980, as older, smaller vessels were withdrawn and scrapping grants became available. Thus a Danish fleet of fewer, but more powerful and larger, fishing vessels has been developing in recent years.

The number of fishermen dropped by a mere 3.5 per cent between 1970 and 1977 to 14,909, of whom some 3900 (26 per cent) were part-timers. Some 2600 were employed in fish processing and several thousand others in ancillary industries. Esbjerg is the principal industrial fishing port and has the largest reduction plant in Denmark. Several other important fishing settlements are scattered around the Jutland peninsula including Thyboren, Hanstholm, Hirtshals, Skagen, Frederikshavn and Grena, and the east coast has fishing ports such as Gilleleje. In a small country the Danish fishing industry is thus of great economic importance in several localities and wields a very significant political influence.

Greenland

Although exercising a large measure of home rule, Greenland is a Danish protectorate that, at the time of writing, is still within the European Community despite the 1982 referendum in favour of withdrawal from it. Fishing is a vital element in the tiny Greenland economy, providing the bulk of its exports and employing some 3000 full-time fishermen in 1981. Its coastal fisheries are seen as a resource upon which further development can be based, so a persistent objective is to ensure that foreign vessels do not take too great a share of the stocks available. By 1981 seven stern trawlers had entered a growing Greenland fleet of some 383 vessels totalling 18,354 GRT. With 87 per cent of these boats under 50 GRT, it is clear that small inshore operations still predominated. The total catch had risen to 88,270 tonnes (live weight) by 1981, of which 52 per cent was cod. High-value halibut, salmon and prawns made up most of the rest. Clearly, a factor producing the narrow majority in favour of EEC withdrawal was a fear, justified or not, that access of other Community fishermen to Greenland waters might jeopardize the growth of this industry.

Faroes

Although the Faroes form a self-governing part of the Danish kingdom, the terms of Denmark's accession to the EEC allowed its 37,000 or so inhabitants to opt out of Community membership. This they eventually did, not least because they did not want to accept the CFP. However, because the Faroese played a significant role in the modification of the CFP during the enlargement negotiations of the early 1970s, it is appropriate to summarize the basic characteristics of their fishing industry. At the time of those negotiations, about one-third of the labour force in these islands was occupied in catching fish, whereas another quarter or so were involved in related processing and trading. Fishing directly produced about 33 per cent of the Faroese GNP and indirectly much more; 90–95 per cent of the islanders' export earnings came from fishery products, underlining the overwhelming importance of this industry.

In the 1960s the Faroese, who had fished waters off North America, Iceland and Norway for centuries, were being forced by national fishing limit extensions to concentrate on grounds closer to their own shores. In 1956, 50 per cent of their demersal catch came from the Barents Sea and Icelandic waters, but by 1965 this proportion had dropped to 8 per cent (Map 2.8). Consequently, the Faroese became ever more concerned to establish wider exclusive fishing rights in the waters around them, to the detriment of EEC and other states that fished there.

IRELAND

Over the last two decades Ireland has viewed its fishing industry as underdeveloped but with potential for generating economic growth and employment, particularly in peripheral areas where jobs are scarce, incomes are low and emigration is high. Government-sponsored policies to capitalize on the fishery resources around Ireland are reflected in the statistics of growth throughout the still small Irish fishing industry during the last two decades (see Figures 2.4–2.7). The total national catch rose by 89 per cent in volume between 1970 and 1980 to 149,000 tonnes (live weight), while the average price of catches increased by more than 500 per cent during the same decade. The total tonnage of the fleet grew by 120 per cent over the period 1970–81, while the number of vessels grew by 54 per cent to 3095. Moreover, the proportion of fishing boats with a fixed engine – 52 per cent in 1981 – was steadily growing.

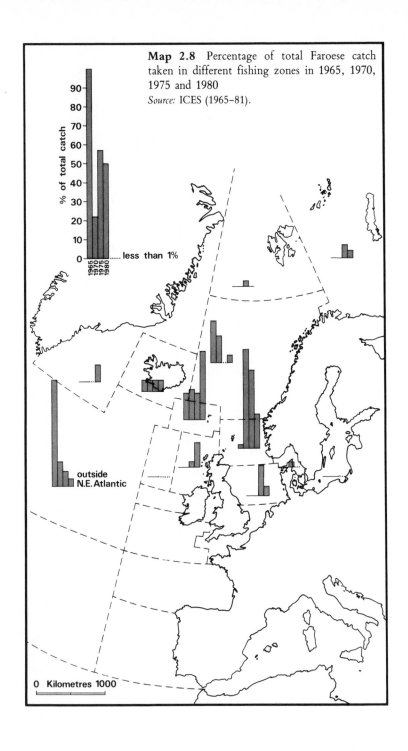

Map 2.8 Percentage of total Faroese catch taken in different fishing zones in 1965, 1970, 1975 and 1980

Source: ICES (1965–81).

% of total catch

90
80
70
60
50
40
30
20
10
0

1965
1970
1975
1980

······ less than 1%

outside
N.E. Atlantic

0   Kilometres 1000

Despite this rapid growth in capacity, Irish fishing remained dominated by small skipper-owned vessels operating in adjacent coastal waters (Map 2.9). In 1981, 36 per cent of the fleet tonnage was in the 0–50 GRT class, with another 28 per cent between 50 and 100 GRT. The national catch was composed mainly of high-value species for human consumption – cod, saithe, whiting, haddock and plaice. The hopes of basing substantial growth on the herring fishery proved a little too optimistic in the wake of overfishing and subsequent conservation controls during the 1970s, but a massive increase in the mackerel catch – from 1055 tonnes in 1970 to 52,971 tonnes in 1980 – provided compensation. An important objective of Irish fishermen during the 1970s was to increase their share – some 14 per cent in 1978 – of the total catch in the fishing zones around the country.

The hope that development of fishing would generate more employment has been justified. In 1958 there were 1700 full-time fishermen, plus 4500 part-timers; by 1981 there was a total of 8740 fishermen, of whom 3464 were in full-time employment. Investment in shore-based activities related to fishing continued to grow, so that by the late 1970s some fifty sea-food distribution and processing establishments employed more than 2500 people. This generated jobs in other sectors as well. Although fishing communities are dispersed around the entire Irish coast, this growth was most marked in the western, less developed regions. Killybegs, Burtonport and Fenit are important centres on the west coast, with Howth and Clogher Head among the largest landing points to the east. The fishermen in these areas formed an important pressure group within bodies like the Irish Fishermen's Organization. Given the massive increase of investment in this industry – from I£5 million in 1970 to I£53.5 million in 1979 – the Irish government was obviously concerned to protect the interests of this sector.

UNITED KINGDOM

The UK has long possessed one of Europe's most important and diverse fishing industries. In general, it maintained a total national catch in excess of one million tonnes (live weight) during the turbulent 1970s, but between 1978 and 1980 there was a sharp drop of some 20 per cent to 902,100 tonnes. However, even this reduced quantity was substantially above any other Community country except Denmark with its massive industrial fisheries. The value of landings rose fourfold

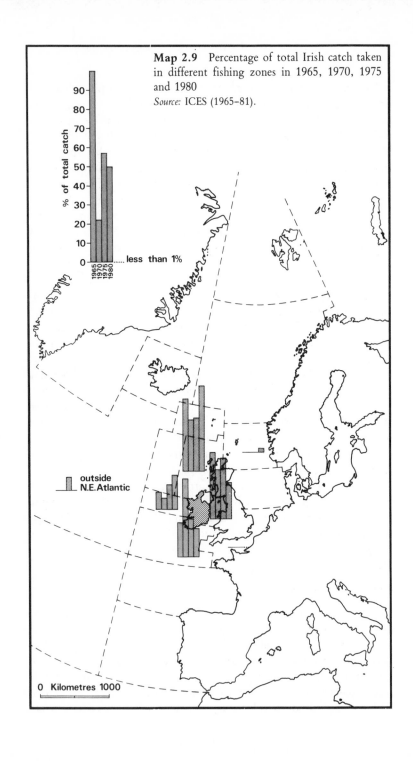

Map 2.9 Percentage of total Irish catch taken in different fishing zones in 1965, 1970, 1975 and 1980
Source: ICES (1965–81).

% of total catch

90
80
70
60
50
40
30
20
10
0 ...... less than 1%

1965
1970
1975
1980

outside
N.E.Atlantic

0 Kilometres 1000

during the 1970s, with the average catch prices rising considerably faster than consumer prices in general. There was, unusually for northern Europe, a growth in the numbers of fishermen from 21,651 in 1970 to 23,927 in 1981. However, the proportion of part-time fishermen grew over the same period from 19 to 31 per cent of the total. During the same decade the number of fishing boats with engines increased by a quarter, to reach 7351 in 1981, while total engine capacity was similarly enlarged.

However, this statistical picture of apparent stability in the British fishing industry masks great changes in the structure of the fleet as well as in the distribution of fish-related activities both on sea and on land after the loss of fishing rights off Iceland, Norway and Canada. These losses led to a sharp decline in the number of distant-water boats; in 1972 there were 168 such vessels, but by 1980 a mere 50 remained. It is this fact that largely explains the 33 per cent drop in total fleet GRT between 1970 and 1981 (see Figure 2.6). The severity of the cutback in distant-water capacity was counterbalanced to some extent by a large increase in small and medium-sized vessels. Between 1970 and 1981 the numbers and tonnage of boats in the 0–50 GRT range rose by 27 per cent. There was also a noticeable increase in the number of somewhat larger vessels in the 50–100 GRT category. In 1980 the White Fish Authority reported that all these changes had produced a British fleet structure as follows: 1982 inshore boats (under 24.4 m); 110 near-water vessels (24.4–33.5 m); 85 middle-water vessels (33.5–42.7 m); and 50 distant-water trawlers (over 42.7 m). A sub-stantial remodelling of the fleet to concentrate on grounds in the British 200-mile/median line fishing zone had clearly taken place, leading, furthermore, to a substantial reduction in its overall age. The trend towards smaller vessels also meant that skipper-owners were growing in importance relative to large company ownership.

This restructuring of the fleet had a marked impact on the geographical distribution of onshore activities as well. The elimination of much distant-water fishing led to substantial economic damage in certain ports. Hull had 90 vessels designed for fishing in faraway grounds in 1972, but only 35 in 1980. In neighbouring Grimsby the total fell from 50 to 9 over the same period, while in Fleetwood the equivalent drop was from 10 to 3. Such vessels disappeared altogether from Aberdeen. Figure 2.10 shows the severe impact this had on the employment of fishermen in these localities. These ports lost jobs in ancillary fishery industries as well, although imports kept much of the

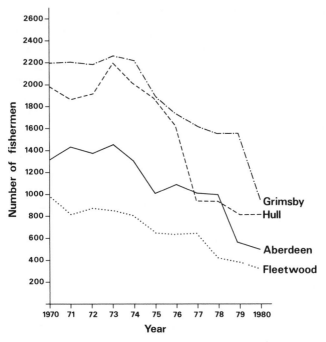

Figure 2.10 Numbers of regularly employed fishermen in UK distant-water ports, 1970–80
Source: White Fish Authority (various).

processing and distribution sectors in operation. In 1975 the White Fish Authority reckoned that, in addition to some 6000 full-time fishermen, there were about 26,000 employed in fish-related industries in the five main ports of Grimsby, Hull, Aberdeen, Peterhead and Fraserburgh.

In contrast, other fishing communities around the British Isles held their own or developed during the 1970s. The number of deep-water (i.e. not necessarily distant-water) boats operating outside the traditional main ports grew from 18 in 1975 to 42 in 1980. In Scotland, where some 45 per cent of Britain's full-time fishermen were to be found in 1980, employment remained broadly static over the last decade. In some regions and localities there were job increases; for example, employment of fishermen in Northern Ireland increased from 600 to 700 in the single year 1979–80.

Despite the radical changes in British fishing patterns over the last few years (Maps 2.10 and 2.11), the national catch – about 87 per cent of it in 1980 – remained largely for direct human consumption. However, the loss of distant-water rights produced marked changes in the species composition of the catch. For example, Atlantic cod used to make up about one-third of the national catch in the first post-war decades but had declined to a mere 14 per cent of the total in 1980. The catch of herring, once the mainstay of many Scottish and east coast fishermen, fell from 168,199 tonnes (live weight) in 1971 to a tiny 11,428 tonnes in 1980 after massive overfishing. Such losses were made good in volume, if not value, by switching to other species such as whiting, saithe and, most notably, mackerel. The catch of mackerel rose from a miniscule 3647 tonnes (live weight) in 1969 to a massive 352,574 tonnes in the peak year of 1979. Something over a quarter of this catch was taken in grounds off North West Scotland, but the bulk came from waters around South West England, where this stock has flourished in recent years.

The shift in UK fishing effort from distant grounds towards nearer waters obviously altered the political balance of forces weighing on British government as well. The distant-water sector, powerfully organized within a few large companies and articulately represented by the British Trawlers' Federation, had long been most influential in moulding UK fishery policy, as successive 'Cod Wars' with Iceland demonstrated. However, the ultimate victory of the Icelanders in the last of these conflicts in 1975, followed by the generalized spread of 200-mile national fishing zones, means that nearer-water interests now have the ascendancy in the corridors of power. The political influence of such interests, based in a range of marginal constituencies around the UK, is not negligible. In addition, British politicians are aware that fishing stirs potentially vote-swaying emotions in patriotic people not associated with the industry. Consequently, fishing matters in the UK can assume a political importance incommensurate with its relatively small contribution to the national economy (*Economist* 1978a, 60).

Fishing industries in the old and new applicant states

NORWAY

Although the Norwegians rejected Community membership in the 1972 referendum, they played a vital role in the modification of the

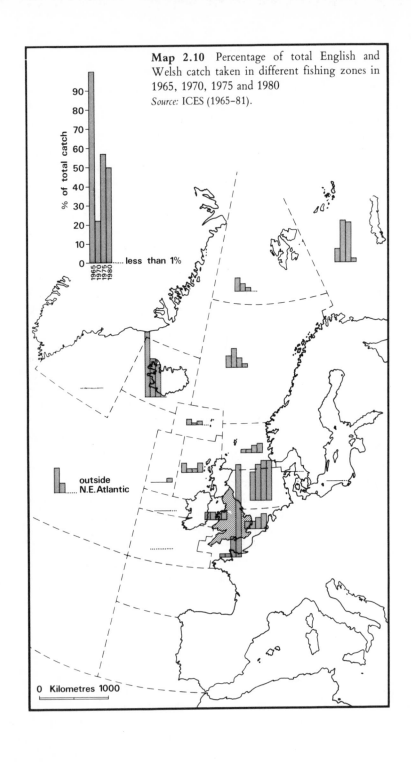

Map 2.10 Percentage of total English and Welsh catch taken in different fishing zones in 1965, 1970, 1975 and 1980
Source: ICES (1965–81).

% of total catch

90
80
70
60
50
40
30
20
10
0 ......less than 1%

1965
1970
1975
1980

outside
N.E. Atlantic

0 Kilometres 1000

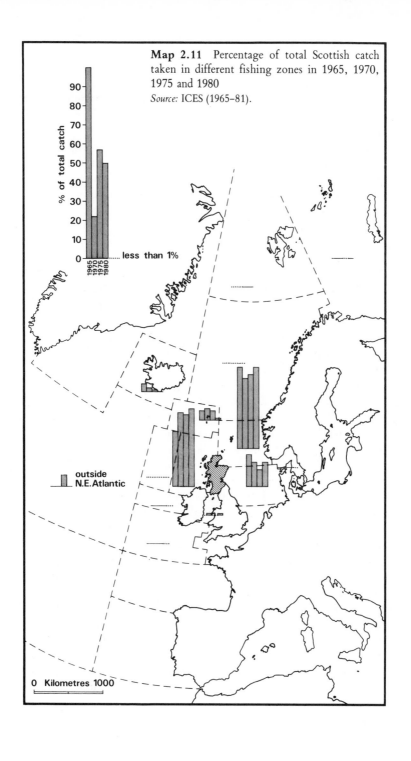

Map 2.11 Percentage of total Scottish catch taken in different fishing zones in 1965, 1970, 1975 and 1980

Source: ICES (1965–81).

% of total catch

90
80
70
60
50
40
30
20
10
0 .... less than 1%

1965
1970
1975
1980

outside
N.E.Atlantic

0 Kilometres 1000

original CFP in the EEC enlargement negotiations of the early 1970s. Consequently a summary of the main features of their fishing industry at that time is required. Of all the countries involved in that enlargement process, Norway had by far the largest fishing industry. Its national catch in 1970 exceeded that of all the original 'Six' Community states together (see Figure 2.4), although about three-quarters of it was used for reduction purposes. With the doubtful exception of Italy (see above), it had the largest number of fishermen among those states involved in the effort to extend the Community; there were 43,000 in 1970, of whom 23,354 were part-timers (see Figure 2.7). The total tonnage of the fishing fleet amounted to 400,000 GRT in 1970; this capacity, in excess of any other national fleet in North West Europe, had grown substantially during the 1960s (see Figure 2.6). With a total of some 36,200 in 1970, Norway had more fishing boats in operation than any other European country outside the Mediterranean. The 2.5 per cent or so of the Norwegian GNP produced by fisheries during the 1960s was far above the levels existing elsewhere, with the exceptions of Iceland and the Faroes. Moreover, annual export earnings – some 10 per cent of the total – from this industry were exceptionally high.

The importance of fishing was most pronounced in the northern and western coastal regions, where some 95 per cent of the country's fishermen inhabited numerous, often small, communities. The harsh, isolated environments prevailing in many of these areas meant that alternative employment to fishing was limited. Generally speaking, fishermen became poorer and economic opportunities scarcer the further north they lived. It is vital to grasp that the Norwegian fishing industry was still dominated by the individual skipper-owner or farmer-fisherman exploiting adjacent coastal waters (Map 2.12). This socio-economic structure had long been protected by a range of governmental measures. For example, there were: laws restricting the number of Norwegian trawlers; laws severely limiting the rights of those from outside the traditional fishing communities to own fishing vessels; laws confining the use of Norwegian inshore waters to local fishermen with small boats, and so on. This highly protective philosophy, deeply entrenched, stemmed from a desire to maintain a substantial population in these rugged, peripheral regions for various nationalistic, cultural, strategic and planning motives. It was this reality that was to clash so sharply with the common market principles of the European Community.

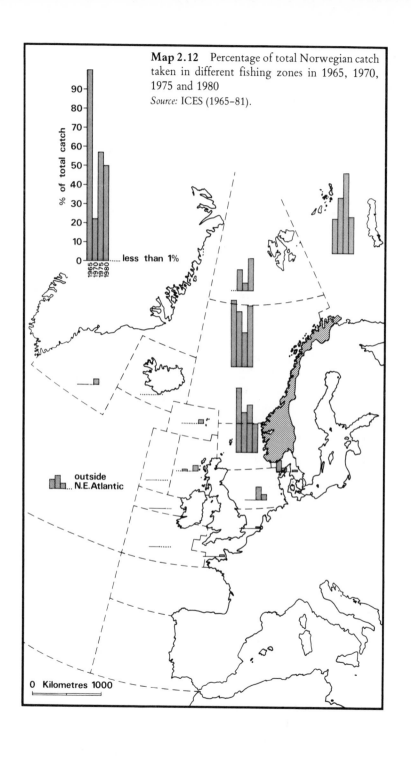

Map 2.12 Percentage of total Norwegian catch taken in different fishing zones in 1965, 1970, 1975 and 1980
Source: ICES (1965–81).

% of total catch

90
80
70
60
50
40
30
20
10
0

..... less than 1%

1965
1970
1975
1980

outside
.... N.E. Atlantic

0 Kilometres 1000

In the 1980s three Mediterranean countries – Spain, Portugal and Greece – became serious applicants for Community membership. On 1 January 1981 Greece entered the EEC, and the prospective adherence of the other two countries gradually became a factor in the protracted efforts to reform the CFP.

GREECE

Like other Mediterranean countries, Greece had numerous fishermen (an estimated 45,000 in 1981, of whom 31,500 were reportedly full-time) using a very large number of boats (some 25,000 in 1981) to catch a relatively small amount of fish (a live-weight catch of 120,000 tonnes in 1981). The numbers of fishermen and the national catch had been steadily growing in the decade before Community membership (see Figures 2.4 and 2.7). However, statistics about the Greek fishing industry must be treated with caution; for example, some estimate that only 20 per cent of the inshore catch is officially recorded (White Fish Authority 1979). This lack of precision stems from the geographically scattered and unorganized nature of the inshore industry. There were an estimated 25,000 boats in this sector at the beginning of the 1980s. Such boats were usually operated (by two or three persons) out of a multitude of ports dispersed around the whole mainland coast and the islands. Inshore fishing officially contributed about one-quarter of the national catch. It is often closely related to tourism and/or farming on a part-time basis. Although this mixture of small-scale activities seems inefficient to some, it can help provide an adequate income for families in poor areas often far from the main centres of economic growth.

A so-called 'Mediterranean' fleet of some 850 vessels in 1980 ventured further from Greek shores to exploit grounds off Libya and elsewhere, producing around 60,000 tonnes annually in the late 1970s. In addition, an ageing deep-sea fleet of some 45 vessels were catching about 25,000 tonnes each year, principally from grounds off North West Africa. It sought species popular on the domestic market such as sea-bream, squid and octopus which had been overfished in waters nearer home. Both the Mediterranean and deep-sea sectors had obviously suffered from the extension of 200-mile/median line zones.

SPAIN

Spain took a larger catch – 1,240,000 tonnes (live weight) in 1980 – than any EEC country with the exception of Denmark (see Figure 2.4). In 1981, 108,414 commercial fishermen were recorded, with a further 18,600 in fish processing (see Figure 2.7). ECOSOC estimated that, out of a national population of around 37 million, some 700,000 Spaniards were dependent on fishing to one degree or another, in the early 1980s. The comparable estimate for the Community of 'Nine' was only 600,000 out of a total population of 260 million (ECOSOC 1982, 46). As Spain moved towards EEC entry, the total tonnage of its fishing fleet was greater than that of the British, French, Danish, West German, Dutch and Belgian fleets combined (see Figure 2.6). Much of this enormous fishing capacity had traditionally been deployed in distant- and middle-water grounds off the Atlantic coasts of Africa and the Americas, as well as Portugal, France and the British Isles. The extension of 200-mile national fishing limits during the 1970s had led to the eviction of Spanish vessels from many of these areas, thus producing excessive pressure on the limited stocks of Spain's narrow continental shelf, as well as acute problems of overcapacity and unemployment. The Spanish were able to alleviate these problems to some extent by negotiating a continuation of access rights in certain foreign waters; thus in 1979 only 40 per cent of the national catch came from Spain's fishing zone, about 9 per cent from both EEC and Portuguese waters, with the remaining 40 per cent or so coming from African and American fisheries (ECOSOC 1982, 46).

Dependence on fishing was particularly high on the north and west coasts. The fate of San Sebastian in the politically sensitive Basque region was similar to that endured by Britain's Humberside ports in the 1970s and underlines the critical situation confronting many fishing communities in Spain. In the early 1970s this large port possessed newly developed facilities for about 200 fishing vessels, the majority of which operated in what became the French 200-mile/median line zone. Ten years later, after successive evictions from this and other areas, a mere three dozen boats, often under-utilized, were still based there.

PORTUGAL

Most of Portugal's 37,251 commercial fishermen in 1981 were small inshore operators using some 15,500 boats of less than 50 GRT on a full- or part-time basis (see Figures 2.4–2.7). Out of a total fleet of around 16,000 vessels, only 5296 had fixed engines in 1981. The larger of these powered craft made up the middle- and distant-water sector exploiting grounds off North West Africa, Namibia and the USA. In the early 1980s the capacity of the Portuguese industry was still growing in terms of vessel numbers, fleet tonnage and fishermen. However, the national catch had fallen substantially from 437,000 tonnes (landed weight) in 1971 to 241,920 tonnes in 1979. But this downward trend was being sharply reversed in the early 1980s as Portugal enjoyed more exclusive use of the vast 200-mile/median line fishing zone that had fallen under its jurisdiction, particularly around its island territories of Madeira and the Azores. In 1981 a national catch of 320,187 tonnes (landed weight) was reported, putting Portugal more or less on a par with West Germany and the Netherlands. However, the species caught were, in general, very different from those exploited by more northern states, with the sardine predominant and fish such as horse mackerel occupying an important position. As in other southern countries, the great bulk of the catch is used for direct human consumption. Like its Irish counterparts, Portuguese governments saw the fishing industry as underdeveloped, thus representing a source of economic growth and employment in some of the poorest regions on Europe's western maritime fringe. Moreover, like Ireland and the UK, Portugal was determined to increase its share of the catch in the immense tract of sea space that had fallen under its sovereignty during the 1970s (White Fish Authority 1978).

The problem of overfishing

Despite the complex diversity of the fishing industry in western Europe and the sharply conflicting interests within it, all fishermen were concerned, to a greater or lesser extent, with the problem of overfishing. Many important stocks in the North East Atlantic have been overfished in recent decades, including cod and herring. The fate of the latter species provides a dramatic, albeit exceptional, example of the effects of excessive exploitation. Herring is a particularly relevant case, in that it is exploited in waters adjacent to the European Community and has traditionally been of great importance to most member states (Map 2.13).

There are several different stocks of herring in the North East Atlantic. One community of stocks – the Atlanto-Scandian – migrates between Iceland, Norway and Spitzbergen, while another is associated with waters to the west of the British Isles. Within the North Sea, three major stocks can be distinguished, each having its own migration

Map 2.13   Herring in the North Sea and Irish Sea
Source: ICES (1974).

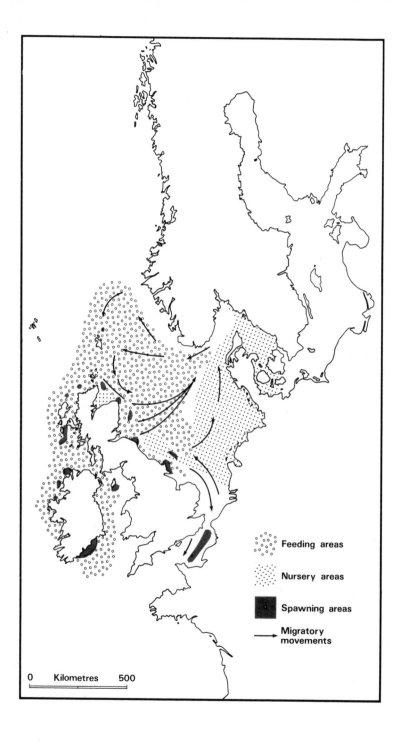

	Feeding areas
	Nursery areas
	Spawning areas
	Migratory movements

0   Kilometres   500

patterns but being interrelated to some extent. The Buchan stock spawns off the Shetlands and Scotland's east coast before migrating to winter on the edge of the Norwegian Deep and the Skagerrak. The Bank herring spawn on the Dogger Bank in autumn, move to wintering grounds in the Skagerrak and migrate westwards again to spring nursery areas before returning to their original breeding ground. The Downs herring spawn in autumn and winter in the eastern Channel and Southern Bight, then move north-eastwards into the North Sea before returning to spawn. The exploitation of these complex North Sea stocks provides a classic example of overfishing.

As an international common property resource moving around a highly accessible sea area, North Sea herring attracted a very large number of competing sectional, regional and national fishing interests all trying to increase or maintain their share of the total catch. In an essentially uncontrolled, open-access situation, fishing effort from many countries kept growing, eventually leading to a massive increase of the catch in the first half of the 1960s (Figure 2.11). However, after 1965 catch levels fell sharply as overfishing led to a collapse of the stocks.

The great increase in fishing effort, particularly in the early 1960s, was primarily due to the rapid development of the Danish and Norwegian fleets designed to supply factories making fish meal and oil. Denmark's share of the herring catch in the North Sea and Skagerrak rose from 21 per cent in 1960 to 34 per cent in 1970 and 43 per cent in 1977. Norway's share rose from 2 per cent in 1960 to a massive 42 per cent in the peak year of 1965. The catches of most other countries fell in both absolute and relative terms (ICES 1971a). New techniques were a significant element in this large expansion of fishing effort. Drift-nets were replaced by the purse-seine and mid-water trawls which were extremely efficient catching devices, especially when used in conjunction with acoustic fish-detection equipment.

Symptoms of overfishing were apparent before the post-1965 decline in catch levels; international teams of scientists working within the ICES (see Chapter 3) pointed to falling catches per unit of fishing effort. Such deteriorations in yield were first most apparent in the accessible southern North Sea zone, where the Downs herring became severely depleted. As effort was diverted northwards, so stocks in other parts of the North Sea yielded lower and lower catches per unit of effort as well. This diversion of fishing activity is typical of overfishing; by moving to new grounds and increasing the intensity of

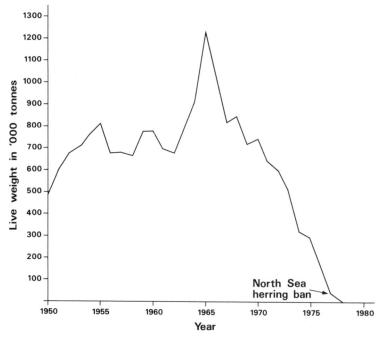

Figure 2.11   North Sea herring landings, 1950–78
Source: Eurostat.

their operations, fishermen can, in the short run, keep up, or even increase, total catches. But, as the eventual collapse of North Sea herring demonstrates, the consequences of excessive effort cannot be avoided in the long run.

Another classic symptom of overfishing is the capture of an increasing proportion of immature stock; the North Sea herring fisheries illustrate this perfectly. An ICES working group calculated that, in 1968, 81 per cent of the total catch consisted of immature herring less than 3 years old, whereas mortality rates were in the order of 68 per cent per year, indicating a very high level of overfishing (ICES 1971a). In simple terms, such a high rate of exploitation leads to the following: catches composed of fish of lower average age, length and weight than before; reduced catch weight (biomass) for increased effort; a smaller proportion of large-sized herring suitable for human consumption; an increase in the reduction of herring to meal and oil; a young herring population composed of few year-classes (age groups) which fluctuates greatly in size from year to year in response to natural factors (a more mature, balanced stock with a more even distribution of year-classes can absorb natural yearly fluctuations, remain more stable in population size and permit more consistent, sustainable catches). Having accumulated evidence that all these characteristics had become associated with North Sea herring in the 1960s, the ICES working group estimated that this species could, if carefully managed, produce a maximum sustainable yield of around 700,000–800,000 tonnes per annum. However, to achieve this, they calculated that fishing effort would have to be reduced by some 50 per cent from its late 1960s level! The enormous economic, social and political difficulties of achieving such reductions are another crucial element in the overfishing syndrome (see Chapter 3).

The easiest response to such problems of overfishing is not to reduce effort but to divert it elsewhere. This in fact happened to some extent, as more fishermen turned their attention to Atlanto-Scandian herring stocks as well as those found off the western coasts of the British Isles. Soon ICES scientists were detecting signs of excessive exploitation in these fisheries as well, and urging limitations on catching activities (ICES 1970, 1971b).

Clearly, the North Sea herring provides an exceptionally severe example of overfishing, and unduly simplistic generalizations based upon it should be avoided. However, it was an extreme case of a widespread problem, as a mid-1970s report on the North Sea made clear: 'Nearly all stocks of high value fish are now heavily fished and many are overfished, resulting in reduction of yield, wasted fishing effort and the risk of reduced potential for reproduction of the stock' (Sibthorp et al. 1975, 14–15). OECD, wary of overstatement in such matters, was reporting overfishing of important North Atlantic stocks, such as cod, from the late 1950s onwards, and the first so-called 'Cod War' at the end of that decade was, in part, stimulated by Icelandic fears that stocks around their shores were being depleted by the activities of distant-water vessels from the UK and elsewhere.

Not everyone viewed overfishing of a stock as an unmitigated disaster. There were those in Denmark, for example, who felt that the general reaction to overfishing was often more emotional than rational. After noting that 'the words "industrial fisheries" have been used by those who oppose this fishery with an almost religious undertone of abusing the resources of the sea for some dubious purpose', the Director of the Danish Institute for Fishery and Marine Research commented on the decline of North Sea herring as follows:

The herring stock has been depleted and so has the stock of mackerel. In the beginning of the sixties the total biomass of fish in the North Sea was about 8 million tonnes, of which 5 million tonnes were herring and mackerel. Today these two species constitute only about 1 to 1.5 million tonnes, but the total biomass of the North Sea is still estimated to be 8 million tonnes. Other species like sprat, sandeels and Norway pout seem to have taken the place in the ecosystem which was left open when the large quantities of herring and mackerel were caught. It must (moreover), be more than a coincidence that together with the depletion of pelagic fish stocks in the North Sea an unprecedented increase in recruitment also took place in gadoid stocks like cod, whiting and especially haddock. (Christensen 1977, 4)

Such dynamic views of stocks waxing and waning in complex, poorly understood ecosystems were based on evidence from beyond the North Sea too. For example, the appearance of vast mackerel shoals off South West England during the 1970s – for reasons not fully comprehended – provided a large, unpredicted compensation for some British fishermen faced with disaster after the collapse of herring stocks (Figure 2.12).

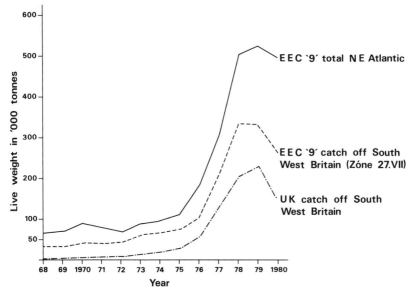

Figure 2.12 Mackerel catches by the EEC 'Nine', 1968–80
Source: Eurostat.

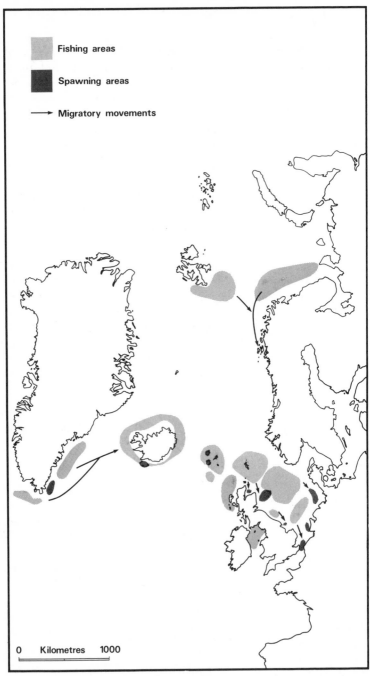

Map 2.14 Fishing and spawning areas for cod
Source: ICES (1974).

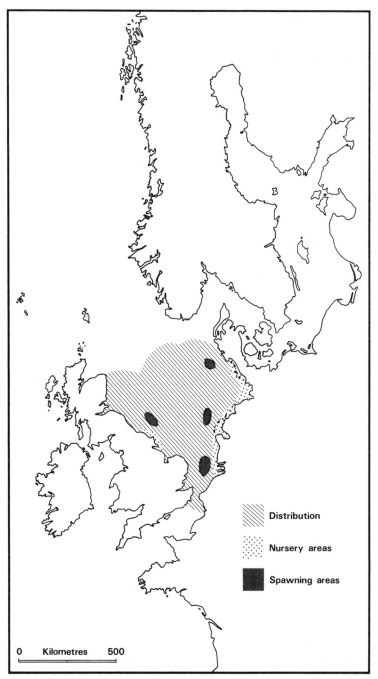

Map 2.15 Distribution, nursery and spawning areas for North Sea plaice
Source: ICES (1974).

However, despite these divergent views on the precise significance of overfishing, all those concerned with fisheries were increasingly forced to face up to resource management problems. The international dimension of these problems can easily be underlined by examining the geographical distribution of major fish stocks (Maps 2.13–2.16). Such realities brought diverse fishermen and their representatives from all over Europe progressively closer together, often in conflict, but sometimes in co-operation as well. The following chapter surveys the major results of this contact and sets the European Community's CFP firmly in its historical setting.

Note: The general surveys of fishing industries in this chapter have been based on the following sources: Agra Europe (1981), Eurostat, *Fisheries* (various editions), FAO (1960–80), ICES (1965–81 and 1974), OECD (1969–82), White Fish Authority (Various).

Map 2.16   Fishing and spawning areas for haddock
Source: ICES (1974).

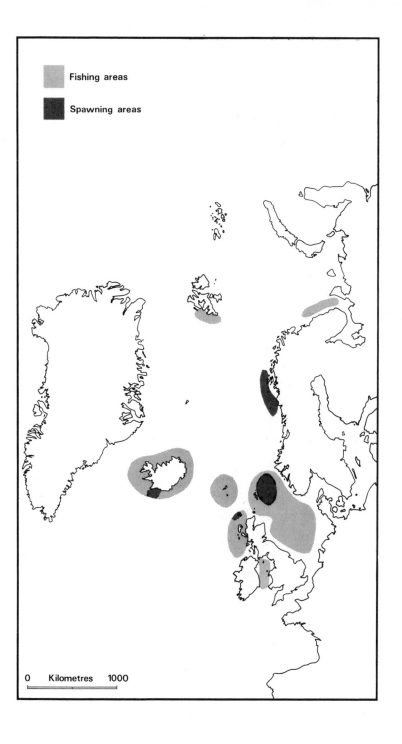

Fishing areas

Spawning areas

0   Kilometres   1000

3 The control of European fisheries before the CFP

> For centuries, because of the vastness of the sea and the limited relationships between states the use of the sea was subject to no rules: every state could use it as it pleased. (Alvarez 1951)

The CFP forms a part of the long evolution of systems to allocate and control European fishery resources. The history of international conflict and co-operation over European fisheries has focused on the following political–geographical issues: first and foremost, the fundamental question about how marine space and its fishery resources should be allocated among states; secondly, the development of effective regimes to conserve stocks.

The development of national fishing limits

State claims to control adjacent sea areas stretch back to antiquity. Sometimes these claims have entailed the demand to exercise sovereignty over *all* activities; in such cases the state is making claim to 'territorial sea'. In other cases, a state may claim jurisdiction over particular activities in the offshore zone; control over military activities, trade, navigation and fisheries provide major examples of these more restricted claims to what is usually referred to as the 'contiguous zone' beyond the territorial sea (Alexander 1966, 38–9). Claims to exclusive national fishing zones have generally been much more ambitious in spatial terms than claims to territorial waters.

The fishing limits off Europe have changed frequently since medieval times, with a recurrent theme being the effort of Scandinavian countries, sometimes followed by those of the British Isles, to repel fishermen from further south (Alexander 1966, 6–18). During the nineteenth century, the development of distant-water fishing by large trawler fleets exacerbated these disputes. In particular, inshore fishermen resented the 'intrusion' of large modern vessels into 'their' fishing grounds. Thus, for example, in 1869 the Norwegians delimited a baseline that enclosed vast bay and fjord areas for the exclusive use of Norway's fishermen. Such actions antagonized the growing distant-water interests of the large industrial countries to the south. These conflicts led to the first attempt to find a 'European' solution to the problems of marine resource allocation.

THE NORTH SEA FISHERIES CONVENTION

In an effort to regulate an increasingly confused situation eight countries – Britain, France, Germany, Denmark, Norway, Sweden, Belgium and the Netherlands – produced the North Sea Fisheries Convention in 1882 which established 3-mile territorial and fishing limits off the North Sea coasts of signatory countries. This limit was measured from a baseline composed of the low water mark and, in the case of bays, 'a straight line drawn across the bay, in the part nearest the entrance, at the first point where the width does not exceed 10 miles' (UN 1957). Norway and Sweden refused to sign the Convention. They unilaterally persisted with a 4-mile limit drawn, in the case of Norway, from long straight baselines that enclosed vast exclusive fishing areas landwards of the baseline. Denmark accepted the general 3-mile limit, but it was nineteen years before the provisions of the Convention became applicable in two of Denmark's territories – Iceland and the Faroes – where opposition to foreign fishermen in 'their' coastal waters was long established.

The principles embodied in the North Sea Fisheries Convention were not sufficient to settle all disputes. Norway, in particular, insisted that broad fishing limits were justifiable when a coastal community was heavily dependent upon fishing. Norwegian objections to the norms generally accepted elsewhere in Europe became stronger as heavy capital investment in steam-trawler fleets with long-range capacity led to British, German and other foreign vessels taking larger and larger catches off Norway's coasts from the early years of this century onwards. A long series of claims and counterclaims ensued with all sides invoking 'historic rights', but the Norwegians also pointing to the 'dependence' of their inshore fishing communities and convicting many foreign trawlermen for 'trespass'. Such conflict eventually led to the Anglo-Norwegian Fisheries Case which marked a major step in the evolution of international fishery policy in Europe.

THE ANGLO-NORWEGIAN FISHERIES CASE

In 1935 the Norwegian government responded to the pressure of fishing interests in the economically vulnerable region of North Norway and officially delimited a 4-mile exclusive fisheries zone north of 66°28.8′ N measured from a series of straight baselines that passed between a mere 48 points (Johnson 1958). They did not follow the low-water mark anywhere along the coast, were frequently based on tiny offshore islets and drying rocks, and thus were often further seawards than the headlands of individual bays. Eighteen of these baselines exceeded 15 miles in length, thus enclosing large sea areas on their landward side.

The British government refused to recognize these new baselines and referred the dispute to the International Court of Justice in 1935, although the case was not considered until 1951. In essence, the British rejected the manner in which the Norwegians had used the straight baselines to shut off access to large coastal fisheries, arguing that their use should be limited to the generally accepted 10-mile closing line for bays and indentations established in the 1882 Convention. In reply, the Norwegians argued that there was no established law on methods of baseline limitation (despite the 1882 North Sea Fisheries Convention which they had refused to sign). Moreover, Norway had always refused to accept limitations to its offshore claims. The Norwegians justified their standpoint on the grounds of 'historic rights' springing from traditional usage, the extremely complex configuration of the Norwegian coast, and the great dependence of their coastal populations on fishing, particularly in the north.

In judgement the Court supported the Norwegian case, ruling that the 10-mile closing line principle for baselines incorporated in the North Sea Fisheries Convention had not acquired the authority of a general international law. It also enunciated some very broad principles for the establishment of baselines which allowed a large degree of freedom to the coastal state when delimiting its baselines (Alexander 1966, 52). This judgement sprang in large part from acceptance of 'socio-economic' criteria as primarily relevant in deciding the validity of an offshore claim. The 'historic rights' of Norway were given priority over the similar 'rights' of other states because of the economic dependence of Norwegian coastal communities on inshore fisheries. Furthermore, the decision of the Court over this issue was significant in that it implied that uniform rules for determining the extent of exclusive fishery limits in very different physical, economic and social situations did not and could not exist.

The outcome of the Anglo-Norwegian Fisheries Case provided a stimulus for further claims to fishing limit extensions in regions and countries 'dependent' on fishing. In Norway itself, a further 74 straight baselines were established in 1952 to cover the southern section of the coastline not involved in the 1935 decree. Pressure from Norwegian fishermen for a further extension of the national fishing limit to protect the coastal population and stop overfishing also grew. Thus in May 1960 the Norwegians unilaterally claimed a 12-mile exclusive fishery limit (Fleischer 1965, 93–6). In so doing Norway pointed to the resolutions adopted by the 1958 UN Geneva Conference which, without being very specific, suggested preferential treatment in certain cases for coastal populations 'dependent' on fishing (UN 1958).

In reaction, the British called for negotiations, but could only postpone the effects of Norway's decision in the Anglo-Norwegian Fishery Agreement of 1960. This stipulated that British vessels would cease to operate within 6 miles of the Norwegian baseline immediately, and that after 1 October 1970 they would stop fishing within the 12-mile zone. In April 1962 the Soviet Union, which also had a large fleet operating off Norway, signed a similar agreement and acceptance of Norway's 12-mile fishing limit became general, although not always official.

THE ANGLO-ICELANDIC FISHERIES CASE

The Anglo-Norwegian Fisheries Case facilitated claims to ever larger national fishing zones, thus exacerbating the conflicts between 'fish-surplus' and 'fish-deficient' states in Europe (Alexander 1966, 107–25). One of the most important of these disputes arose between Iceland and Britain. With its rich coastal fisheries, its large export capacity and its heavy socio-economic dependence upon the fishing industry, Iceland's fishery policies have had important repercussions for fishing industries and policies elsewhere in Europe.

In 1952 Iceland delimited 47 straight baselines that enclosed vast bay areas as 'internal waters'. From these new baselines – which were sometimes 30 miles from the nearest shoreline – the Icelanders unilaterally extended their exclusive fishery limit from 3 to 4 miles.

The UK government, concerned about the fate of its distant-water fleet which depended heavily on Icelandic grounds and had just lost access to large areas of Norway's coastal fisheries, protested, and the British fishing industry prevented landings of Icelandic fish in Britain. Such action was not effective, for Iceland was able to redirect this lost trade elsewhere, mainly to the Soviet Union and eastern Europe. Later, in September 1958, Iceland unilaterally extended her exclusive fishing limits from 4 to 12 miles, but the UK – which had the largest foreign fleet operating in these waters – refused to withdraw its trawlers from the newly claimed zone and sent warships into the area to protect British vessels. The first 'Cod War' had begun.

The Icelanders justified their action by invoking the familiar arguments; first, the very heavy dependence of the national economy on coastal fisheries, and second, the need for restrictions to prevent overfishing in coastal waters. The British retorted by citing the principle of the 'freedom of the seas' and arguing that the Icelanders had not scientifically proved that British activities were leading to overfishing of major commercial species such as cod and haddock.

After two years of confrontation, negotiations between the two sides began and led to the Anglo-Icelandic Agreement of 1961. In this, Britain accepted the 12-mile limit 'in view of the exceptional dependence of the Icelandic nation upon the coastal fisheries for their livelihood and economic development' (Johnston 1965). In return Britain claimed assurances that any Icelandic proposal for further fishing limit extensions would be referred to the International Court of Justice (the second Anglo-Icelandic 'Cod War' of the early 1970s revealed the meaningless nature of this undertaking). Britain's acceptance of Iceland's 12-mile limit led other European countries with fishing interests in this area to do likewise.

FISHING ACCESS INCREASINGLY RESTRICTED

The success of the Norwegians and Icelanders in extending their control over adjacent fishery resources encouraged other countries to follow. The Faroese, semi-independent under the Danish crown, were one such case (Johnston 1965; Alexander 1966, 103). In 1901, the fishing limits around the Faroes were reduced to 3 miles by Denmark in accordance with the criteria established by the North Sea Fisheries Convention of 1882. After the Second World War the local Faroese parliament began to claim a 12-mile limit from a series of straight baselines which themselves enclosed large new areas as 'internal waters'. In 1959, the Danish government responded to this pressure and decreed a 12-mile limit around the Faroes measured from straight and curved baselines which favoured the islanders. The British, who were once again the main protagonists of distant-water interests, negotiated 'historic rights' in parts of the 6- to 12-mile zone, but no other states were granted access to the new zone.

However, this concession to the British did not last long. In 1961 the Danish government, in response to Faroese pressure, followed Norway and Iceland in unilaterally declaring a 12-mile limit around the Faroes from which all foreign fishermen were to be excluded after March 1964. The British government refused to accept this new limit officially, but decided not to oppose its enforcement. At the same time the Danes recognized the dependence of Greenland (also under Danish sovereignty) upon coastal fisheries and declared a 12-mile limit to replace the old 3-mile zone, again causing considerable difficulties for Europe's distant-water fleets, which had been turning to this area in increasing numbers to compensate for reduced catches elsewhere.

The developing interest of the Irish Republic in its coastal fisheries as a source of economic growth was manifested in 1959 when 49 straight baselines were delimited. Some of them were 20 miles from the mainland in places, enabling Ireland to claim vast new areas of exclusive fishing without actually extending its 3-mile fishing limit (Alexander 1966, 74–5).

Thus, the decade following the Anglo-Norwegian Fisheries Case in 1951 was characterized by the successful attempts of northern European states to extend their exclusive fisheries jurisdiction over 12-mile zones measured from straight long baselines. Other states, led by the UK, tried to resist these extensions in order to protect the interests of their distant-water fishermen, but their efforts met with little success. The threat of restricting access to fish export markets was not powerful enough to prevent the 'fish-surplus' states of the north from restricting access of foreign fishermen to their coastal waters. Also the fear of antagonizing strategically important Nordic countries in the Atlantic alliance prevented states such as Britain from pressing their case too hard; this was particularly so in the case of Iceland.

Britain's call for a new 'European' settlement

By the early 1960s the North Sea Fisheries Convention of 1882 was irreversibly broken. Britain, in its disputes with Norway and Iceland, had been the champion of the 3-mile limit system set down in the 1882 Convention. This reflected the pre-eminence of Britain's distant- and middle-water interests in the UK and its general interest in maintaining the international character of the seas for various strategic and economic reasons. However, Britain also has a very significant inshore fishing fleet based on substantial coastal resources that attract foreign as well as local fishermen. Thus, although British distant-water interests militated against the extension of exclusive fishing limits, British inshore interests became more concerned with extending theirs. Having failed to stop Nordic states from extending their control over adjacent marine resources, the UK government made some- thing of a volte-face in the early 1960s and decided that, owing to the exclusion of their fishermen from distant coastal waters, they no longer felt justified in refusing British fishermen greater protection from foreign fishermen in 'their' inshore waters.

This change of British policy was accompanied by a call for a new 'European' settlement of the fishing-limit question. In April 1963, Mr Edward Heath, then within the Conservative government, called for a European conference to establish new common principles according to which the fishery resources off Europe might be allocated. Britain did not want to establish new limits unilaterally, but as part of a general European agreement on fishery limits and related problems. Referring to the failure of the 1958 and 1960 UN Conferences on the Law of the Sea to reach international agreement on fisheries jurisdiction, Mr Heath asked for a European settlement in the following terms:

> Again, at the time of the Brussel's negotiations [i.e.: concerning Britain's original demand to join the EEC] *Her Majesty's Government made clear their interest in the settlement of common fishery problems on a European basis.* Although the negotiations were not concluded, our objective remains to secure a reasonable livelihood for fishermen and stable markets in western Europe. (my emphasis)

> Her Majesty's Government believe that these questions and the special problems of fisheries must be looked at as a whole and can best be settled by discussion. We are, therefore, inviting those countries affected, the members of the EFTA and the EEC, Iceland, the Irish Republic and Spain, to a conference in the autumn.

> We propose that this conference should consider the questions of trade in fish and access to fishing grounds. We hope by this means to arrive at an equitable settlement on a European basis which will

have regard to the interests of all sections of the fishing industry.
(Commons 1963–4)

THE EUROPEAN FISHERIES CONVENTION, 1964

The British initiative led to the European Fisheries Conference held in
London from December 1963 to March 1964. The Conference was
attended by 16 states; those of the EFTA, the EEC, Ireland, Spain and
Switzerland. The Commission of the EEC was also represented in the
capacity of observer and it is interesting to note that some of the first
steps in the formulation of the CFP were being taken at this time.
Despite the growing importance of their fishing activities in the North
East Atlantic, the USSR and the other fishing states of the Eastern
Bloc were not invited.

The most important feature of the Final Act of the European
Fisheries Conference was the European Fisheries Convention within
which the old 3-mile exclusive fisheries zone of the 1882 Convention
was abandoned for a new two-zone system; a 0- to 6-mile belt and a
6- to 12-mile belt (Final Act 1964). In the 0- to 6-mile zone the coastal
state was given absolutely exclusive fishery rights (Article 2). In the
6- to 12-mile zone the exclusive rights of the coastal state were
modified in that foreign states that had 'habitually' fished within this
belt between 1 January 1953 and 31 December 1962 could continue to
do so (Article 3). However, within the 6- to 12-mile zone, these states
enjoying 'historic rights' could not 'direct their fishing effort towards
stocks of fish or fishing grounds substantially different from those
which they have habitually exploited' (Article 4). The primacy of the
coastal state in the 6- to 12-mile zone was further underlined in Article
5:

> Within the belt mentioned in Article 3 the coastal state has the
> power to regulate the fisheries and to enforce such regulations,
> including regulations to give effect to internationally agreed measures
> of conservation, provided that there shall be no discrimination in
> form or in fact against fishing vessels of other Contracting Parties
> (i.e.: states) fishing in conformity with Articles 3 and 4.

The Convention also included a more liberal straight baseline policy
based on the practices that had been unilaterally adopted by Norway
and Iceland (see above) before their general acceptance in the 1958 UN
Convention on the Territorial Sea and Contiguous Zone. In effect, this

meant that 'bays' could be closed by baselines up to 24 miles in length instead of the 10-mile maximum permitted in the now defunct 1882 Convention. This was especially welcome to British inshore fishermen for the indented nature of the UK coastline meant that large areas of water not covered by the new 12-mile zone were enclosed as national 'internal waters'. This was particularly true of the west coast of Scotland with its many indentations and islands.

Although certain non-coastal states were granted specific 'historic rights' in the outer 6-mile belt, no such rights were given to foreign fishermen who had habitually fished up to the old 3-mile limit. However Article 9 permitted foreign fishermen who had habitually fished this inner zone to continue doing so for a limited time. As a result two *Agreements as to Transitional Rights* (Final Act 1964, 30–2, 34–6) were concluded: one was between the UK on one side and West Germany, France, Belgium, Ireland and the Netherlands on the other; the other was made between Ireland on one side and Belgium, France, West Germany, the Netherlands, Spain and the UK on the other. These Agreements led to the phasing out of all historic rights in the 3- to 6-mile zones around Britain and Ireland by 31 December 1966. In the context of later developments over the CFP, note that it was the continental states of the original EEC that suffered from this reduction of traditional rights and had fought hard to maintain them in the 6- to 12-mile zones around the British Isles (see Appendix Map 1.1).

Obviously disputes could arise over the interpretation of several of these provisions. For example, difficulties could arise in defining 'habitually fished'. Article 13 provided for an arbitration machinery to settle such disputes; this, in principle at least, marked an important step forward. If one signatory state requested arbitration other signatory states were obliged to submit themselves to the same process. The disputing parties had to accept the decision of the Arbitral Tribunal which was to be composed of five members nominated by the disputing states or the International Court of Justice.

NORWAY, ICELAND, THE FAROES AND GREENLAND REJECT THE CONVENTION

However, the Convention was obviously only binding on signatory states and, true to their independent tradition in such matters, Norway, Iceland and Switzerland refused to sign. Moreover, although

Denmark signed the Convention, the offshore zones of the Faroes and Greenland were specifically excluded from the terms of the Convention. Thus, once again, the Nordic states with the richest coastal fisheries had refused to accept a general West European agreement on fishery limits. The reasons for their refusal were, as usual, related to the importance of the fishing industry to their national or regional economies and their rejection of such notions as 'historic rights' for foreign fishermen. Dr Fleischer of the University of Oslo clearly expressed these Scandinavian viewpoints when explaining the negative Norwegian attitude to the Convention:

> It should be obvious that Norway could not accept a regime of fisheries according to which traditional fishing should continue between six and twelve miles for more than twenty years or even without limit of time (the Convention provided for possible revisions after a twenty year period). Such an arrangement would entail great hardships for the coastal population of Norway, for whom fishing is the predominant source of living. This population would be deprived of the protection which had been accorded by the extension to twelve miles in 1960.... During the Conference the argument was brought forward that Norway is not dependent on her coastal fisheries to the same extent as for example Iceland. While this may be true with respect to the Norwegian population as a whole it should be quite clear that Norway represents a special case with regard to her coastal population, in particular as compared with most other countries, which took part at the Conference. The special case of Norway has even been recognized by the International Court of Justice in its judgement of 1951. (Fleischer 1965, 107)

Britain's original hope of a 'European' settlement of 'common fishery problems' dealt with 'as a whole' was thus thwarted. The Convention had other limitations. It focused almost entirely on fishing limits; the declaration concerning conservation and trade were of a general exhortative nature. The Conference urged the Commission of the North East Atlantic Fisheries Convention (see below) to pursue its conservation task, but accepted that resource management, although linked to the questions of resource allocation and fishery limits, be dealt with by a separate organization (Final Act 1964, Annex 2, 5). Similarly with respect to international fish trade, the European Fisheries Conference contented itself by passing a Resolution on Access to Markets that supported the efforts of the OECD and other organizations to liberalize trade in fish and fish products (Final Act 1964, Annex 3). Britain's original proposal that the Conference 'should consider questions of trade in fish and access to fishing grounds' in a comprehensive fashion, thus failed to fructify.

Despite the Convention's concentration on allocating fisheries authority over marine space, it can be criticized on this issue as well. First, apart from the need to 'balance' inshore and distant-water interests, there was no 'rational' justification in economic or biological terms of the 'inner' and 'outer' 6-mile belt system laid down by the Convention. Also, the Convention ignored the problems of control on the high-seas off western Europe where overfishing was a recognized problem. Furthermore, the exclusion of the eastern European countries lessened the scope of the Convention. As Johnston concluded:

> The Convention is a diplomatic accomplishment but does not help, and indeed may hinder, the development of rational schemes of fishery management, unless supplemented and modified by other arrangements that deal directly with the economic and biological problems of fishery use in the region. (Johnston 1965)

The development of European fishery conservation regimes

The first attempt to set up some form of 'European' conservation authority was during the North Sea Fisheries Conference of 1881-2 (see above). The overwhelming preoccupation of this conference was to establish territorial waters and fishing limits around the North Sea, but the German delegation tried to broaden the scope of the Conference by proposing a common European policy to protect small fish. But narrower conceptions of fishery policy-making prevailed and the initiative was dropped (Johnston 1965).

THE INTERNATIONAL COUNCIL FOR THE EXPLORATION OF THE SEA (ICES)

However, evidence of overfishing began to accumulate, leading to another conference of European states at Stockholm in 1899, which set in motion a process leading to the creation of the ICES in 1902. Despite its name, ICES is European in character, being financed by member states and confining its activities to the North East Atlantic. The foundation members were Denmark, Finland, Germany, the Netherlands, Norway, Russia, Sweden and the UK, with France, Belgium, Italy, Spain, Portugal, Iceland, Poland and Ireland joining later. It is a scientific research body whose various committees – composed of scientists from member states – study problems related to the exploitation of North East Atlantic fisheries. Although the ICES has no decision-making powers, its research provides a relatively impartial data basis for management of Europe's offshore fishery resources.

However, despite the work of the ICES, international ideas of managing Europe's offshore fisheries in a biologically 'optimum' manner have been far less influential than national interests in moulding the manner of fishery exploitation. This was clearly illustrated by the events following the First World War. In 1919, after four years of greatly reduced fishing, the average landing per day's absence of an English trawler from the North Sea was 30.6 cwts compared with 14.3 cwts in 1913; moreover, the average size of fish had increased. The ICES scientists documented this carefully and argued for the long-term benefits of controlling fishing effort in order to obtain optimum yields. However, instead there was a 'trawler boom', with boats being bought at high prices to exploit the replenished stocks. A period of high returns was inevitably followed by decreasing yields and depressed financial conditions among European fleets (Engholm 1961, 41).

THE INTERNATIONAL CONFERENCE ON OVERFISHING, 1946

The Second World War led to another replenishment of fish stocks as warships replaced fishing boats around Europe. To prevent a new era of excessive exploitation, the International Conference on Overfishing was held in London in 1946 between Belgium, Denmark, France, Iceland, Ireland, the Netherlands, Norway, Poland, Portugal, Spain, Sweden and the UK. This Conference produced a 'Convention for the regulation of the meshes of fishing nets and the size limits of fish' which applied to the activities of signatory states in the North East Atlantic (Johnston 1965, 361). All signatory states agreed to enforce its regulations. A permanent Commission was set up to administer the Convention and put into effect recommendations accepted unanimously by the member states. The importance of international scientific advice was recognized by the setting up of a Liaison Committee between the Permanent Commission and the ICES.

This Convention lacked, however, adequate political authority. Consequently overfishing, particularly in the North Sea, soon followed the immediate post-war boom. As always the basic problem was to get separate national and sectional interests to forsake individual short-term gains for the development of catch levels related to maximum sustainable yields. National governments find it difficult to withstand the socio-economic pressures that inevitably stem from attempts to reduce fishing effort, particularly if there is the justifiable fear that fishermen from other states will take advantage of moderation in an open-access fishery and increase their share of the resource. The existence of such problems and fears was clearly illustrated by the fact that it was not until 1954 that the Convention was finally ratified by all the members of the 1946 Conference as well as West Germany and the Soviet Union.

The Convention had other weaknesses. Firstly, its provisions did nothing to protect herring stocks. As herring fishing was one of the major elements of European fisheries and subject to serious overfishing, this was a major omission. Secondly, enforcement of regulations for those stocks covered by the Convention was weak. However, the most fundamental fault was the failure to limit the quantity of fishing. Some delegations recognized the necessity for international control of fishing effort, and proposed measures such as: fleet capacity reduction, catch quotas and closed areas. However, agreement on such radical proposals proved impossible. This is not surprising given that the allocational problem of defining 'equitable ' catch quotas for different producers remains an intractable problem.

THE NORTH EAST ATLANTIC FISHERIES CONVENTION, 1959

During the 1950s it became apparent that the mesh and fish-size regulations of the 1946 Convention were too limited to deal with growing overfishing. Hence, in 1955, Belgium, Denmark, France, West Germany, Ireland, Iceland, the Netherlands, Norway, Poland, Portugal, Spain, Sweden, the UK and the Soviet Union began consultations which eventually produced the North East Atlantic Fisheries Convention (NEAFC 1963), which widened the scope of the 1946 agreement in several ways.

Firstly, the area to which the new Convention applied was

greater than that of its predecessor; it was extended along the north coast of Russia from 36°E to 51°E and from 48°N to 35°N in the south. The Baltic and the Mediterranean were still dealt with under separate organizations, but this new areal scope meant that virtually all the main 'European' fisheries were subjected to the regulations of the Convention. Secondly, a North East Atlantic Fisheries Commission (the NEAFC) was set up. Article 7 permitted it to make recommendations to contracting states over a far wider range of conservation matters than permitted by the 1946 Convention:

1 . . .

    (a) any measures for the regulation of the size of fishing nets;

    (b) any measures for the regulation of the size limits of fish that may be retained on board vessels, or landed, or exposed, or offered for sale;

    (c) any measures for the establishment of closed seasons;

    (d) any measures for the establishment of closed areas;

    (e) any measures for the regulation of fishing gear and appliances, other than regulation of the size of mesh fishing nets;

    (f) any measures for the improvement and the increase of marine resources, which may include artificial propagation, the transplantation of organisms and the transplantation of young.

2 Measures for regulating the amount of total catch, or the amount of fishing effort in any period, or any other kinds of measures for. the purpose of conservation of the fish stocks in the Convention area, may be added to the measures listed in paragraph 1 of this Article on the proposal adopted by not less than a two-thirds majority of the Delegations present and voting and subsequently accepted by all the Contracting States in accordance with their respective constitutional procedures.

Article 7 also permitted recommendations to relate to *any* species of fish and shellfish. Article 11 recognized the importance of obtaining impartial international scientific information upon which to base recommendations by emphasizing the need for close co-operation between NEAFC and ICES.

All these provisions marked a further step towards using European fisheries more 'rationally' in biological terms. However, the crucial problems of enforcement remained. The Commission could only make recommendations to member states. According to Article 8 of the

Convention, if a recommendation was accepted by a two-thirds majority of the member states then all the signatories 'undertake to give effect' to this recommendation. However, this 'undertaking' was subject to several conditions (contained in Articles 7-10) which in effect left each member state complete freedom of action. Paragraph 2 of Article 8 provided the key condition:

Any contracting state may, within 90 days of the date of the notice of a recommendation ... object to it and in that event shall not be under any obligation to give effect to the recommendation.

Similar 'escape clauses' undermined Article 13 which envisaged international enforcement of conservation measures in both national and international waters. Furthermore, no arbitration machinery was provided for in the Convention to deal with disputes arising out of the application of conservation measures. Whether the NEAFC's recommendations were applied or not depended on the will of individual sovereign states. A brief survey of NEAFC's activities during the 1960s illustrates this political reality.

On the positive side the Commission was able to promote agreement among member states on various recommendations related to mesh size, net type, fish size, restricted areas and closed seasons (NEAFC 1971, 79-87). These conservation methods were most susceptible to general acceptance in that they avoided the difficult problems of reducing effort and determining quotas, thus permitting all fishermen to continue their activities, albeit with different nets or in different areas. But such measures were often too limited and too late, as the problem of North Sea herring conservation demonstrates.

The problem of herring conservation

The 1964 NEAFC meeting had before it a report from the ICES concerning the overfished North Sea herring stocks (NEAFC 1964) from which catches of adult herring had been declining since the early 1950s (Chapter 2). The report argued that mesh regulations were of little use in this situation; only a reduction of fishing effort could increase yields and improve the numerical stability of the stock from year to year. However, 'after thorough discussion' the Commission merely passed a resolution inviting ICES to continue research in order that the matter might be discussed further at the next annual meeting. Thereafter, the problem of herring fisheries was brought up regularly with ever increasing urgency, but action was deferred and yet further study called for. Thus at the 7th meeting of the NEAFC in May 1969 (NEAFC 1969, 2, 12–15) the ICES–NEAFC Liaison Committee produced a very pessimistic scientific report on the levels of overfishing for North Sea herring, and the Commission took 'a very serious view' of the situation. Consequently, a Working Group of administrators, economists and fishery scientists was set up to consider all possible measures to protect the herring stocks, including the establishment of catch quotas. A year later at the 8th meeting of the NEAFC (NEAFC 1970, 14) this group reported that a 50 per cent reduction in catch rate was necessary to return to maximum sustainable yield conditions (Chapter 2). Moreover, there was general accord that some catch-quota system of limiting catches would be the effective solution. However, the North Sea Working Group was unable to agree on a scheme to recommend to the Commission. It was pointed out that 'the constitutional position of the Commission prevented the early introduction of a quota system' and indeed Article 7(2) of the Convention (see above), which envisaged the possibility of total catch and effort regulations, required a two-thirds majority vote in the Commission and the subsequent acceptance of all member states before such regulations could be applied. Given the difficulties involved in trying to introduce such regulations, various less effective short-term measures were proposed. However, agreement still proved difficult to reach as various delegations complained about 'inequality of sacrifice' and 'the need for exemptions to avoid disruption' (NEAFC 1970, 13). Finally, a majority agreed to introduce closed seasons in May 1971 and from 20 August 1971 to 30 September 1971. However, this measure applied for one year only and there was general agreement that it fell far short of what was required to prevent the depletion of North Sea herring. Subsequently, overfishing of North Sea herring intensified, leading to its virtual collapse in the mid-1970s and a total ban imposed by the EEC and Norway in 1977 (see Chapters 2 and 9).

Conclusion

It became increasingly evident that a satisfactory solution to Europe's conservation and fishing access problems required an approach that took into account all aspects of the fishing industry. For example, the sorts of allocational issues which prevented agreement on effective conservation measures included: the degree of fishing access preference that should be allowed to coastal states with large fishing populations in remote areas; the rights of distant-water fishermen exploiting stocks far from their home base; the rights of 'fish-deficient' states to supply a large proportion of the domestic market with the catches by their national fleets; disputes over how fish catches should be used (for example, many European states resented the high proportion of Norwegian and Danish catches used for reduction purposes rather than direct human consumption); conflicts over international trading arrangements; and the problem that individual producers are not prepared to reduce their catches in the general interest of conservation if they fear that, given the absence of effective common controls over all fishermen, this would lead to sacrifice of their incomes for the benefit of their competitors. The limited constitutional scope and authority of the NEAFC prevented it from dealing with these broader issues of resource allocation that underlie conservation problems; consequently its effectiveness was limited. For example, it could not propose 'package-deals' whereby concessions on a conservation measure could be matched by concessions on fishing rights, fish trade restrictions, etc. Moreover, it could not compensate for losses imposed by some conservation measure (e.g. quotas) by offering financial aid of some sort (e.g. grants to encourage new forms of employment in fishing communities). The following chapters will indicate whether the political structures of the EEC had more scope than those of the NEAFC to facilitate the development of effective policies to deal with the related problems of fishing rights allocation and fisheries conservation which confronted both its actual and would-be member states.

4 The original CFP in the Community of Six

France alone has insistently demanded the establishment of a CFP.
(Thibaudau, French fishery official, 1971)

In 1966 . . . the Commission . . . clearly explained . . . the inextricably
interrelated character of the various elements of the CFP; for this
reason it does not seem possible to treat the problem of fishing rights
separately.

Since 1966 a new element has emerged; that is, the prospect of the
enlargement of the Community. In this respect it would be in the
greatest interest of the Community to be able to present, at the time
when the negotiations are opened, the existence of a Community law
on the application of fishing rights, the extension of which would later
give access to the territorial and reserved waters of the countries
applying for membership (waters, moreover, from which Community
fishermen have been evicted in recent years, at least with respect to
important fishing grounds). (Representative of the European Commission, Council 1970b)

According to the European Commission (EC), the CFP was a legal
obligation imposed by the Treaty of Rome (Simonnet 1967). But what
sort of 'common policy' was it to be? Here the scope for interpretation
of the Rome Treaty was large. Article 38.1 required the free
movement of fresh and processed fish within the internal EEC market
and a common customs tariff (CCT) on fish imports. Article 38.4
suggests that some form of common policy for fisheries (as part of
agriculture) be developed within the framework of the overall CAP,
but there is no mention of a separate CFP within the Treaty of Rome.
   The objectives of a CAP in which fisheries would be presumably
included were set out in Article 39:

(a) to promote agricultural productivity by promoting technical
    progress and by ensuring the rational development of agricul-
    tural production and the optimum utilization of the factors of
    production, in particular labour;
(b) thus to ensure a fair standard of living for the agricultural

community, in particular by increasing the individual earnings of persons engaged in agriculture;

(c) to stabilize markets;

(d) to assure the availability of supplies;

(e) to ensure that supplies reach consumers at reasonable prices. (*Treaties Establishing the European Communities* 1973)

In its initial statement of goals for a CFP, the Commission quoted these very general aims verbatim, merely substituting the word 'fisheries' for 'agriculture' (Commission 1966, 34). In pursuit of these general goals, Article 40.2 of the Treaty permitted a range of possibilities between two basic alternatives; at one extreme, a very simple policy establishing rules of competition within a common market, at the other, an elaborate, comprehensive market organization administered at Community level. The Commission not only proposed a market organization of the most integrated 'Community' character possible, but also called for radical 'structural' and 'social' policies affecting all aspects of the fishing industry. Why did the Commission propose this very comprehensive policy? Much of the answer can be found by looking at problems then confronting the French fishing industry.

French fishing interests and demands

The liberalization of internal EEC fish trade and the gradual establishment of a CCT was generally welcome in all Community states except France where the dismantling of what had previously been a very high degree of national protection led to cheaper foreign fish products depressing domestic price levels. Before the application of the Treaty of Rome, the levels of customs duties varied greatly among the individual member states (Commission 1966, 60–2). France had the highest levels of protection, with customs duties of between 25 and 30 per cent imposed on major fish imports. In the case of processed cod and halibut the duties rose as high as 50 per cent. Consequently, prices in France were often double those in neighbouring states. This was in sharp contrast to the much more liberal import regimes in West Germany and Benelux. Benelux countries had no duties on fresh, frozen, salted, smoked or dried fish, shrimps or crab. In West Germany the major types of fresh and filleted fish bore an import duty of 5 per cent, and non-filleted fish (other than herring and sprats which were exempt) generally carried a levy of 10 per cent. At certain times of the year the main white fish species were imported free from duties. Like most of its partners, West Germany imposed relatively high tariffs (14–30 per cent) on preserved and prepared fish, crustaceans and molluscs. Italy was a case apart. As regards tariff protection it occupied an intermediate position between France and other member states. Locally caught species of fish, such as anchovies and sardines, enjoyed a high level of protection with duties of 27 per cent. But these species are not caught in northern waters and this protection was not directed against other members of the EEC. Italy was generally prepared to import fairly freely from northern European states, because its essentially Mediterranean fishing industry could not produce the species they caught.

The harmonization of these very diverse national systems began on 1 January 1962 when member states applied a duty against non-EEC countries that had the effect of reducing by 30 per cent the difference between the individual national duty applied on 1 January 1957 and that provided for under the CCT. This difference was reduced by another 30 per cent on 1 January 1966. The Community aimed ultimately to establish a CCT of between 15 and 25 per cent on fish and fish products. With reference to intra-Community trade, customs duties on fish and fish products were also gradually reduced. By 1 January 1966 they had fallen to 35 per cent of their 1957 level and the following year they dropped a further 10 per cent.

So, the French fishing industry found itself increasingly threatened by the competition of cheaper foreign imports from both other member states and non-EEC countries which found the Community's CCT easier to cross than the original high French national tariff barriers. Fish trade was also being progressively liberalized within the framework of OECD and GATT agreements to which France, as an EEC member, was signatory. As a result, imports into France rose rapidly, passing from 95,000 tons in 1957 to 242,000 tons in 1962 and 282,000 tons in 1966 (Commission 1966, 60). This lowered domestic fish prices and led the French government to seek an EEC CFP that would help France's fishing industry to cope with increased competition from other states (Thibaudau 1971). In March 1963 the French persuaded the Council of Ministers to invite the Commission to make proposals for such a policy. However, progress was slow because French enthusiasm was not shared. Nevertheless they kept up pressure whenever the occasion presented itself. For example, in 1964 the Commission approved a decision to remove administrative barriers preventing the fishing vessels of one member state from landing their catches directly at the ports of other EEC states. These barriers were hindering the free circulation of products within the common market. French fishermen, dismayed at the prospect of foreign vessels landing fish in France, saw little compensation in the right to land their catches in the ports of neighbouring states which had much lower price levels. Thus, the French government demanded a postponement of the new system. The other member states refused to agree, but France obtained an undertaking that the Commission would proceed as fast as possible towards proposals for a comprehensive CFP which would, among other things, channel EEC funds into the French fishing industry (*E* 1964).

The interests of France's EEC partners

In general France's partners favoured a simple liberalization of fish trade within the framework of the EEC and the GATT without a comprehensive CFP which would involve a large degree of centralization and the expenditure of considerable Community funds (Michielson 1971; Mocklinghoff 1971; Tienstra 1971). Many were reluctant to help French fishermen adapt to a more competitive situation, reasoning that they had already made substantial efforts to modernize their fishing industries and that it was unreasonable to expect them to approve Community financing which would be of principal benefit to the French (Gueben and Keller-Noellet 1971). The Dutch were most in favour of fish trade liberalization. They were the only net exporters in the original Community with a national fisheries policy that encouraged open international competition. Thus, they welcomed the new export opportunities, protesting strongly each time the French prevented the import of fish from elsewhere in the EEC.

Proposals for a comprehensive CFP

Responding to these pressures, the Commission broadly supported the French argument that the introduction of a comprehensive CFP dealing with the industry's problems as a whole would be the best way to prevent the recurrent clashes over fish trade (Commission 1968a). Consequently, the Fisheries Division of the Directorate-General for Agriculture gradually constructed a package of proposals. In 1966 it produced a report that contained proposals in embryonic form, including the equal-access concept (Commission 1966); these were later modified and formally proposed to the Council in 1968 (Commission 1968c, 1–19). This slow progress expressed the lack of enthusiasm in all member states except France. The low-order priority generally accorded to fisheries was also reflected in the small staff – 5 or 6 persons – of the Fisheries Division, albeit led energetically by M. Simonnet, a Frenchman, who combined a sympathetic understanding of the problems confronting France's fishermen with a desire to create a coherent 'European' fishery policy. Given that the initial stimulus for the fisheries policy arose from trade issues, the market proposals are presented first.

A COMMON ORGANIZATION OF FISHERY MARKETS

Firstly, fish-quality standards were to be fixed for the whole Community to ensure that Community price regulations applied to the same product throughout the common market. Secondly, the establishment of Producers' Organizations (POs) was to be encouraged in order to centralize market supply in major centres and contribute to the stabilization of fish prices. Fifty per cent of the cost of setting up these POs would be met by the Community's EAGGF 'guidance' fund. Thirdly, a price-support system was proposed similar to those applying to other products within the general CAP. 'Guide' and 'intervention' prices would be fixed by the Council of Ministers each year. In addition, the proposed POs could fix 'withdrawal' prices below which they would not sell their members' products. These prices would have to be between 60 and 90 per cent of the guide price. When prices fell below the intervention price for three successive days, member states would have to grant compensation for the products withdrawn from the market up to a point not exceeding 90 per cent of the costs incurred in withdrawing the product. This system of market support would be financed by the Community's EAGGF 'guarantee' fund. Thus, the market proposals entailed the setting up of a complete organization going far beyond the mere abolition of internal customs and the erection of a CCT.

A COMMON STRUCTURAL POLICY

The structural proposals contained the fishing rights and conservation provisions that have consistently been at the heart of conflict over the

CFP. However, the other aspects are first examined because these much publicized provisions cannot be understood outside the context of the structural proposals as a whole. The crucial element in these proposals was the insistence that the great disparities between the fishing industries of the member states made it impossible to apply the customs union provisions of the Treaty of Rome without a common policy that dealt simultaneously with market and structural problems. Indeed, in their original enunciation of principles for a CFP the Commission even envisaged a distinctive social policy for fisheries, although this was later merged in the structural proposals. In proposing such a comprehensive policy financed by Community funds, the Commission was strongly supporting the French position.

As an integral part of this all-encompassing CFP, the structural proposals were designed to equalize conditions of competition between the Community's diverse fishing industries over a transition period. The Commission argued that to put everyone on 'equal terms' in facing the challenge of open-market competition, various structural and social actions were required. For example, it proposed that national fishery policies and aids be harmonized so that 'distortions' in the free movement of economic factors could be progressively eliminated. A whole series of measures was designed to ensure this co-ordination, entailing the use of EEC funds, the establishment of common rules governing the granting of national aids, and so on. Community financing would be based on the guidance section of the EAGGF which would be able to intervene in virtually all aspects of the production and distribution process.

EQUAL CONDITIONS OF ACCESS TO FISHING GROUNDS

The preamble of the structural regulation proposal also insisted that 'Community fishermen must have equal access to and use of fishing grounds in maritime waters coming under the sovereignty or within the jurisdiction of member states'. Article 2.1 of these proposals articulated this principle of so-called 'equal access' (n.b. not 'free access') in more precise terms:

> Rules applied by each member state in respect of fishing in the maritime waters coming under its sovereignty or within its jurisdiction shall not lead to differences in treatment of other member states.

Member states shall ensure in particular equal conditions of access to and use of fishing grounds situated in the waters referred to in the preceding subparagraph for all vessels flying the flag of a member state and registered in Community territory. (Commission 1968c, 2)

This Article did not mean that the member states would be deprived of all authority in their exclusive national fishing zones. They would remain free to apply national fishing laws, rules and regulations within them, providing that these measures applied equally to all Community fishermen regardless of nationality. Article 2.3 made it clear that these equal-access provisions would apply whatever the extent of national fishing limits 'described by the laws in force in each member state'. Thus, if a member state unilaterally established a 50-mile exclusive national fishing limit, the fishermen of other member states would continue to have the right of equality of access to such a zone. However, Article 4.1 of the proposed regulation envisaged the possibility of regional exceptions to this national non-discrimination principle:

1 By way of derogation from the provisions of Article 2, access to certain fishing grounds situated in the maritime waters ... falling under the sovereignty or jurisdiction of member states ... may be limited to the local population of the coastal region concerned if that population depends primarily on inshore fishing.

2 The fishing areas referred to in paragraph 1 shall be specified and fixed by the Council, acting in accordance with the procedure provided for in accordance with the procedure provided for in Article 43(2) of the Treaty on a proposal from the Commission. (Commission 1968c, 2)

Note that in this original proposal there was no mention of exceptions to equal access being limited in time, whereas in the adopted regulation such exceptions became very temporary in nature and restricted to a narrow coastal belt.

The Commission presented these access proposals as an integral part of the whole structural policy designed to equalize conditions of competition, eliminate national discriminations and to encourage a 'rational use of the biological resources of the sea' within the common market:

> Fishing rights must be formulated and applied following the fundamental principles of the Treaty (of Rome) concerning the free movement of people, products, services and capital. (Commission 1966, 42)

Just as the Treaty of Rome insisted on the removal of national barriers to fish trade, so it was logical, argued the Commission, to eliminate similar discriminations preventing the free movement of fishing boats (i.e. a means of production).

CONSERVATION

Article 5 of the structural proposals envisaged the possibility of action against overfishing in the fishing zones of member states equally open to all Community states, but a concern with conservation did not play an important role in the initial formulation of the CFP. Although a more 'rational' exploitation of fishery resources was one of the stated objectives of the policy, the Commission never clearly defined what it meant by 'rational' in this context or how these objectives might be achieved. The 1966 Report contained a brief section devoted to resource conservation and international fisheries co-operation, but did not examine such questions in depth (Commission 1966, 52).

INTERRELATED PROPOSALS

The fishing access and conservation provisions formed an integral part of the whole comprehensive policy formulated by the Commission. They cannot be understood outside of this context. The Commission adopted the French argument that the simple liberalization of fish trade within the common market was not acceptable without market and structural policies that harmonized conditions of competition within the EEC and enabled the weaker sectors of the fishing industry to adapt to freer trade. The access provisions formed a logical part of the resultant structural policy, in that they eliminated a national source of discrimination 'distorting' conditions of competition among the fishing vessels of the EEC; the free movement of products within the common market was to be matched by the free movement of the means of production.

However, the 'Community principles' underpinning the access proposals are not always adopted so wholeheartedly. It requires concrete national or sectional interests to ensure their rigorous application. For example, the comprehensive policy proposals for the fishing industry formulated by the Commission materialized because of pressure applied by the French government. Similarly, national interests within the 'Six' helped to mould the equal-access proposal. But there was no government in the original Community pressing for a rigorous common conservation policy. Consequently, this element of the Commission's proposals remained superficial.

Reaction in the European Parliament and ECOSOC

ECOSOC and, more importantly, the European Parliament played an essentially consultative role in the making of the CFP. They articulated in public identical arguments to those expounded in the far more crucial, but private, Council of Ministers where the final decisions are taken. Consequently, there is no need to describe the deliberations of these institutions in detail, particularly as both the Parliament and ECOSOC Reports on the Commission's original proposals were generally very favourable, with neither body putting any serious brake on their passage through the Community institutions. It is noteworthy that the equal-access proposals, which were to cause so much strife in later negotiations in the Council of Ministers, were welcomed as 'an integral part of the CFP' (ECOSOC 1967; European Parliament 1968a). Furthermore, the Parliamentary Report insisted that any regional exceptions to the equal-access principle must be genuinely 'local limitations' and not widespread (European Parliament 1968b; 1968c). In contrast, the Parliament and ECOSOC paid virtually no attention to the Commission's limited conservation proposals. Their members were almost totally pre-occupied with the details of market-support mechanisms, external trade and structural aids (European Parliament 1968d).

Conflicting objectives

The vital decision-making centre of the Community is the Council of Ministers. Here, the Commission's proposals are either converted into Community regulations or disregarded. Here, the mass of converging and diverging demands emanating from the Community meet, conflict and sometimes merge into policies that are acceptable to all member states. The objectives pursued by the various governments in these original CFP negotiations were far from identical, so agreement was difficult to achieve.

FRENCH OBJECTIVES

France insisted on completion of the CFP before beginning enlargement negotiations with Norway, Denmark, the UK and Ireland for several reasons. First, the problems posed by the liberalization of fish trade within the EEC would become more acute in an enlarged EEC including the 'Four' applicants; it was already proving hard to get a fisheries policy to cope with such difficulties within the 'Six'. Furthermore, there was a general French strategy to complete the CAP (of which the CFP was a part) before enlargement so that it would be part of the 'acquis communautaire' (established Community policy and law) that had to be accepted by the applicants as the basis of their entry into the Community. The French government knew that several applicants were hostile to the CAP and wanted to protect their interests from a position of strength.

By the beginning of 1970 the French had developed 'reservations' about the provisions relating to equal access. Manipulating the ambiguities of the Rome Treaty with great skill, they argued that fishing rights did not fall within the legal competence of the Community. More particularly, they maintained that equal access would be a cause of 'discrimination', in that it would permit any fishermen not established in a member state to exploit the territorial waters and reserved fishing zones of that country without being subjected to the various obligations stemming from its legislation. They accepted that the 3-mile zone of territorial waters was an extension of the national territory and thus subject to the Treaty of Rome. However, by referring to the 'right of establishment' provisions of Articles 52 and 59 in that Treaty, they argued that other Community fishermen could enjoy equality of access to this French territorial zone only if they belonged to enterprises established in France, thus bearing the same legal and financial obligations as French fishermen. A different solution was proposed for the reserved national fishing zones of the 3- to 12-mile belt which, according to France, fell outside the Rome Treaty's competence; this involved the creation of a system based on the 'most favourable one defined in the European Fisheries Convention of 1964'. This access regime, based essentially on the 'status quo', should, in French opinion, be incorporated in a separate agreement among member states outside of the Rome Treaty and the CFP (Council 1969b, 1970a, 1970b).

What motivated French objections to the equal-access proposals? It would be a mistake to emphasize their 'legal' nature. Juridical conflicts within the EEC can obscure the politico-economic interests that motivate them. As these interests differ, so legal interpretations of the Rome Treaty differ. Furthermore, it would be wrong to exaggerate a French interest in protecting inshore fishing communities by exclusive national fishing limits. French members of the European Parliament had defended France's fishing interests with great vigour, but none had expressed any anxieties over the equal-access provisions. As a French government fishery official argued:

> the common regime for the carrying out of fishing does not involve any damaging consequences since no fishing fleet of any of the Member States (i.e.: the original 'Six') has indicated any intention to frequent the reserved waters of its partners. (Thibaudau 1971, 971)

In fact, French objections to equal access were essentially a tactical manoeuvre in the pursuit of other objectives. France knew the importance that its partners attached to acceptance of the equal-access provision before enlargement. Consequently, it used its 'reservations' on this issue as a form of leverage to gain agreement on the structural aid, market support and external trading elements it wanted elsewhere in the CFP, but which its partners, notably the West Germans, were very reluctant to concede.

The French argument that a separate convention was needed to determine access to exclusive fishing zones was rejected by France's partners and the Commission. If the equal-access provisions were based on such a convention (an 'international act') rather than a CFP regulation (a 'Community act') they would not automatically extend to the new members of the envisaged Community of 'Ten' as part of the vital 'acquis communautaire'. Given that these provisions, applied in an enlarged Community, were one of the few aspects of the proposed policy attractive to France's partners, they did not want access to coastal zones treated as a separate issue outside the framework of Community law (Commission 1970a).

Having built up this strong negotiating position around the access issue, the French used it to pursue their primary objectives. They were ready to admit the principle of equal access after a transition period in exchange for immediate Community aid to facilitate specific structural modernization programmes in sectors of the French fishing industry facing difficulties as a result of EEC membership (Council 1970c; Commission 1970b). In particular, France sought help for its outdated salt-cod and tuna fleets which were having severe problems coping with increasing competition. Other states, reluctant to increase EEC spending, merely wanted to adopt the 'principle' of Community structural aid without any firm commitment (Council 1970d, e, f).

The French initially wanted a fully 'European' market organization for fish with a common system of prices and marketing almost totally supported by Community funds (EAGGF). However, they later declared themselves ready to accept that the financial support of fish markets should primarily be the responsibility of POs. However, this acceptance depended upon substantial Community support to help establish such POs (which hardly existed in France and Italy) and the intervention of EAGGF funds to help support markets during the 'transition' to a system based upon them (E 1970a).

The French government could do little to prevent the ultimate freeing of fish trade within the EEC, but pressed for external Community trading arrangements that would give an 'adequate' level of protection to French producers. The Commission had proposed a generally liberal external trading regime that included the suspension of import tariffs on cod, tuna and herring in which the 'Six' were deficient. This was generally welcomed by the 'Five', but feared by the internationally uncompetitive fishermen of France (Council 1970g; E 1970b).

WEST GERMAN OBJECTIVES

West Germany often opposed French objectives involving EEC expenditure, and, to a large extent, debate was focused on the opposing interests of these two major member states. The equal-access proposal was the only one implying significant gains for West Germany; consequently its representatives 'insisted strongly' on the 'necessity' of equal access to both territorial waters and exclusive fishing zones (Commission 1970c; Council 1970a). The national interests underpinning this firm attitude were very well summarized thus:

> Germany, by her geographical position, does not control any important stretch of sea. Since the loss of her colonies in the First

World War, she is confined to the remotest corner of the North Sea and to a coast along the still more secluded Baltic. On the other hand, her maritime trade is important, and her fisheries must provide for a population of over 60 million ....

All this would urge her to advocate maximum freedom of the sea, defined as regulated freedom for all, with the self-evident limitations protecting the marine environment from pollution and the living resources of the sea from depletion. (Munch 1973, 253)

In pressing for equal access as an integral part of the CFP, the West Germans rejected the French thesis that rules of entry to fishing zones should be defined under a separate international convention that could not be imposed on the applicant states as part of the 'acquis communautaire'. The West German government insisted that it would not make financial efforts to support structural modernization unless its fishermen could benefit from equal access to the exclusive national fishing zones of both the 'Six' original member states and the 'Four' applicants for Community membership (i.e. Norway, Denmark, the UK and Ireland). There could be 'no question' of 'splitting off' the *one* aspect of the CFP proposals that held out the prospect of positive gains for West Germany (Commission 1970a, b). The West Germans supported their case with detailed legal arguments to counteract those of the French, maintaining that the Articles in the Treaty of Rome forbidding discrimination on grounds of nationality, required equal access of Community fishermen to the territorial waters *and* exclusive fishing zones of member states. They were, nevertheless, ready to envisage temporary exceptions to equal access if these were limited to restricted areas, as well as being subject to Community, rather than national decision (Commission 1970c; Council 1970h).

The West Germans also opposed the French over the use of Community funds to renovate outdated fishing industries. The French and the Italians would be the major beneficiaries of such provisions, for West Germany had already spent much in modernizing its national fishing industry during the 1960s. Consequently, the Germans merely wanted a 'simple co-ordination' of national structural policies without the wide-ranging, potentially costly, 'social' objectives cited in the Commission's proposals. These financial reservations were also related to the rising costs of the CAP as a whole. West German concern about EEC costs also moulded their attitude to the market proposals. The Federal Republic's market was based on self-financing POs. Consequently,

the West Germans did not want EEC funds used to support
markets in France and Italy where such POs were either non-existent
or in an embryonic form (Council 1969a, 1970g; E 1969; Commission
1970d). Moreover, the West German government welcomed the
generally liberal orientation of the Commission's external trade
proposals:

> The German fishing industry has been used to strong international
> competition for many years. Competition compels constant vigil-
> ance and is the motor of progress. That is why we remain supporters
> of a liberal fisheries policy. (Mocklinghoff 1971)

ITALIAN OBJECTIVES

The Italians were of secondary importance in the formulation of the
CFP. In general, they supported the Commission, West Germany and
the Benelux countries on the equal-access and external-trade issues, but
aligned themselves with the French over the question of aid for
structural reform and market support. With its largely poor inshore
fishing industry, Italy obviously wanted Community funds to finance
modernization and support fishermen's incomes.

BENELUX OBJECTIVES

Of the Benelux countries, only the Netherlands had a really significant
interest in the CFP. For the most part, they supported the West
German standpoints on Community funds, market organization
and external trade, whereas, with their short coastlines, the Dutch
and Belgians obviously welcomed the Commission's equal-access
proposals.

So a complex pattern of diverging and converging interests existed
amongst the 'Six' in the Council of Ministers (Table 4.1). Clearly, the
Commission had to revise its proposals in order to facilitate the
achievement of a generally acceptable compromise.

Compromises

MARKET ORGANIZATION

The Commission first sought to resolve the conflict between these
different aims by modifying their market proposals. As a concession to

West Germany and the Netherlands, it suggested that self-financing POs should assume prime responsibility for supporting market prices. However, to win French and Italian acceptance, the Commission made some compensatory recommendations. Firstly, these producers' organizations would have to operate according to Community rules and a common price system. Secondly, Community aid would help set up such organizations. Finally, Community funds would support prices during a three-year transition period. Eventually all the member states declared their readiness to accept such a compromise. But this issue formed only one strand of the complex CFP negotiation; final agreement on markets depended on the outcome of other issues, such as structural aids and access provisions.

STRUCTURAL AIDS

Despite West German and Dutch opposition, the Commission continued to insist that structural aid policies were an essential element of the CFP as a whole, and supported the demand for immediate measures to help France's salt-cod fleet and inshore fishermen. Eventually, a few days from the deadline presented by the opening of the enlargement negotiations, the Commission proposed a compromise designed to: (i) appease the West Germans and the Dutch by an assurance that Community spending in this area would be strictly limited by existing CAP regulations; (ii) satisfy the Dutch by an insistence on common rules governing national aids; (iii) ensure, on the other hand, that the French would obtain at least some of the aid they required (Council 1970f). Thus here, as in the market sphere, the 'Six' were moving towards compromise. One major problem – that of access to fishing zones – remained to be settled before the final adoption of the CFP as a whole.

ACCESS TO FISHING ZONES

The Commission insisted unswervingly on equal access; indeed, its proposals for exceptions to this principle became much more limited in time and space as the negotiations progressed. This was clearly in response to West German, Benelux and Italian demands. The Commission argued that the right to fish in various maritime zones of member states had nothing to do with the 'right of establishment' (as the French suggested) for fish were mobile common property resources. Moreover, the absence of equality of access would

Table 4.1 Simplified matrix of objectives among the 'Six'

Objectives	France	Italy	W. Germany	Netherlands	Belgium	European Commission
1 Equal access to fishing zones	√	√	√	√	√	√
Exceptions to equal access	√?	×	×	×	×	√?
Equal access as part of the 'acquis communautaire'	√	√	√	√	√	√
2 Substantial and comprehensive Community structural aid from EAGGF	√	√	×	×	×	√
Limited or no Community structural aid from EAGGF	×	×	√	√	√	×
3 Strict harmonization of structural policies of member states	√	–	×	√	--	√
Simple co-ordination of structural policies of member states	×	–	√	×	–	×
4 Community-financed market support	√	√	×	×	–	√
Self-financing POs	×	×	√	√	–	×
5 Liberal external trade regime	×	√	√	√	√	√
Protective external trade regime	√	×	×	×	×	×
6 Final agreement on the CFP before enlargement	√+	?√	?√	?√	?√	√
7 Common community conservation policy (Article 6)	×	×	×	×	×	√

Note: √ Perceived gain; × perceived loss; ? ambiguity/uncertainty; – lack of evidence.

Table 4.2 Simplified matrix of elements in agreement among the 'Six'

Basic elements of agreement amongst 'Six'	France	Italy	W. Germany	Netherlands	Belgium	European Commission
1 Equal access to fishing zones	√	√	√	√	√	√
Temporary exceptions to equal access	√?	√	√	√	√	√
Equal access as part of the 'acquis communautaire'	√	√	√	√	√	√
2 Specific Community structural aid linked to liberalization of fishing access and trade	√	×	×	×	×	√
Limitations on Community structural and social aids in general	×	×	√	√	√	×
3 Simple co-ordination of structural policies of member states	×	–	√	×	–	×
4 Partial Community market support from EAGGF	√	√	×	×	×	?
Some degree of self-financing in POs	×	×	√	√	√	?
5 Essentially liberal external trade regime	×	√	√	√	√	√
Limited measure of trade protection for certain products	√	–	–	–	–	√
6 Final agreement on the CFP before enlargement	√ +	√	√	√	√	√
7 No common EEC international conservation policy (no Article 6)	√	√	√	√	√	×

Note: √ Perceived gain; × perceived loss; ? ambiguity/uncertainty; – lack of evidence.

discriminate on national grounds and thus be contrary to the Treaty of Rome. These arguments were not presented in purely legal terms. For example, the Commission dropped all juridical niceties when insisting that the 'Six' had the 'greatest interest' in completing the equal-access provisions before the enlargement negotiations with the UK, Ireland, Norway and Denmark, so that the creation of a Community law on equal fishing rights would later give the 'Six' access to the exclusive national fishing zones and territorial waters of the fish-rich applicant states. The importance of this was underlined by reminding the member states of the 'Six' that they had recently been 'evicted' from important fishing grounds around those now seeking entry to the Community. The Commission also reaffirmed constantly that the equal-access provisions formed part of an inextricably interrelated package and could not be hived off without upsetting a delicate balance of different interests. France excepted, this frank statement of motives received the vigorous support of all member states who also insisted on the 'political and economic opportunities' presented by the equal-access proposals in the 'prospect of Community enlargement' (Commission 1970a; Council 1970b).

Despite protestations to the contrary, the French government also accepted the essence of these arguments; its legal 'reservations' on equal access were, in large part, a tactical ploy to force concessions in other areas. It became clear that these objections would be lifted if Community funds were made available to modernize sections of the French fishing industry threatened by increasing international competition (Commission 1970a).

Eventually, this common interest in establishing a CFP before Community enlargement led the Council of Ministers to reach a somewhat incomplete agreement late in the night of 30 June 1970, the very day entry negotiations with the UK, Ireland, Denmark and Norway began! This agreement involved a complex balancing of interests in a familiar Community 'package-deal' (see Table 4.2) composed of the following elements.

A finely balanced agreement

FINAL AGREEMENT BEFORE ENLARGEMENT

It was agreed that the final market, trade and structural regulations of the CFP must be formally adopted by the Council before 1 November

1970 along the lines of the general accord reached on the night of 30 June 1970. Thus French insistence that a CFP be adopted in time to become part of the 'acquis communautaire' to be accepted by the applicants for Community membership was met by the finest of dubious margins in that enlargement negotiations on fisheries were not due before that date!

EQUAL ACCESS WITH LIMITED EXCEPTIONS

Having attained this basic objective, the French lifted their reservations about equality of access to fishing grounds which was thus firmly established in both territorial waters and exclusive national fishing zones as an integral part of Community law automatically applying to new member states. Obviously this satisfied West Germany, Benelux and Italy, but France would also gain from a liberalization of access within an enlarged Community and later became the most ardent defender of this provision (see Chapter 5).

The full acceptance of equal access as part of the 'acquis communautaire' was slightly tempered by the possibility of exceptions to it. But these exceptions were extremely limited both in time (five years) and space (a 3-mile coastal zone for regions primarily dependent on fishing). The limited nature of these exception provisions was accepted by the French on condition that Community structural aid would be introduced during the transition period to ensure a 'fair' standard of living for fishermen adversely affected by the application of the equal-access principle. This linkage of the equal-access and structural-aid provisions was a crucial element of the compromise between the 'Six'. The French obtained the prospect of Community aid for their inshore fishermen, and the West Germans and the Benelux countries achieved a far weaker exception provision than had originally been proposed by the Commission.

COMMUNITY STRUCTURAL AIDS

The French also succeeded in getting Community funds to help their fishermen adapt to the more competitive fish-trade situation involved in common market membership. Some 15 million EUA (approximately 15 million US dollars) were to be made available for such purposes over a 3- to 5-year period. However, the French, supported by the Italians, did not achieve the high level of structural aids originally sought. Measures of a 'social character' would not qualify, thus satisfying the West Germans and the Dutch who were afraid that such provisions would allow France and Italy to obtain increased sums from the Community budget in a multitude of ill-defined areas. So measures aimed at the retraining of fishermen, improving working conditions, pensions, etc., were to remain the responsibility of national governments. Again it can be seen how agreement was based on a delicate balancing of interests.

COMMUNITY SUPPORT FOR DECENTRALIZED MARKET SYSTEM

In this area a balance was struck between the interests of the French and Italians on one side, and the West Germans and Dutch on the other. The former achieved a measure of Community financial intervention, whereas the latter ensured that a substantial degree of responsibility for market support was conferred on POs. The West German and Dutch desire for flexibility in market arrangements was also satisfied, in that fishermen were to be encouraged, rather than obliged, to join these bodies. However, financial support from the Community would be dependent on belonging to one. For a transition period of three years the formation of POs was to be encouraged by financial aids; 50 per cent from the EAGGF and the rest from national governments. France and Italy would be the major beneficiaries of this provision, but the West Germans and Dutch were pleased that the amount of Community aid available was limited.

The system of market intervention adopted resembled those elsewhere in the overall CAP. First, guide and withdrawal prices were to be set by the Community. When the market price fell below the withdrawal price, POs could withdraw their produce and qualify for financial compensation from the Community's EAGGF Guarantee Fund. This financial compensation would amount to 55 or 60 per cent of the guide price. The remaining compensation payments for withdrawn fish had to come from levies on catches. This degree of self-financing was intended to stop fishermen abusing the Community system. The system only applied to the major commercial species of the Community, namely herring, cod, saithe, haddock, whiting, mackerel, redfish and plaice. Market support for other species would be financed purely by the POs. For tuna fish production, a deficiency payment was introduced to compensate Community producers (mainly in France) when their income was reduced by cheaper foreign imports. This met the demands of the French who wanted adequate protection for their fishermen following the EEC decision, primarily in response to Italian interests, to abolish import duties on tuna destined for the canning industry. Italian concerns also led to the creation of a separate system of direct EAGGF market support for anchovies and sardines without the intermediary of POs, which would be difficult to create among the numerous, scattered and economically backward 'peasant' fishermen found in much of Italy. In general terms the market organization provisions ensured that POs would be responsible for about 25 per cent of the costs of market support for the major species and 100 per cent of the costs of withdrawing other species.

EXTERNAL TRADE WITH NON-COMMUNITY COUNTRIES

As regards external trade, a system similar to that employed elsewhere in the CAP was adopted for the major commercial species. A reference price would be set at a level that ensured that the products of non-member countries could not enter the Community at a lower price than the withdrawal price set for the internal market system. However, in general, all quantitative restrictions on fish imports were to be abolished. To quell French fears, a 'safeguard clause' was maintained that allowed restrictions to be imposed if the Community market was severely perturbed by large quantities of cheap fish imports.

Finally, on 21 October 1970 it was decided to implement the whole CFP on 1 February 1971, thus ensuring that all aspects of the policy would be operating before fisheries were dealt with in the enlargement negotiations (Council 1970j, k). On this last point, the Council also agreed that any future revision of the policy must be made by the Foreign Ministers, responsible for the enlargement negotiations as a whole, rather than their Agricultural counterparts who would normally deal with fishery matters. Here, the 'Six', particularly France, were indicating that the CFP was to be an important bargaining component of the whole negotiation strategy with the 'Four' applicants (Council 1970l; E 1970c).

Conservation: 'A final problem'

In the Council of Ministers on 21 October 1970, when all the outstanding issues remaining among the 'Six' were finally resolved, the Dutch delegation raised a 'final problem', that of conserving fishery resources (Commission 1970e). In the complex bargaining across the whole range of fishery matters that led to eventual agreement on a CFP the truly common problem of fishery conservation played little or no part (Table 4.2). In fact, even this 'last-minute' intervention was of a limited nature, being essentially concerned with Norwegian 'industrial fishing' in the North Sea which, according to the Dutch, was harming Community producers, especially those from the Netherlands. Given the likely entry of Norway into the Community, the Dutch wanted to include provisions in the CFP that would curtail this type of fishing. The problem was quickly resolved by adopting a supplementary preamble to the market regulation which blandly stated that

> implementation of this common organization must also take account of the fact that it is in the Community interest to preserve fishing grounds as far as possible. (Council 1970k, 5)

Such a partial and irresolute provision typified the general approach of the 'Six' to the conservation problem, and was in marked contrast to the resolute effort expended on the equal access, aid and market issues!

Despite the reservations of the West Germans and the Dutch, the limited provisions of Article 5, which, as we have seen above, would allow common conservation measures in the national fishing zones of member states, were eventually included in the structural regulation. However, the more comprehensive provisions of a proposed Article 6, which required the Council to define 'the principles and means of common action to be pursued in the sphere of international relations for all the problems relating to the sea and particularly those concerning access to fishing grounds and conservation of the biological resources of the sea' (Commission 1968c, 3), were rejected completely by the governments of the 'Six'. They argued that Community institutions had no power beyond the territorial boundaries of member states; therefore common policies to help conserve stocks in waters outside of their 12-mile fishing limits were legally impossible. The Commission replied that the fish upon which the CFP was based came mainly from such waters beyond the jurisdiction of the 'Six'; therefore it was logical for the Community to act as a unit in international efforts to conserve fisheries. However, the individual member governments, although prepared to surrender sovereignty on the issue of access to national fishing zones, were not yet ready to co-ordinate their efforts as a Community in order to protect the fish stocks of the high seas (Commission 1970f; Council 1968, 1970f, m). Again one can see how perceptions of national interest moulded legal interpretations of the Rome Treaty!

Conclusions

The European Commission proposed an interrelated CFP with provisions touching on virtually all aspects of the fishing industry from the extraction of the basic natural resource to its consumption. It found it difficult to maintain this comprehensive approach in negotiations with the Council of Ministers where specific national interests surged to the fore. The process of policy formulation within the Council and its related institutions was characterized by vigorous defence of narrowly defined national interests allied to a bargaining process where one interest was 'traded-off' against another in the search for some mutually satisfactory compromise among the member states. These interests were not confined purely to the fisheries field. Whether a proposal was accepted, modified or rejected depended upon the divergence and convergence of specific national interests rather than some synoptic 'European' analysis of what was necessary 'to promote harmonious and balanced development of this industry within the general economy and to encourage the rational use of the biological resources of the sea' (Article 1 of the structural regulation). It is crucial to remember that the final 'bargain' between these diverse interests depended to a large extent on the equal-access question in the perspective of Community enlargement. In the lengthy process of negotiation over the Commission's proposals, the imminent prospect of Norway, Denmark, UK and Ireland entering the Community had been consciously used by both individual member states and the Commission to put pressure on each other to compromise and thus capitalize on their common interest in adopting the equal-access principle before enlargement. On 30 June 1970, the very day negotiations with the 'Four' were officially opened, this 'enlargement factor' finally galvanized the 'Six' into common accord.

5 Enlargement negotiations of 1970–2

> The liberalization of access to fishing grounds formed part of a 'package': certain French concessions on this question were compensated for by the concessions of other delegations in the area of 'market organization'. One cannot modify one element without upsetting the overall balance. (Dutch delegate, *E* 1971a)

> This (fishing access) regime … must permit the establishment of a new and satisfactory balance among the legitimate interests of each of the member countries both new and old. (European Commission, (*E* 1971b)

On the very day agreement among the 'Six' was reached on the CFP, the UK, Ireland, Denmark and Norway began negotiations to enter the Community. The original member states insisted that a basic condition for membership was that applicants accept existing EEC policies. Any problems encountered would have to be solved by use of transitional measures rather than modifications of existing rules. It was made clear that the CFP was included in this 'acquis communautaire' to be accepted by the 'Four'.

When the enlargement negotiations began to deal with fisheries in June 1971, attention rapidly focused on the equal-access provisions that had finally been implemented by the 'Six', along with other CFP regulations, in February of that year. The market and trade provisions of the fisheries policy presented some problems, but satisfactory compromises were reached without excessive difficulty. However, the divergence of interests on fishing access rights was so great, that it proved to be one of the major stumbling-blocks in the whole enlargement process.

Norwegian interests

The Norwegians, who would become by far the largest producers of fish in an enlarged Community, were irritated that the CFP had been so recently defined without their participation and called for a fundamental renegotiation of it. In particular, they found the very limited and temporary exceptions to equality of fishing access totally unacceptable. They wanted larger zones exempt from this provision on a permanent basis. Norway had extended its exclusive fishing limit to 12 miles in 1961 to protect its inshore fishermen and deemed it of vital importance that this remain, in order to maintain an active population in its remote coastal regions for various economic, social, nationalistic and strategic reasons. In response to the argument that limitations on access to fishery resources would discriminate on national grounds, it was stressed that Norway's protective fishery policies formed part of a 'social philosophy' which discriminated against other Norwegians let alone foreigners. For example, only Norwegians actively engaged in fishing were usually allowed to own fishing vessels; special government permission was needed to gain an exception to this law. Such 'discriminatory' legislation

> has as its objective to prevent capital interests from outside fishing communities and outside the fishing districts from obtaining a dominant position in the fishing industry. (Int. doc. 1971a)

Such domination would, in Norway's view, lead to the elimination of the independent inshore fishermen and provoke rural depopulation. Norway also argued that a permanent exclusive fishing zone at least twelve miles wide was essential to conserve coastal fishery resources. Equal access of EEC fishermen into Norway's exclusive fishing zone would, they believed, increase overfishing (Int. doc. 1971b).

Norway's demands ran counter to the provision that any exceptions to equal access must be temporary. However, the Norwegians refused to accept that their demands were contrary to principles in the Treaty of Rome. They argued that a solution existed that took account of both Norwegian interests and Community principles. Thus, they presented a proposal based on the 'right of establishment' incorporated in Articles 52-58 of the Treaty of Rome. This, in their opinion, overcame the Community's objection that Norway's demands violated Article 7 of the same Treaty which prohibits 'discrimination on grounds of nationality'. According to this proposal, citizens of other EEC states would be free to fish within Norwegian fishing limits provided they were resident in Norway. More specifically, the Norwegians demanded that the Community rules of establishment would have to ensure that the fishing enterprises and vessels concerned were registered in Norway. Moreover, at least 50 per cent of the capital involved would have to be held by people living in the country and the majority of the directors would have to be resident in Norway. In other words:

> those who want to exploit these limited resources should share the lot of those who live there and ... the exploitation of these resources should be undertaken on equal terms. (Int. doc. 1971a)

A solution based on the 'right of establishment' was also justified by Norway on the grounds that it alone would permit an effective control of conservation measures within the coastal zone:

> the long nature of the Norwegian coastline makes it impossible to control fishing effort unless the fishing fleet which is allowed to fish here is attached to the coast by establishment there. (Int. doc. 1971b)

Norway suggested that these 'establishment' proposals could be extended to other member states. However, the French had presented similar arguments during negotiations among the 'Six' and had been vigorously opposed. In the delicately balanced 'package-deal' underpinning the CFP, France abandoned this position in exchange for concessions elsewhere. This helps explain why Norway's proposals received a negative response from the Community. Nevertheless, the Norwegians insisted that they had conceded their maximum. The only alternative to the 'right of establishment' procedure was the complete exclusion of non-Norwegian fishermen from Norway's national fishing zone.

The Norwegian government certainly had severe constraints on its freedom of manoeuvre. While trying to win approval for its access proposals in Brussels, strong opposition was being voiced by fishermen and anti-common market circles in Norway; the president of a Norwegian fisheries co-operative was unequivocal:

> Why enter the European Community? We are happy as we are. We have absolutely no desire to be governed by Brussels. What does the common market represent for us? The arrival of foreign trawlers in our waters, the end of our means of existence. (*Le Monde* 1972)

Such problems were exacerbated by the extremely fragile nature of the parliamentary situation in Norway. When the enlargement negotiations were opened in June 1970, Norway was governed by a minority conservative coalition headed by Mr Borten, leader of a Centre Party dependent on rural support. Within the country a finely balanced debate between those for and against common market membership was developing. In March 1971 Mr Borten, personally hostile to Norway joining the EEC, was forced to resign. He was succeeded by a minority Social Democratic government led by Mr Bratteli, who, like the majority of his party, favoured membership of the Community if 'adequate' conditions of entry could be achieved. However, Mr Bratteli faced much opposition within the Parliament. At least thirty-seven deputies stated that they would oppose membership and only thirty-eight 'anti-market' votes were required to block it. The position was further complicated in that Norway had decided to hold a consultative referendum on Community membership. Clearly, a finely balanced Storting could be decisively swayed by the outcome of this referendum. Thus, the Norwegian negotiators in Brussels had to achieve an enlargement agreement that was very obviously favourable, particularly on emotive issues like the protection of fishermen in remote regions of Norway.

Whereas equal access to fishing grounds was perceived as a 'loss' for Norway, free access of Norwegian fish products to the large fish-deficient markets of the Community was obviously a potential 'gain'. Furthermore, market support from the EAGGF was something from which Norwegian fishermen could benefit. But some changes in the market regulation were demanded to take account of Norway's 'special' difficulties arising from its 'geographical' characteristics and its position as Europe's major exporter of fish (Int. doc. 1971a).

Norway's membership would convert the EEC from a net importer to a net exporter of fish and this, argued the Norwegians, would require a more liberal import system. Protective measures taken by the Community were likely to stimulate retaliatory action elsewhere and damage Norwegian export prospects. As regards the internal market organization, the Norwegians insisted that most commercial fish must be sold through POs. Given the large number of scattered landing points around the lengthy, fragmented Norwegian coastline, such an 'extension of discipline' was considered of 'fundamental importance' by the Norwegian government if effective market stabilization was to be achieved. They could not accept the CFP provisions which gave fishermen freedom of choice whether or not to join a PO.

The dispersed and isolated nature of Norwegian fishing communities also led to a demand for the 'regionalization' of the market support mechanisms. The existing regulation only applied to fresh fish. Given that many Norwegian producers were far from the main centres of consumption and had to process their catch before marketing, Norway demanded that processed fish products be eligible for Community support as well. Furthermore, it argued that the system of price support should not operate uniformly throughout the whole Community. Remote Norwegian fishing communities had to pay greater transport costs than those nearer the large markets of Europe. It was therefore essential to apply a flexible system of market support.

However, Norwegian demands on market organization and external trade called for *adaptations* of the CFP's provisions, rather than radical *revisions* of basic principles. Many Norwegians knew that they exported 80–90 per cent of their fish catch and that, if a satisfactory answer could be found to the fishing access problem, benefits could accrue to Norway's fishing industry as a result of EEC membership.

Finally, Norway wanted Community recognition that, in fishing, it was a 'special case' requiring separate treatment. This conformed to its history of independent action in international fishery policy. Consequently, the Norwegians always refused to co-operate with the other applicants in the negotiations over equal access to fishing grounds.

British interests

The UK's negotiating posture on the CFP was more flexible than that of Norway. This, to a large extent, reflected the British government's subjection to various conflicting pressures within the national fishing industry. British inshore fishermen vociferously pressed the government to reject the equal-access provisions. They wanted to keep the 12-mile exclusive national fishing zone established by the 1964 European Fisheries Convention (Hamley 1971). But Britain's distant-water fishing industry had a different view of the CFP's access provisions. For an industry increasingly eliminated from the rich traditional fishing grounds of Scandinavia and North America, the equal-access principle in a Community including Norway had an obvious attraction. Furthermore, the possibility that united common market strength might gain more fishing access to these increasingly restricted grounds was an additional potential advantage. Mr Laing, the Director-General of the British Trawlers' Federation, admitted that:

it would seem that inshore fishermen on this issue can hardly look for the support of distant-water fishermen because the latter seek – within the bounds of equity and properly observed conservation measures designed to preserve maximum sustainable yield – the utmost freedom of access to waters everywhere. Stated in this way, distant-water fishermen find Article 2 (i.e. the CFP's equal-access provision) perfectly acceptable. (Laing 1971-2)

However, Mr Laing accepted that inshore fishermen should be given 'fair and clear-cut protection' by an inshore fishing limit. But, whereas the British inshore fishermen were insisting on a 12-mile limit, Mr Laing argued for 'the reservation of the inner 6 miles for the exclusive use of local inshore fishermen' (Laing 1971-2). In what he termed the 'common waters' beyond six miles, Mr Laing pressed strongly for equality of access. In fact, he thought the CFP's existing provisions inadequate to ensure such freedom from national discrimination. He noted that the individual member states remained free to determine their national fishery zones and the regulations operating within them. This led him to fear that a member state would be able to declare a 12- or even 50-mile limit and then devise a series of 'conservation' measures that 'in fact' if not 'in form' restricted entry of fishermen from other common market countries. Consequently, the Community should assume responsibility for all conservation measures, both within 6-mile national zones and in what he thought should be the 'common waters' beyond them (Laing 1971-2). Thus, as one observer of the CFP negotiations stated:

In these negotiations the UK government tended to suffer from schizophrenia. On the one hand a powerful inshore fishing lobby was pressing for nothing less than a 12-mile limit, in other words, a maintenance of the status quo, while an equally vociferous distant-water fishing lobby wanted fishing grounds opened up so that its members could go trawling in the rich Norwegian grounds. (Churchill, Simmonds and Welch 1973, 286)

Such contradictory pressures were not the only factors producing flexibility among British negotiators. The determination of Mr Heath's government to achieve British entry into the Community made the thought of such a major goal foundering on a relatively minor fisheries problem difficult to entertain. Although the parliamentary position of the UK government was not as precarious as that of its Norwegian counterpart, there were powerful 'anti-market' forces in both major political parties and in the public at large. Fishing access was an emotive issue that EEC opponents could use to support their arguments about loss of sovereignty, failure to protect national interests, and so on. Thus, the British government needed a settlement of this dispute that would not alienate parliamentary and public support.

In pursuit of such a settlement, the British government was reluctant to accept that the CFP formed part of the 'acquis communautaire' given that it had been adopted at a most 'inopportune' moment. Its negotiators pointedly observed that equal access among the 'Six' was not important given their limited inshore resources, whereas the fishing grounds of the 'Four' were rich and would endure 'real effects of great political significance' if national barriers were removed (Int. doc. 1970). They stressed the importance of the British inshore fleet operating from ports widely scattered around the coast and producing some 40 per cent of the UK's catch for human consumption. They insisted that inshore fisheries under British jurisdiction had been carefully conserved, but were now being exploited at maximum level. Equal access would lead to overfishing and lost jobs, which was unacceptable (Int. doc. 1971c).

But, as already seen, the British government was also under pressure from a distant-water fishing industry attracted by the equal-access provisions. Consequently, it sought an arrangement that, although rejecting complete equality of access free from national discrimination, would be more liberal than the 'inner 6–outer 6' 12-mile exclusive fishing limits permitted in the 1964 European Fisheries Convention. Britain therefore proposed 'that waters within a 6-mile limit only, measured from the usual baselines, should be reserved for vessels genuinely belonging to the ports from which such waters are being fished' (Int. doc. 1971d). It will be noted that this proposal involved an 'establishment procedure' similar to the one favoured by the Norwegians and bore a strong resemblance to the ideas put forward by Mr Laing of the distant-water British Trawlers' Federation (see above). But the Secretary of the Inshore Fisheries Organization Society was very hostile to this British proposal; he articulated a widespread feeling among his members:

> Mr Rippon's team (without prior consultation with the industry) made a quite startling 'offer' to the 'Six' on fisheries on 1 June

1971.... Thus in this complicated 'bartering' on fishing rights, if all the applicants join the EEC, the 6- to 12-mile waters around our coastline could well be opened up for almost unlimited exploitation by nine other countries, as compared with only marginal historical access rights now granted to a few countries on strict international agreements.... Thus our stocks of fish and the breeding grounds for future supplies could well be decimated in a short time by over-exploitation and a virile forward looking industry in Britain could rapidly be brought to economic disaster. (Hamley 1971)

This reaction from inshore fishermen, and the impact it had on parliamentary attitudes in Britain, led the UK government to modify its initial proposal and advocate the maintenance of the 'status quo' on fishing limits (i.e. the 1964 Convention regime) until after enlargement, when a permanent settlement could be sought. Once in the Community the British government knew that it would be in a stronger bargaining position and have the *de facto* power of veto.

The British government, under pressure from inshore fishermen, also became increasingly determined that Norway should not receive more 'favoured' treatment than other applicants on the access question and pressed for multilateral negotiations on the issue involving the whole 'Ten' states (Int. doc. 1971c). However, for tactical reasons, the Norwegians and the 'Six' preferred to negotiate within the separate bilateral 'Community-applicant' frameworks established for the enlargement negotiations in general.

Britain also wanted some modification of the CFP's market provisions. Like Norway, Britain basically wanted a regionalization of the Community price levels which determined when fish would be withdrawn and what levels of compensation would be available from EAGGF funds (Mackintosh 1972). But these demands did not threaten any fundamental elements of the CFP.

Irish interests

Irish attitudes to the CFP were moulded by the inshore, underdeveloped character of their fishing industry and centred overwhelmingly on the issue of equal access. There was a fear that such access to Ireland's coastal zones would adversely affect the growing inshore fishing industry. Thus, the Irish refused to abandon their

12-mile national fishing limit, as the President of the Irish Sea Fisheries Board made clear:

> It is because they know that these resources are available to them and not threatened in the near future that Irish fishermen have invested their money in this industry. If Ireland accepted, in its present form, the common market provisions, concerning the equality of access to fishing grounds, all these advantages would be reduced to nothing and the growth of the industry would be immediately and forever stopped by the destruction of our coastal resources . . . as for the possibility of European fishermen respecting Irish resources, it is rather unlikely. (O'Kelly 1971)

This would entail 'grave consequences' for Ireland's fishermen who, in general, lived in areas heavily dependent on fishing, had incomes below the national average, were often farmer/fishermen whose income from fishing was essential for economic survival, had few alternative forms of employment, and lived in poor peripheral regions where the rate of emigration was high. The Irish also pointed out that they were not equipped to fish away from home waters and therefore could not hope to benefit from reciprocal access to the fishery waters of other member states.

Furthermore, it was a 'prime aim of Irish government policy' to enlarge its fishing industry which, unlike others in western Europe, was 'still at an early stage of development' (Int. doc. 1971f). In consequence, the Irish government thought it best to maintain existing fishing rights until after Community enlargement and then seek an 'equitable' solution. This 'status quo' proposal was later taken up by the British (see above).

The Irish did not accept that this approach was contrary to Community principles. They reminded the 'Six' that an objective of the CFP was to provide a 'fair standard of living for all'; their access proposals were designed to achieve this end! Moreover, argued the Irish, who were quickly becoming adept manipulators of Community principles, Article 39.2 of the Rome Treaty specifically provided that account shall be taken of 'the structural and natural disparities between various regions'. Surely this lifted the obligation to apply identical treatment to all areas? On a similar point, the Irish were aware of Norway's claim for 'special treatment' and insisted that 'there is absolutely no question of Ireland accepting a solution less favourable than that offered to other applicant states' (Int. doc. 1971g). All these demands were reinforced by the fact that the Irish government needed public as well as parliamentary support for the terms of EEC entry, especially as the whole issue was to be subject to a referendum and fisheries had become an emotive issue in Ireland's 'common market' debate.

Danish interests

Denmark's objectives were moulded by two basic sets of interests. First, those of Denmark itself and, secondly, those of its semi-independent territories of the Faroes and Greenland. Denmark's large fishing industry depends heavily on waters beyond its adjacent coastal zone; in particular, it has a fundamental interest in maintaining freedom of access within the North Sea. Consequently, mainland Danes sought to keep access to fishing grounds as international as possible. On the other hand, the Faroes and Greenland had important coastal fisheries and were increasingly dependent upon them. As a result, the Danish government had pursued policies restricting access of foreign vessels to the coastal zones of these territories. Such protective policies had become more pronounced as the Faroese were progressively excluded from their traditional distant-water activities around Iceland, Canada and elsewhere.

The Danish government reconciled these divergent interests by proposing two different access regimes. First, a 'general regime' requiring that all member states should gradually move towards acceptance of the equal-access principle during a transition period not exceeding ten years in which exclusive national fishing zones of six miles could be maintained. Secondly, a 'special exception regime' should be created for regions such as the Faroes and Greenland where alternative employment was 'very limited' or 'non-existent' and the threat of depopulation was great. The Danes proposed that such regions should have exclusive use of a 12-mile coastal zone for at least ten years. If after ten years the degree of dependence on fishing remained high, then the 'special exception regime' should continue. Furthermore, they argued that if the conditions governing fishing in one of these 'exception' regions were 'modified' by the extension of limits elsewhere in the world, the Community would have to find 'appropriate solutions which might include an extension of the 12-mile limit'. In acting thus, the Danes emphasized the special constitutional position of the Faroes and demanded that the Faroes enjoy a three-year interim period from 1 January 1973 during which time they would decide whether or not to join the enlarged European Community after seeing the CFP in operation (Int. doc. 1971h).

As for Denmark itself, equality of access 'presented no problem' (Norgaard 1971); indeed, it resisted an unwelcome trend towards ever larger exclusive fishing zones. The Danes were prepared to accept 'special exception regimes' for regions like the Faroes and Greenland, but were firmly opposed to less 'dependent' fishing communities (e.g. those in the UK) getting similar treatment. They especially wished to maintain the idea of national non-discrimination in the North Sea upon which Danish fishing was overwhelmingly focused. Opposing the extension of special exception status to eastern Britain and southern Norway, they were adamant that 'coastal regions bordering the same waters must receive the same treatment; otherwise, fishermen exercising their activities in the same zone would be subjected to different conditions of competition' (Int. doc. 1971h).

The Danes broadly accepted the market and trade regulations of the CFP, although they wanted some modifications. The entry of Norway and Denmark would turn the Community into a large net exporter of fish and more attention would have to be given to encouraging overseas sales and liberalizing the international trading arrangements. Again like Norway, they also wanted market support by the EAGGF to extend to processed fish products not included in the original regulations; this clearly reflected Denmark's position as a major processor of fish. Such demands challenged nothing fundamental.

Interests of the 'Six'

The 'Six' negotiated as a single Community in the enlargement negotiations after agreeing common positions in co-operation with the Commission. Such agreement was difficult to achieve, but the fact that they had adopted a CFP meant that there was a basic 'package' of interests in which everyone had some stake. This enabled the 'Six' to maintain a more or less common front on fisheries throughout the enlargement negotiations.

In meeting the objections of the applicants, the Community insisted that the equal-access provisions stemmed directly from a fundamental principle in the Rome Treaty and were thus inviolable. Furthermore, the proposal made by some applicants, notably Norway, that the access provisions should be modified according to another fundamental principle of the Rome Treaty – the right of establishment – was firmly rejected (Int. doc. 1971i). Why did the 'Six' adopt such an uncompromising position?

It will be recalled that the CFP agreement among the 'Six' was based on complex 'bargaining' in which a series of interlinked compromises was made to conciliate very divergent objectives. The prospect of equal access to fishing grounds in an enlarged Community of 'Ten' formed an important part of this finely balanced 'package deal'. Thus, elimination or substantial modification of the equal-access principle in the enlarged Community would threaten the delicate equilibrium upon which the CFP was based. If West Germany lost the prospect of freer access to the waters of the enlarged Community, its reluctance to sanction the use of Community funds in the fishing industry would intensify to the cost of the French. If the French lost the prospect of freer access to the waters of the enlarged Community their reluctance to accept the freer access of fish products into France would be increased to the cost of the fish-exporting states such as the Netherlands.

It is also important that the French in particular had a strong interest in maintaining the CFP in its entirety. France had most reservations about Community enlargement in general and had blocked it in the past to the regret of its five partners. Therefore an additional factor weighing on the fisheries negotiations was the fear that France might use the conflict over the access issue to prevent entry of the applicants on the grounds that they were not prepared to accept fundamental Community principles.

Negotiations between the 'Six' and the 'Four'

Official negotiations about the CFP began in June 1971 when agreement on most of the other major 'enlargement' questions was close. However, the 'Four' had been registering their objections throughout the year preceding June 1971. Gradually the basic negotiating positions described above and presented in simplified form in Table 5.1 had evolved. It is important to stress the simplifications in Table 5.1. Most delegations maintained a certain ambiguity about their objectives as they sought some generally 'satisfactory' settlement based on an 'overall balance of interests' within the enlarged Community. Moreover, time was an important factor in the process of decision; the attitudes of various delegations changed as parliamentary deadlines were passed, other issues were settled, and a process of

Table 5.1 Simplified matrix of objectives among the 'Ten'

Objectives	France	Italy	W. Germany	Netherlands	Belgium	The 'Six'	Commission	UK	Ireland	Denmark Den	F/G	Norway
1 Enlargement of the EEC	√?	√	√	√	√	√	√	√	√	√	?	√
2 Need to win public/parliamentary support for enlargement	×?	×	×	×	×	×	×	√+	√	√	√	√+
3 Protect the 'acquis communautaire'	√+	√	√	√	√	√	√	×	×	√?	×	×
4 Equal access based on national non-discrimination	√	√	√	√	√	√	√	×	×	√	×	×
Access based on the right of establishment	×	×	×	×	×	×	×	?	–	×	–	√
Access based on other EEC principles (eg: conservation)	×	×	×	×	×	×	×	√	√	×	–	–
5 Exceptions to equal access strictly limited in time	√	√	√	√	√	√	√	×	×	–	×	×
Exceptions to equal access as long as 'necessary'	×	×	×	×	×	×	×	√	√	√	√	–
Exceptions to equal access on a permanent basis	×	×	×	×	×	×	×	–	–	–	–	√
6 Exceptions to equal access for areas where fishing important	×	×	×	×	×	×	×	√	√	×	–	√
Exceptions to equal access for areas 'essentially dependent' on fishing	√	√	√	√	√	√	√	×	×	√	√	×
7 No preferential access regime for particular states	√	–	?	?	?	√	?	√	√	√	√	×
Special access regime for particular states (Norway)	×	×	?	?	?	×	?	×	×	×	×	√
8 'Status quo' access regime with decision in enlarged Community	×	×	×	×	×	×	×	√	√+	×	–	×
9 Preservation of national veto on access decisions in enlarged Community	×	×	×	×	×	×	×	√	√	–	√	√
Definite progress towards common Community access regime during transition period	√	√	√	√	√	√	√	×	×	?	×	×
10 Community aid to compensate for loss of exclusive fishing zones of member states	√+	√	–	–	–	√	√	–	–	–	–	–
11 Common Community conservation measures beyond scope of original CFP	×	×	×	×	×	×	√	√	–	√	–	√
12 More liberal EEC external fish trade regime	×	–	–	–	–	–	–	–	–	√	–	√
13 Adjustments to internal CFP market regulations	?	–	–	–	–	–	–	√	√	√	√	√

Note: √ Perceived gain; × perceived loss; ? ambiguity/uncertainty; – lack of evidence.

Table 5.2 Simplified matrix of elements in agreement among the 'Ten'

Basic elements of agreement amongst the 'Ten'	France	Italy	W. Germany	Netherlands	Belgium	The 'Six'	Commission	UK	Ireland	Denmark Den	F/G	Norway
1 Enlargement of EEC	√	√	√	√	√	√	√	√	√	√	?	√
2 Agreement capable of winning public/parliamentary support for EEC membership or Community enlargement	√	√	√	√	√	√	√	√	√	√	?	?
3 Protection of 'acquis communautaire'	√	√	√	√	√	√	√	×	×	√	×	×
4 Equal access based on principle of non-discrimination on grounds of nationality	√	√	√	√	√	√	√	×	×	√	×	×
8 Some liberalization of access to national fishing zones in enlarged EEC	√	√	√	√	√	√	√	?	×	√	?	×
Maintenance of 'historic rights' in enlarged EEC	√	√	√	√	√	√	√	–	–	√	√	–
5 6 Widespread area exceptions to equal-access provisions during 10-year transition period in areas where inshore fishing important	×	×	×	×	×	×	×	√	√	×	?	√
9 Ambiguity/uncertainty about how, when and where equal-access provisions to be applied after 10-year transition period ending 31/12/82	×	×	×	×	×	×	×	√	√	×	×	×
7 No preferential treatment for Norway (apart from minimal 'concessions' in the special protocol)	√	√	√?	√?	√?	√?	√?	√	√	√	–	× (√?)
11 Common conservation measures beyond scope of original CFP within 6 years of enlargement	–	–	–	–	–	–	√	√	–	√	–	–
12 13 Modifications to CFP market and trade regulations within enlarged EEC	×	–	–	–	–	–	–	√	√	√	√	√

Note: √ Perceived gain; × perceived loss; ? ambiguity/uncertainty; – lack of evidence.

'attrition' took effect. Norway, however, formed a notable exception by sticking rigidly to the demand for unequivocal guarantees to protect its inshore fishermen.

THE COMMUNITY MODIFIES ITS POSITION

Faced with the opposition of the 'Four' and torn by internal dissension about how to deal with it, the Community eventually relaxed its original position in the following package of proposals:

1   A new agreement would have to 'respect the principles and objectives' of the existing CFP.
2   Fishing-access arrangements would have to apply equally to both old and new member states. .
3   A transition period of 10 years could be allowed before equal access was introduced. This was 5 years more than allowed under the existing CFP regulation.
4   This transition period would be divided into two stages. During the first 5 years member states could reserve an exclusive 6-mile national fishing zone on condition that the existing traditional rights of all Community fishermen were respected. During the second 5-year stage member states would be able to reserve a 6-mile zone for local fishermen *if* they depended 'essentially' on inshore fishing. This 6-mile zone was larger than the 3 miles permitted in the existing CFP regulation.
5   For the second 5-year stage it would be the Council of Ministers that determined the nature, extent and application of restrictions in the 6-mile coastal zone, *not* individual member states. Thus a definite step towards establishing a common Community system of access was envisaged.
6   At the end of the 10-year transition period, the Commission would report to the Council of Ministers on the social and economic situation in fishing regions and the state of fish stocks. If this report maintained that the introduction of equal access at that time was likely to produce 'unfavourable' developments in certain regions that 'depended essentially' on inshore fishing, the Council of Ministers would take appropriate 'social and economic measures'. However, if there were no such circumstances the equal-access provisions would henceforth be implemented.
7   In addition to these arrangements a 'special exception regime' could be permitted in certain 'strictly limited geographical zones'

that lacked alternative resources and employment. The zones proposed were as follows: Norway, north of Trondheim; the Faroes and Greenland; the Orkneys and Shetlands. In these regions a 12-mile exclusive fishing limit would be allowed during the first 5 years of the transition period. During the second 5-year period, this 12-mile belt might be continued, but it would be the Council of Ministers, not the individual member states concerned, who would decide on this. This emphasized the determination of the 'Six' to make access to fishing grounds subject to Community rather than national decision. The traditional rights of all EEC fishermen in these 'special exception zones' would have to be respected.

8   With regard to market organization, the Community agreed to the demand that withdrawal prices could be adjusted regionally so that fishermen in remote areas would obtain satisfactory access to major markets. It also conceded Norway's insistence on an 'extension of discipline' for POs. Moreover, the desire of the Scandinavian applicants for common market support systems for deep-frozen fish, fish-meal and fish-oil was conceded (E 1971c).

THE REACTION OF THE APPLICANTS

Despite these concessions the reactions of the applicants were uniformly hostile. Predictably, the Norwegians completely rejected the access proposals but agreed that their market demands had been largely satisfied. The British could not accept the provisions designed to bring control of fishing access more fully within the scope of common Community decision. They insisted that the system proposed for the first five years must apply to the whole ten-year transition period. Aware of the demands of inshore fishermen in regions such as South West England, they rejected the notion that only regions 'essentially dependent' on fishing should have a 12-mile special exception regime. Britain also stressed the importance of using resource conservation as a criterion for determining these exception zones. In particular, it emphasized the importance of conserving shellfish in certain regions, such as South West England. And the UK negotiators insisted that some clearer notion of the access regime to follow the transition period be elaborated during the enlargement negotiations. It could not accept that equal access would become the rule after ten years unless the Council of Ministers decided otherwise. It was essential to have provisions that would permit individual member states to maintain exclusive national fishing limits. What the British wanted were fishing-access arrangements on some 'continuing basis subject to review'. These arrangements would have to be 'more than transitional' but 'not necessarily permanent' (Int. doc. 1971j) whatever that might mean!

So, the UK government declared itself 'flexible' in search of a 'fair balance' among the different interests of the 'Ten' and, one might add, between the conflicting demands of inshore and distant-water fishermen within Britain. Thus, despite its objections to Community access to inshore zones, the British delegation wanted to keep fishing grounds beyond six or twelve miles as open as possible. Here it was clearly thinking of possible future fishing limit extensions by Norway and the interests of British deep-sea fishermen. British flexibility was also determined by a desire to agree quickly because of the adverse effect the issue was having on parliamentary opinion and the wish to sign the Treaties of Accession before Christmas 1971. Thus on 9 November 1971, Mr Rippon suggested a multilateral negotiation involving the whole 'Ten' in order to break the various deadlocks blocking the separate bilateral discussions. But the 'Six' rejected this proposal, as did the Norwegians who, determined to emphasize their 'special' position, rejected such a communal 'bargaining' session.

The Irish government unambiguously rejected the Community's proposals, surprised that Ireland had not been accorded any 12-mile special exception zones and suggesting that such a regime should be applied to the whole of its coast. There was absolutely no question of the Irish accepting a solution less favourable than that offered to other applicants. They also supported the British in refusing to accept that their national powers to maintain exclusive fishing limits after the transition period be reduced as the Community wanted.

Denmark's response to the new proposals reflected the conflicting interests it had to represent. The Danes themselves welcomed the Community's determination to move towards the full implementation of the equal-access principle. On the other hand, the Faroese and Greenlanders welcomed the offer of a 12-mile special exception regime, but rejected the idea that equal access remained the ultimate goal. In order to escape from this uncomfortable position, the Danish government proposed a 'regionalized' access system. In the more southerly parts of offshore Europe, movement towards a genuine equal-access regime was thought essential to get an equitable balance of interests between member states. However, in regions 'truly dependent' on fishing – such as the Faroes and Greenland – exceptions to this principle should be assured for as long as necessary without reference to the transition period! This proposal neatly maximized all Denmark's objectives by liberalizing access to the fishing grounds of the North Sea upon which Danish fishermen depended, but restricting access in the regions whose populations the Danes wanted to protect (Int. doc. 1971h).

FURTHER COMMUNITY CONCESSIONS

Following rejection of the Community's proposals by the applicants, the Commission advocated further concessions. But the Council of Ministers insisted that the principle of equal access must remain; any exceptions to it must be temporary in juridical character. However, some of the 'Six' favoured rather loose provisions that would clearly allow exceptions to continue after the transition period, whereas others wanted a much stricter agreement whereby transition to an equal-access regime after ten years would be difficult to avoid. In particular, the French insisted that temporary exceptions must not become permanent. France had most to lose if the fragile equilibrium of national interests underpinning the original CFP agreement was shattered. Eventually the Council put a new set of proposals to the applicants.

1 Despite the resistance of the Dutch, the British demand for a single-stage ten-year transition period was conceded, thus reducing the rate of progress towards a Community access regime to be decided by the Council of Ministers.

2 In addition to the 12-mile special exception zones proposed by the Community on 9 November 1971 (see above), similar zones could be extended to shellfishermen in Ireland and certain regions of Britain. The north west coast of Ireland was accorded this special exception for all types of fishermen.

3 The 'Six' still insisted that any such exceptions must not interfere with traditional fishing rights.

4 For those regions that did not qualify for a continuation of a 12-mile zone at the end of the transition period, but where fishing was still of special importance, the Community suggested the 'possibility' of social and economic aid from EEC funds to deal with any remaining problems of adaptation to a common regime.

5 The Council also stated that these new concessions on the access

problem did not affect the market proposals of 9 November 1971 upon which general agreement had been reached between the 'Six' and the 'Four'. The possibility of trying to 'trade-off' concessions on market organization against fishing access rights was thus rejected by the 'Six'.

6 Finally, in response to the conservation arguments of the 'Four', the Community proposed that not later than six years after enlargement the Council of Ministers would determine measures necessary to protect the sea fishery resources upon which the EEC depended. (*E* 1971d)

Another all-night 'marathon' negotiating session based on these proposals failed yet again to find an agreement through fatigue! None of the applicants thought the concessions adequate, but the degree of dissatisfaction varied greatly. At one extreme, the Norwegians refused to budge from their long-established positions. At the other, the Danes thought that most of the Community's proposals were acceptable, but, aware of the Faroese and Greenlanders, they still maintained certain 'reservations' about the decision-making procedures that would determine what would happen at the end of the transition period. Would the Community decision have to be unanimous? Would the Norwegians get more privileged treatment? The Irish restated their preference for maintaining the status quo, but were prepared to reach agreement before enlargement, provided its provisions applied equally to all the enlarged Community of 'Ten'. Moreover, as a minimum, they insisted that the whole of the west coast of Ireland must be granted special exception status. Furthermore, all herring fishing around Ireland would have to be protected by a 12-mile exclusive national limit. Finally, the Irish were adamant that any settlement would have to provide clearly for continuing exceptions to equal access beyond the transition period if that should prove necessary.

However, the bulk of the negotiations on 29–30 November 1971 took place between the Community and the UK. The British government, worried about the ultimate success of the whole enlargement process, was determined to reach an agreement and made strong diplomatic efforts to get the other applicants to do likewise. In particular, Mr Heath, the British Prime Minister, sent a personal letter to his Norwegian counterpart, Mr Bratteli, encouraging him to be more 'flexible' in dealings with the Community so that final agreement with all the applicants could be reached together (*E* 1971e).

Mr Heath expressed his fear that the Community's negotiators would abandon the flexibility they had been showing, arguing that the adoption of strictly rigid positions on matters where Community principle was at stake could be counterproductive. In his view, the 'Six' were ready to concede the substance of what Norway wanted, even though they were unwilling to grant it in unequivocal legal form. Given the way the Community functioned, Norway (and the other applicants) would be able to protect their fishing interests once they were members of it. Mr Heath also pointed to the risk of prolonging the negotiations too long and reminded Mr Bratteli that certain groups had an interest in seeing the negotiations fail.

However, Mr Heath's attempt to make the Norwegians more accommodating came to nothing. So the UK government made counterproposals to those of the Community in an attempt to take the initiative away from the Community and put the 'Six' in the position of being 'demandeurs'. They were as follows:

1   A special 12-mile exception regime be extended to 95 per cent of Britain's coast! In effect, this meant the maintenance of the 'status quo' which the 'Six' had earlier rejected and was much more than the British government had asked for at the start of the fishery negotiations in June 1971! This increased demand was partly in response to the growing pressures within Britain and partly a strategy to outflank the Norwegians (and the Community) by demanding the sort of maximum special treatment that Norway was insisting upon.

2   Although not rejecting the 'principle' of equal access, exclusive national fishing zones would not automatically finish at the end of the transitional period. It was essential not to prejudge any final access regime, but simply provide that the Council of Ministers would decide what to do in ten years' time. (E 1971d)

The 'Six' rejected these British proposals on the following grounds:

1   The quasi-totality of British coastal regions would be thus accorded 'special exception treatment'.

2   The idea of a genuine transitional period was negated. The Community, following the French argument, insisted that transitional periods must be truly transitional and that there must be no ambiguity that the final objective of the CFP's fishing rights provisions was to ensure equality of access to fishing grounds free from national discrimination. (E 1971d)

At this point Mr Rippon at the head of the UK delegation made a reportedly angry effort to take the debate out of the realms of 'legal' intricacies into what Community politicians rather oddly call the 'political' and 'economic' spheres (as though the juridical nit-picking had no economic and political base!). Did the Community really want to threaten the livelihood of certain regional populations? If the Community did not want to leave the nature of the post-transition regime an open question, then it was essential to define its characteristics by taking account of 'real situations' rather than abstract Community 'principles'. Furthermore, Mr Rippon declared his astonishment that such an historic event as British entry into the European Community could be held up by a relatively minor problem. Moreover, one could not regard the CFP as part of the real 'acquis communautaire' for everyone was aware that it had been rushed to partial conclusion just before enlargement negotiations had begun (E 1971d).

Following this attempt to raise the negotiations from the morass of legal ambiguities into which they had sunk, the Council made further concessions which included the following main points:

1   The whole Scottish coast was added to the growing list of regions benefiting from a 12-mile 'special exception regime'.
2   A rather more subtle concession concerned the sorts of actions that might be permitted to help fishing communities. The 'Six' had initially proposed Community 'measures of a social and economic nature' to help any fishing populations in difficulty at the end of the transition period. This implied that the continuation of exclusive national inshore zones would not be one of the means permitted to help such communities. The new proposal enabled the Community to introduce 'any measure' to help inshore fishing communities at the end of the transition period; this implicitly admitted the possible continuation of exclusive national fishing zones. (E 1971d)

However, the 'Six' still insisted that such measures would have to be taken up by unanimous vote in the Council of Ministers. If such unanimity did not exist then the equal-access provisions would be implemented! This was impossible for Britain (and the Irish and Danes) to accept. Moreover, the Community's continued insistence that any special measures after ten years could only apply to those regions 'essentially dependent' on fishing prevented a settlement at this stage despite the eagerness of the British to conclude.

It is noteworthy that the Commission, which had always tended to be more conciliatory in its proposals than the 'Six' member states, had wanted to eradicate the 'unanimity' and 'essentially dependent' clauses in this arduous attempt to reach agreement with the British, Irish and Danes. But France, in particular, refused to make more concessions. The battle to find a compromise combining balanced doses of commitment and ambiguity was to continue for at least another round.

Final agreement among all except Norway

While the Norwegians refused to budge from their initial objectives, the 'Six' and the 'Three' (without Norway) eventually reached an agreement after an arduous Ministerial meeting lasting from 9.30 a.m. on 11 December 1971 to 7.00 a.m. on 12 December 1971. The Norwegians apart, it was clear that none saw advantage in prolonging the negotiations further; the costs of failing to agree were now perceived as outweighing any possible future gains. In particular, the cost of jeopardizing the major goal of Community enlargement was seen as too great a price to pay for possible benefits in the restricted field of fisheries. The final text of the agreement ultimately incorporated into the Treaty of Accession read as follows:

Article 100
1   Notwithstanding the provisions of Article 2 of Regulation (EEC) No. 2141/70 on the establishment of a common structural policy for the fishing industry, the member states of the Community are authorized, until 31 December 1982, to restrict fishing in waters under their sovereignty or jurisdiction, situated within a limit of six nautical miles, calculated from the base lines of the coastal member state, to vessels which fish traditionally in those waters and which operate from ports in that geographical coastal area; however, vessels from other regions of Denmark may continue to fish in the waters of Greenland until 31 December 1977 at the latest.
    Member states may not, insofar as they avail themselves of this derogation, adopt provisions dealing with conditions for fishing in those waters which are less restrictive than those applied in practice at the time of accession.
2   The provisions laid down in the preceding paragraph and in the Article 101 shall not prejudice the special fishing rights which

each of the original member states and new member states might have enjoyed on 31 January 1971 in regard to one or more other member states; the member states may exercise these rights for such a time as derogations continue to apply in the areas concerned. As regards the waters of Greenland, however, the special rights shall expire on the dates laid down for these rights.

3 If a member state extends its fishing limits in certain areas to twelve nautical miles, the existing fishing activities within twelve nautical miles must be so pursued that there is no retrograde change by comparison with the situation on 31 January 1971.

4 In order to permit a satisfactory overall balance of fishing operations to be established within the Community during the period referred to in the first paragraph, the member states need not make full use of the opportunities presented by the provisions of the first subparagraph 1 in certain areas of the maritime waters under their sovereignty or jurisdiction.

The member states shall inform the Commission of the measures which they adopt for this purpose; on a report from the Commission, the Council shall examine the situation and, in the light thereof, shall, where necessary, address recommendations to the member states.

Article 101
The limit of six nautical miles referred to in Article 100 shall be extended to twelve nautical miles for the following areas:
1 Denmark
   – the Faroe Islands;
   – Greenland;
   – the west coast, from Thyboren to Blaavandshuk.
2 France
   – the coasts of the départements of Manche, Ille-et-Vilaine, Côtes-du-Nord, Finistère and Morbihan.
3 Ireland
   – the north and west coasts,from Lough Foyle to Cork harbour in the south west;
   – the east coast, from Carlingford to Carnsore Point, for crustaceans and molluscs (shellfish).
4 United Kingdom
   – the Shetlands and Orkneys;
   – the north and east of Scotland, from Cape Wrath to Berwick;

- the north east of England, from the River Coquet to Flamborough Head;
- the south west from Lyme Regis to Hartland Point (including twelve nautical miles around Lundy Island);
- County Down.

Article 102
From the sixth year after accession at the latest, the Council, acting on a proposal from the Commission, shall determine conditions for fishing with a view to ensuring protection of the fishing grounds and conservation of the biological resources of the sea.

Article 103
Before 31 December 1982, the Commission shall present a report to the Council on the economic and social development of the coastal areas of the member states and the state of stocks. On the basis of that report, and of the objectives of the common fisheries policy, the Council, acting on a proposal from the Commission, shall examine the provisions which could follow the derogations in force until 31 December 1982. (*Treaties Establishing the European Communities* 1973)

The 'Six' and the 'Three' also agreed that this solution to the fishing access problem did not alter the agreement of the common organization of fishery markets reached earlier on 8 November 1971. There was no question of the 'Six' restricting access of fish products to their markets to counterbalance the access restrictions placed on their fishing vessels.

This accord was reached after demands were lessened on all sides and an acceptable level of ambiguity was found on several contentious issues. In particular, the 'Six' conceded more 12-mile special exception regimes to the applicants, and the 'Three' accepted the principle of equality of access, albeit in an equivocal manner.

CONCESSIONS BY THE 'SIX'

12-mile special exception zones
The demands of the British and Irish for 12-mile special exception regimes increased throughout the negotiations as domestic pressures built up and a determination to get parity of treatment with Norway became a prime objective. The Danes had persisted with similar claims

on behalf of the Faroese and the Greenlanders. At this final meeting the Community conceded most, but not all, the demands of the applicants. About one-third of the UK coast was granted a 12-mile limit (Map 5.1), although the north west coast of Scotland was excluded because baselines in this area already enclosed large inshore zones for the exclusive use of British fishermen. This agreement conceded considerably more than the original British demands in June 1971 (see above)! The British government did give a little in the north east of England; at the beginning of the final meeting the British had claimed a 12-mile zone from Berwick to Spurnhead, but this zone was trimmed down a little in the final 'bargaining' and extended the shorter distance from the River Coquet to Flamborough Head (Int. doc. 1971k).

Although only about a third of the UK coast received the special exception regime in addition to the generalized 6-mile limit, the British negotiators claimed that these zones accounted for about 95 per cent of the value of the British inshore catch (Hansard 1971). The British negotiators based this claim on the fact that about 95 per cent of the inshore landings took place in ports adjacent to these 12-mile zones. This logic conformed to the 'regional' principle of restricting access to inshore waters to 'vessels which fish traditionally in those waters and which operate from ports in that geographical coastal area' (see Article 100.1 above). The Irish succeeded in getting a 12-mile limit for about 70 per cent of their coast (Map 5.1) according to the same non-national principle and claimed that 90 per cent of the catches of Irish fishermen were thus protected (E 1971f).

Denmark had won a 12-mile special exception regime for the Faroes and Greenland at the earlier meeting of 29 November 1971. However, in this final agreement Denmark itself, a champion of the equal-access principle, obtained a 12-mile limit for a small part of its coastal region (Map 5.1). Moreover, France, the most fervent defender of the equal-access provisions during the enlargement negotiations, obtained a special exception regime for a substantial part of north west France, particularly Brittany (Map 5.1). Having seen the balance of the original agreement among the 'Six' upset and the prospect of freer access to the coastal zones of the applicant states whittled away, the French government insisted on re-establishing a 12-mile limit in the regions where inshore fishing was a major activity. The establishment of the very limited Danish 12-mile zone was similarly motivated; there was no point in abandoning national protection if greater reciprocal advantages were not forthcoming.

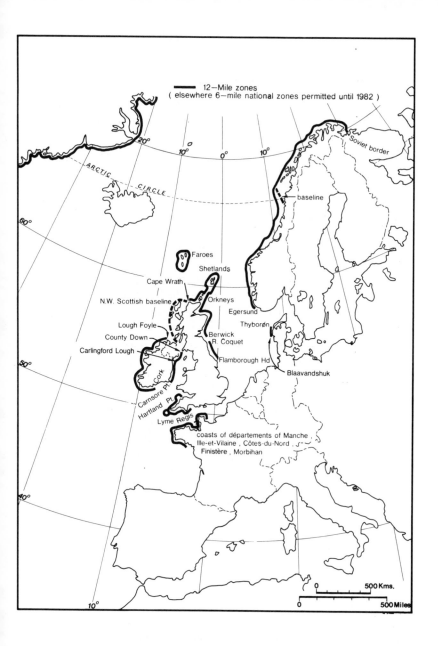

Map 5.1 The 12-mile special exception fishing zones permitted until 1982 by the EEC Treaty of Accession 1972

Source: Treaties Establishing the European Communities (1973).

Arrangements following the transition period

The 'Six' also gave ground on the nature of the access regime to be adopted at the end of the transition period, although less than most of the applicants would have liked. Agreement was finally struck on the basis of a statement (see Article 103 above) that was open to various interpretations. The 'Six' softened their insistence on a formula that would make the equal-access provisions widely, if not universally, applicable after the transition period; thus the Council of the *enlarged* Community would 'examine' what provisions 'could' follow 31 December 1982. There were no stipulations insisting, as the 'Six' had previously wanted, that any decision by the Council to continue exceptions to equality of access would have to be unanimous.

The British and Irish immediately clarified their interpretations of these rather vague clauses. Mr Rippon of the UK government publicly stated that the agreement made it 'clear' that what had been decided concerned not only the transition period, nor merely those regions that had been accorded special treatment (*E* 1971f). At the appropriate moment, according to him, the whole question would be re-examined and the final access system decided upon by the enlarged Community. This system might differ from the one established by the original CFP regulation. Mr Rippon stressed that as fishing represented a 'vital interest' for certain countries a 'reasonable solution' would doubtless be found. If the UK government considered that its fishermen needed reserved zones beyond the transition period, they would get them. Moreover, he concluded, the British would not be alone in wanting to protect its fishermen and the fish resources upon which they depended. Mr Hillery, for the Irish government, considered that the agreement provided adequate protection for Ireland's fishermen and would allow the local fishing industry to develop. He also stressed that the enlarged Community now had ten years during which it could formulate a permanent fishing-access regime; there was little point in being specific at this stage (*E* 1971f).

No 'special' status for Norway

The 'Six' also promised to accord 'special' treatment to Norway on the equal-access issue (*E* 1971f). A fear that Norway would obtain a favoured status, either *de facto* or *de jure*, had been an important factor blocking compromise between the 'Six' and the 'Three'. After the final meeting Mr Hillery explicitly declared that the Community had given formal assurances that the provisions governing what would follow the transition period (Article 103) were final and would apply to Norway as well.

CONCESSIONS BY THE 'THREE'

Although the 'Six' had retreated far from their original positions in reaching agreement with the 'Three' (Table 5.2), they did attain some of their objectives.

Maintenance of the equal-access principle

Although none of the applicants, save Denmark, was willing to incorporate the equal-access principle, they were forced to accept a policy of which it was still, however modified, a fundamental part. This point was stressed by the Ministers of the 'Six' after the final meeting. In sharp contrast to the interpretative statements of the British and the Irish Ministers (see above), the 'Six' insisted that the equal-access provisions still formed the legal basis of the new arrangements and would be generally applied after 31 December 1982, unless further exceptions could be justified by the institutions of the Community (E 1971f). Article 100 of the Accession Treaty made it clear that the exclusive national fishing zones of member states were temporary exceptions to the equal-access provision. Furthermore, Article 103 stated that the access regime to be established after the transition period should be based, not only on the report cited therein, but on the 'objectives of the CFP' which, of course, still included equality of access. Although the applicants had succeeded in weakening the possibility of attaining this objective, it was still enshrined in the legal foundations of the CFP ready to be employed in later disputes over fishing rights within the Community.

Maintenance of 'historic rights'

The 'Six' also succeeded in maintaining the 'special' rights they enjoyed on 31 January 1971 with regard to the applicant states (see Articles 100.2 and 100.3 of the Accession Treaty above). In essence, this preserved the historic rights established in the European Fisheries Convention of 1964 regardless of the fishing zones established in the Accession Treaty. In a world where access of the vessels of the 'Six' to fishing grounds was being increasingly restricted, this was an important gain.

A marginal liberalization of access

The agreement between the 'Six' and the 'Three' did involve some limited liberalization of fishing access within the Community. The 1964 European Fisheries Convention had permitted a 12-mile exclusive national fishing zone with exceptions granted in the 6- to 12-mile belt based on historic rights (Chapter 3). This meant, for example, that around the UK coastline a 12-mile limit was established with individual West European states enjoying access up to six miles in certain areas (Appendix Map 1.1). However, the new agreement entailed the generalization of access rights for EEC states in the 6- to 12-mile belt outside of the special 12-mile exception regime (Appendix Map 1.2). Whereas the 1964 Convention had established a permanent 12-mile national limit with individual exceptions in particular areas of the outer 6 miles, the new EEC agreement created a temporary 6-mile limit within the Community, with temporary exceptions out to 12 miles in particular areas and generalized access for all Community vessels in the parts of the outer 6 miles unaffected by special exception rights. Inshore fishermen in Britain expressed serious disquiet at this creeping erosion of what had been gained in 1964 (Hamley 1972). Essentially, the 'Six' had slightly improved their fishing access position vis-à-vis the new member states rather than obtained a radical reversal of the trend towards increasing national fishing limits. Furthermore, the applicant country with most important offshore fisheries of western Europe – Norway – was still steadfastly refusing to accept the compromise arrived at among the 'Nine'.

Agreement between the 'Six' and Norway

The Norwegians rejected the settlement made between the 'Six' and the 'Three' because it did not give sufficiently precise guarantees that their fishermen would continue to enjoy the protection of a national fishing limit beyond the ten-year transition period (*E* 1971f). Furthermore, they had persistently tried to separate themselves from the other candidates in order to obtain a distinct agreement that recognized their 'special' status in fisheries. But the agreement between the 'Six' and the 'Three' had been facilitated by an assurance that Norway would not get such favoured treatment. Thus, its chances of achieving substantially greater concessions were now non-existent. Just as the 'Six' had found it difficult to cope with the demands of the 'Four' because of the fear of upsetting the delicate balance of the original CFP agreement, so now the 'Six' knew that substantial concessions to the Norwegians would nullify the agreement they had reached with the other applicants. This was made clear in striking manner at the Ministerial meeting between Norway and the Community on 10–11 January 1972. The Norwegians stressed the vital importance they attached to the session by sending an extremely powerful negotiating team containing the Foreign Minister, the Fisheries Minister, the Trade Minister and a State Secretary. These four Ministers were confronted by land-locked Luxembourg's Foreign Minister, Mr Thorn, and the Italian Minister responsible for fisheries, whose relevance to the issue was extremely minimal! The imbalance between the two sides could hardly have been greater and, one suspects, more deliberate (*E* 1972a).

Despite this diplomatic affront, the Norwegian delegation continued to insist that their 'special interest' in fisheries should be recognized in a special protocol that would be added to the agreement already achieved with the other applicants. This would make it absolutely clear that Norwegian national fishing zones could continue beyond the transition period. But all that the 'Six' were prepared to concede was a special protocol that granted Norway the 'most positive' interpretation of the agreement already reached with the other applicants (*E* 1972b, c, d). This still fell short of what the Norwegian government required, thus leading it into urgent consideration of the larger question about whether or not Norway would or could join the Community. It was now clear that Norway had received the 'maximum' it was possible to offer. If more were conceded, the agreements already reached with the other applicants would become invalidated and the whole enlargement issue thrown into doubt. With the Accession Treaties due to be signed on 22 January 1972 and the 'common market question' delicately balanced in all the applicant states (particularly Britain) this was a risk the Community could not take. The political debate within Norway became intense. Voices were raised urging an end to all entry negotiations. However, the Norwegian government eventually decided to retreat from its original demands. It conceded that achievement of a precise 'legal guarantee' ensuring permanent exceptions to the equal-access principle was beyond its grasp and accepted that a Community decision would determine what fishing rights followed the transition period. But the criteria upon which this decision would be based must, it argued, be precisely defined in the 'special protocol' so that there was a *de facto*, if not *de jure*, assurance that fishermen resident in Norway's coastal regions would have exclusive access to an adequate protected fishing zone beyond 31 December 1982.

Although Norway made these vital concessions at the outset of the meeting on 14 January 1972, the discussions still dragged on into the early hours of the following day as detailed quibbling over the precise (or rather imprecise!) wording of the special protocol took place and the extent of the 12-mile zone to be accorded to Norway was haggled over. Eventually accord was forged along the following lines (*E* 1972f).

NO SEPARATE AGREEMENT FOR NORWAY

The agreement between the 'Six' and the 'Three' of 12 December 1971 was to apply to Norway as well. The 12-mile special exception zone to apply to Norway in the framework of this agreement was to extend from the Soviet border in the north to Egersund in the south. This resulted from yet another crude compromise; Egersund is halfway between the southern settlement of Lindesnes (which Norway wanted as the southern limit of the 12-mile zone) and the more northerly town of Stavanger (which the Community wanted as the southern limit of this zone) (see Map 5.1).

A 'SPECIAL PROTOCOL' FOR NORWAY

In exchange for Norway's vital concession on the point of Community principle, the 'Six' agreed to recognize Norway's particular fisheries problems and the way in which they should influence the Community's decision on fishing access to be taken in ten years' time. The special protocol to be added to the general agreement thus read:

> The High Contracting Parties; recognizing the very great importance that fishing represents for Norway; considering that, because of the particular geographical situation of Norway, fishing and its related industries constitute an essential activity for the population of a large part of the coastal areas where other possibilities of employment are limited; aware of the importance, as much for Norway as for the whole Community, of maintaining a satisfactory demographic equilibrium in the regions of this country which depend essentially on coastal fishing, and sharing the objectives of the Norwegian government in this field, agree to recom-

mend to the Institutions of the Community that they take special account, during the formulation of the report provided for in Article 103 of the Treaty of Accession, of the problems faced by Norway in the fisheries field, as much in the framework of the general economy as for reasons arising out of the social and demographic structures peculiar to this country, so that the provisions it will be possible to adopt at that time are formulated accordingly; these provisions could include, among other measures, a prolongation beyond 31 December 1982 of the exception regime to an appropriate degree and according to rules to be determined. (E 1972e)

Finally, the Norwegian government insisted on adding a unilateral declaration that clarified its interpretation of an agreement which was much less specific than it desired. This read as follows:

The special protocol concerning Norwegian fisheries upon which we have just reached agreement, provides that the Commission will submit proposals about what it is appropriate to do after 31 December 1982. The protocol recognizes the special problems that are faced by Norway in this sector and have recommended to the Institutions of the Community that they ensure that decisions are taken accordingly. The Community is based on the confidence that exists between its Members. My government is convinced that the Council will not take measures contrary to the vital interests of Norway. The Community has just given to Norway the solemn assurance that it will take special account of the Norwegian inshore fishing industry after 1982. My government considers this to be a real guarantee. (E 1972e)

Norway refuses to join the Community

On the basis of the above agreement Norway signed the Treaties of Accession along with the other applicants. However, unlike the other applicants, Norway did not ultimately join the EEC, despite the efforts of the Norwegian government to assure fishermen that 'real guarantees' had been won. Its task was made more difficult by the fact that the Minister of Fisheries resigned over the issue. Eventually, the Norwegian electorate voted 53 per cent to 47 per cent against membership, Mr Bratteli and his government resigned and the whole fisheries agreement with the Community lapsed. West Europe's major fishing country and richest fishing grounds thus remained outside the framework of the CFP. There seems little doubt that the Community's handling of the dispute was a significant contributory factor to the failure of Norway to join the common market. Certainly, the referendum votes from the fishing areas were overwhelmingly against Community membership (Opsahl 1972).

The conservation problem?

The enlargement negotiations on fisheries focused almost exclusively on the question of equal access and, to a much lesser extent, market organization and trade. However, in developing their arguments about fishing limits, the 'Four' laid considerable stress on conserving stocks. This concern was a factor, not only in preserving the reserved coastal fishing zones during the transition period, but in introducing Article 102 of the Treaty of Accession. This called for common conservation policies within six years and required that the access regime implemented at the end of the transition period in December 1982 take account of the state of fish stocks. It was hardly a radical contribution towards dealing with an urgent problem confronting the Community, but a small incremental step had been taken towards the definition of common conservation policies that had failed to enthuse the original 'Six'. The enlargement negotiations had placed the 'conservation problem' more firmly into the 'basket' of issues about which the Community would henceforth negotiate in the formulation of fishery policy.

Conclusion

The process of decision between the 'Six' and the 'Four' closely resembled the one among the 'Six' themselves. National and sectional interests were vigorously pursued and a compromise agreement on the allocation of fisheries authority within the enlarged EEC was reached after complex bargaining procedures. Once again final accord was dependent, in large part, on interests which extended beyond the purely fisheries domain. In particular, the major question of Community enlargement as a whole acted as a 'catalyst'. Whereas the prospect of fish-rich states entering the EEC had been a vital element generating agreement among the 'Six' at the last possible moment, so the prospect of the overriding goal of Community enlargement being thwarted by a relatively minor fishing matter pushed the governments involved into uneasy accord shortly before the Accession Treaty was due to be signed. Norway's ultimate refusal to join the Community reflected the lack of genuine conviction underlying this agreement. No great foresight was required to fear that conflict over the CFP would break out again in the future.

6 The advent of 200-mile fishing zones: the need for a new CFP

The Commission has given primary importance in its proposals to the need for conservation measures and to the need for controls so as to ensure their effectiveness. It has done so for the reason that there is no other internationally recognized justification for claiming 200-mile fishery zones and that the fundamental purpose of the exercise is to preserve and improve existing fisheries in the interests of both fishermen and the consumer. In terms of the Community this includes the sharing both of advantages and of the burdens imposed by this new world geography of fishing. (Commission 1978a, 1)

On 1 January 1973, Denmark, Ireland and the UK became member states of the European Community. In the following years, the conflicts about the CFP became increasingly acute. The fundamental problem still concerned the related issues of allocating and conserving fish stocks. In the arduous struggle to find a new, commonly acceptable fisheries system, the Commission advocated 'a fair, balanced fisheries policy' in which member states would share 'both the advantages and burdens imposed by the new world geography of fishing' (Commission 1978a), the main element of which was the move towards 200-mile/median line national exclusive economic zones (EEZs) around coastal states in conditions of increased overfishing.

The development of 200-mile/median line EEZs

Successive United Nations Conferences on the Law of the Sea (UNCLOSs) (UNCLOS 1958–64) have sought a new framework of international law concerning all sea-use issues, including the allocation of fishery resources and the spatial extent of national jurisdiction over the sea. In UNCLOS III, which began in 1974 in Caracas and continued in New York and Geneva for years afterwards, a key problem concerned EEZs. These EEZs had come to be regarded as a coastal belt extending out to 200 miles or the median line. Landlocked and other 'geographically disadvantaged' countries with short coast-lines opposed this crude national partitioning of marine space. But by the end of an UNCLOS III session in May 1975 most participants had accepted the principle that coastal states should have jurisdiction over the exploitation of natural resources within the EEZs. The 'single negotiating text' drafted at the conclusion of this session also indicated that the coastal state would not have to respect historic fishing rights that others might claim in this zone. A coastal state would only be obliged to grant other states access to exploit that proportion of the available catch it was unable or unwilling to catch itself. By the mid-1970s, support for this concept of the 200-mile EEZ was widespread, not only in the developing world and fish-rich countries, such as Iceland, but also in the influential superpowers of the USA and the USSR. Regardless of what the delegates in the deadlocked UNCLOS III eventually decided, it was clear that such broad EEZs were rapidly becoming the general rule as individual states took successful unilateral action to establish them. For example, Iceland extended its exclusive fishing limit to 200 miles in October 1975 and, despite vigorous opposition from the British government in another 'Cod War', even-tually won general recognition of it. The Norwegian government successfully followed suit on 1 January 1977. In October 1975 the American House of Representatives passed a law requiring a 200-mile exclusive fishing limit, thus pressing the government of the USA one step further towards the final establishment of such a zone in March 1977. Canada quickly did likewise. In November 1975, Mexico declared a 200-mile EEZ, thus joining the large number of Latin American and African states which had already done so, or were about to do so (US Department of State 1975). Consequently, the environ-ment within which the European Community's fishery policy had developed was radically changed, making modification of the CFP inevitable.

The consequences of EEZs for the Community

In 1975 the European Commission assessed the impact of 200-mile/median line EEZs on the Community (Commission 1975a). Basing its analysis on data for 1973, the Commission pointed out that about 87 per cent of the Community's catch came from the North East Atlantic (see Table 6.1). With the exception of Italy, member states

Table 6.1 EEC member-state catches ('000 tonnes) in different zones, 1973 (italic figures are percentages of national totals)

	Belgium	Denmark Inc. Greenland	W. Germany	France	Ireland	Netherlands	UK	Italy	Total EEC
Total catch 1973	49.1	1453.4	418.2	593.9	80.1	220.4	1048.7	289.9	4159.7
Catch in N.E. Atlantic	49.1 *100.0%*	1417.1 *97.5%*	325.3 *77.7%*	478.6 *80.6%*	80.1 *100.0%*	220.4 *100.0%*	1040.3 *99.2%*	– –	3610.9 *86.8%*
Catch in N.W. Atlantic	– –	36.3 *2.5%*	92.9 *22.2%*	36.1 *6.1%*	– –	– –	8.4 *0.8%*	0.8 *0.3%*	174.5 *4.2%*
Catch in own 200-mile zone	25.9 *52.7%*	990.9 *68.2%*	21.2 *5.1%*	159.3 *26.8%*	72.0 *89.7%*	78.6 *35.7%*	667.0 *63.6%*	191.1 *76.1%*	2206.0 *53.1%*
Catch in 200-mile zone of other EEC states	15.4 *31.4%*	263.2 *18.1%*	113.3 *27.1%*	274.7 *46.3%*	8.1 *10.1%*	134.8 *61.2%*	3.4 *0.3%*	– –	812.9 *19.6%*
Catch in 200-mile zones of non-EEC states	7.8 *15.9%*	199.3 *13.7%*	283.7 *67.8%*	159.9 *26.9%*	– –	7.0 *3.1%*	378.3 *36.1%*	98.8 *34.1%*	1134.8 *27.3%*
Catch in Medit.	– –	– –	– –	30.2 *5.1%*	– –	– –	– –	251.1 *86.6%*	281.3 *6.8%*
Catch off Africa	– –	– –	– –	49.0 *8.3%*	– –	– –	– –	38.0 *13.1%*	87.0 *2.1%*

Source: Commission (1975a).

made all or most of their individual catches in this area. The Mediterranean provided some 87 per cent of Italian production, but a mere 7 per cent of the Community total. Another 4 per cent of this total came from the North West Atlantic and 2 per cent from the East Central Atlantic (off West Africa). Very small quantities came from far distant waters in the South West Atlantic, the Pacific and Indian Oceans. On the basis of these 1973 figures (which represented the situation before the widespread introduction of 200-mile zones) the Commission calculated that about 72 per cent of the Community's catch would fall within a 200-mile/median line EEZ around the EEC. However it went on to point out that the pattern of potential gain and loss within this new political geography of the seas was more complicated than this general survey suggested.

First, the Commission analysed absolute gains and losses implicit in the newly emerging situation for the Community as a whole. On the extreme assumption that the entire catch arising within the 200-mile limits of non-EEC states (third countries) would be lost, whereas the entire catch obtained within the 200-mile zone of member states would be allocated to Community fishermen, the Commission calculated that the EEC's net loss, covering all species, would be quite small (some 150,000 tonnes, less than 5 per cent of the total catch in 1973). In the North Atlantic taken alone, almost no change in total catch weight would occur. But, because member states generally made catches with a larger proportion of high-value species in the waters of third countries, the financial loss to Community fishermen would be substantial (see Table 6.2). For example, the highly valued cod represented some 19 per cent of the Community's North Atlantic production in 1973; according to the extreme assumption made by the Commission about potential gains and losses (see above), this proportion would fall to less than 9 per cent under a generalized 200-mile fishing limit regime. Such losses implied various heavy costs. First, there was the direct loss of production value, assessed by the Commission at some 187 million EUA p.a. on 1973 values. Secondly, there would be the costs of reconverting highly capitalized and specialized fishing vessels to exploit different stocks. Thirdly, money would be required to adapt fish-processing plants, marketing systems and consumer tastes to other species. Fourthly, there was a substantial financial burden inherent in what was likely to be an increased Community trade deficit in fish products; for example, British consumers were not likely to switch easily from cod fish fingers (made

Table 6.2   Some estimated potential gains and losses for the EEC under a 200-mile fishing limit regime (based on 1973 figures)

	Gross losses		Gross gains	
	'000 tonnes	'000 EUA	'000 tonnes	'000 EUA
Cod	381.2	187,928	2.3	1,134
Haddock	79.4	31,372	46.0	18,170
Coalfish	183.5	50,277	43.0	11,782
Whiting	13.2	4,415	0.1	44
Scorpion fish	67.4	27,166	2.5	1,008
Herring	67.0	12,125	302.0	54,662
Mackerel	–	–	252.0	43,344
Scad	–	–	118.0	10,266
Lesser sand eel	95.5	5,062	9.3	493
Norway pout	32.3	1,583	44.0	2,156
Total	919.5	319,928	819.2	143,059

Source: Commission (1975a).

increasingly from imports) to the unknown delights of coalfish, redfish and the blue whiting! Finally, however successful a restructuring of the fishing industry might be, substantial redundancy of men and boats was inevitable. There was already overcapacity in the industry leading to overfishing, low yields and high costs. Such problems would increase if, for example, much of the distant-water fleet capacity was converted to increase fishing effort even more in a 200-mile Community zone.

The picture of potential gains and losses for the Community under a 200-mile regime varied greatly among the separate states, as did their perception of them. Again basing its calculations on catches in 1973 and the extreme assumption of a total ejection of Community fishermen from third country EEZs as well as a total exclusion of non-EEC vessels from the 200-mile zones of member states, the Commission concluded that the UK stood to suffer the largest absolute loss. In that reference year, before the implementation of such EEZs, Britain derived about 378,300 tonnes (36 per cent of its catch) from the waters of third countries (notably high-value species from around Iceland and Norway). English distant-water ports, notably Hull and Grimsby, were the most threatened British areas, facing potential

Table 6.3 Estimated potential losses for EEC member states under a 200-mile fishing limit regime (based on 1973 figures for species listed in Table 6.2)

	Loss in tonnes	% of national catch (1973)	Loss in million EUA	% of total EEC losses
UK	378,300	36%	158,884	50%
W. Germany	283,700	68%	89,619	28%
Denmark (inc. Greenland)	199,300	14%	29,403	9%
France	159,900	27%	38,031	12%
Italy	98,800	34%	–	–
Belgium	7,800	16%	2,240	0.7%
Netherlands	7,000	3%	1,751	0.5%
Ireland	nil	nil	nil	–
Total EEC	1,134,800	27% of EEC catch in 1973	319,928	100%

Source: Commission (1975a).

losses of some 300,000 tonnes. Next came West Germany which would lose some 283,700 tonnes in non-Community waters; this represented about 68 per cent of the national catch, clearly making West Germany, and its North Sea ports, the largest potential losers in *relative* terms. Denmark faced a potential loss of 200,000 tonnes, France 150,000 tonnes, Italy 100,000 tonnes (more than one-third of its production), Belgium 8000 tonnes and the Netherlands 7000 tonnes. In financial terms the pattern of loss was similar (see Table 6.3).

Thus, according to the Commission's calculations based on a *Community* view of the potential impact of 200-mile zones, Britain stood out as the largest net loser in absolute terms. However, if a *national* perspective is adopted, the pattern changes radically. The Commission estimated – rather more conservatively than the British – that some 55–60 per cent of the Community's fish resources are to be found in a 200-mile/median line zone around the UK. If the British regarded these stocks as an exclusive national, rather than a common Community, resource, they could perceive substantial gains to counterbalance the heavy losses of their distant-water industry. The temptation to adopt this standpoint was reinforced by the fact that British fishing in the 200-mile/median line limits of other Community states was a negligible 0.3 per cent (see Table 6.1). For Ireland too, the potential gains to be perceived in a national perspective were clear; 90 per cent of its catch came from within 200 miles of its shore.

On the other hand, the Netherlands and France obtained a large proportion of their national catches (61 per cent and 50 per cent respectively) from the envisaged 200-mile/median line limits of their EEC partners, notably the UK and Ireland. They had an obvious interest in developing a common Community concept of fishery resources and maintaining the equal-access principle within the CFP. To a slightly lesser extent, the same was true for Belgium, West Germany and Denmark which took, respectively, 30, 27 and 18 per cent of their national catches from within 200-miles or the median line of other Community states in 1973 and were likely to increase their activities in these areas as they were progressively evicted from waters claimed by non-EEC countries (see Maps 2.3–2.12 and Table 6.1).

This analysis of perceived costs and benefits under a 200-mile/median line regime was complicated by yet more factors that were difficult or impossible to quantify. For example, the British government's temptation to change abruptly from ardent defender of the international status of the seas (as it was in the so-called 'Cod Wars' with Iceland) to vigorous protagonist of 200-mile national fishing zones was tempered by the desire to maintain some degree of access to resources off Iceland, Norway and elsewhere. British demand for cod and other valuable species from such waters was likely to remain strong in the foreseeable future and large, costly sections of the UK fleet were specially adapted to exploit them. A simple switch from faraway expensive Arctic cod to cheaper Cornish mackerel nearby was not economically feasible for much of the deep-sea fleet based on Humberside. To obtain access to rich distant grounds, bargaining power was required; perhaps the combined commercial strength of the common market was more likely to win concessions on fishing access from major fish-exporting countries than unilateral UK action. If so, the British could not afford to be too unresponsive to the fishing-access demands of their EEC partners who had long exploited grounds around the British Isles. Moreover, British fish exports to the common market were increasing (for example, mackerel from the South West). How far could Britain deny Community fishermen to fish in grounds around its shores and yet still maintain access to EEC markets? This was another imponderable factor in the minds of those attempting to assess the costs and benefits to the UK fishing industry inherent in a new partition of the seas. Furthermore, the extent to which Britain could adopt a nationalistic line on fishing rights without harming its other Community interests weighed on deliberations in Whitehall.

Italy was again something of an 'odd-man-out' in the new geography of fishing rights. It caught no fish at all in the actual or potential fishing zones of other member states. But it faced the possibility of losing a third of its catch if, as was likely, it was evicted from waters around non-Community countries (Table 6.1). Some Italians wondered if compensation for these potential losses off Mediterranean and African coasts might be found in a 200-mile Community zone in the North East Atlantic! Why should the Italians be excluded from a reallocation of fishery resources in such a would-be 'Community pond' from which non-EEC fishermen (for example, the East Europeans) would be evicted?

The Commission's proposals for a revised CFP

Having analysed the pattern of potential gains and losses under the projected 200-mile/median line EEZ regime, the Commission developed ideas for a modified CFP. In February 1976, a preliminary outline of its new thinking was sent to the Council of Ministers (Council 1976), to be followed in September of the same year by more detailed proposals that had these basic objectives:

1   to ensure 'the optimal exploitation of the biological resources of the Community zone' in the medium- and long-term interests of both fishermen and consumers;
2   to ensure the 'equitable distribution of these limited resources between member states' while maintaining 'as far as possible the level of employment and income in coastal regions which are economically disadvantaged or largely dependent on fishing activities'. (Commission 1975a, 10; 1976a)

In pursuit of these objectives the principle of equality of access to fishing grounds within the jurisdiction of member states was to be maintained with no question of discrimination according to nationality. However, the Commission recognized that:

the straightforward implementation of the principle of equal access is bound to result in the rapid exhaustion of resources; the ... consequences of such a situation would be unacceptable. (Commission 1975a, 9)

Consequently, the equal-access principle would have to be 'supple-mented by rules limiting and organizing all fishing activities' in the modified CFP. Another fundamental principle – that of common action by member states both inside and outside of the Community – would, argued the Commission, be essential in developing effective policies to exploit fisheries at a sustainable level. The means proposed by the Commission to achieve its objectives are presented separately below, but it is important to stress the close interrelationships linking them.

THE CO-ORDINATED INTRODUCTION OF 200-MILE/MEDIAN LINE FISHING LIMITS

The Commission believed that the trend towards 200-mile fishing zones would lead to a large-scale diversion of fishing effort by both Community fishermen and others into the waters around the EEC. This would 'accelerate the deterioration of stocks' and reduce the 'catch potential of the Community fishermen who traditionally operated there' (Commission 1976a, 1). Therefore, the Commission proposed that all member states simultaneously adopt 200-mile fishing zones on 1 January 1977 to create an enlarged Community 'pond'. This would produce a legal spatial framework within which to develop effective Community regulations to conserve stocks and allocate them 'fairly' among member states.

A 12-MILE COASTAL ZONE FOR INSHORE FISHERMEN

The diversion of fishing effort into waters around the EEC would, thought the Commission, threaten inshore fishermen in particular. Consequently, it proposed (Commission 1976a, 8) to extend the level of 'special' protection already afforded to inshore fishermen in the Treaty of Accession (see Chapter 5). This Treaty provided that within a 6-mile limit fishing could be restricted to vessels that traditionally fish in those waters and operate from ports in that geographical coastal area. In regions where inshore fisheries were particularly important this general 6-mile protection was extended to 12 miles (see Map 5.1), although the traditional fishing rights of fishermen from outside the area would have to be respected in the outer 6-mile belt. These regional exceptions, which, it is important to note, did not infringe the Community principle of non-discrimination on *national* grounds, applied until 31 December 1982; after this date the Council would reconsider the situation. In its new proposals, the Commission suggested that this temporary protection be extended in two ways:

1 by the establishment of an exclusive 12-mile zone for local fishermen around the whole of the Community coastline;
2 by the continuation of such a limit beyond 31 December 1982 for an indefinite period.

In arguing for this increased measure of protection, the Commission (1976a, 8) stressed how inshore fishing had 'considerable economic and social importance for numerous coastal regions, where it is the main if not the only activity'. It claimed that about 80 per cent of the Community's full-time fishermen could be classified as 'inshore'. By including the families of these men and shore workers in related employment, it was estimated that the income of about 60,000 persons was dependent on this sector. The Commission clearly committed itself to the continuation of this sector in the quest for a 'fair balance' between the interests of inshore and more distant-water fishing.

TRADITIONAL RIGHTS IN THE 12-MILE ZONE

In its outline proposals to the Council in February 1976, the Commission proposed that traditional fishing rights granted to non-local fishermen in the 12-mile zone (Article 100.2 of the Treaty of Accession) should be 'gradually eliminated' (Commission 1976b; Council 1976, 7). But this measure to protect local inshore fishermen was strongly resisted by continental fishermen and their governments. Consequently, by the time it made its fuller proposals in September 1976, the Commission had retreated and merely suggested that such rights be 're-examined' by 31 December 1982.

COMMON 'FRAMEWORK AGREEMENTS' ON ACCESS RIGHTS

Beyond the proposed 200-mile EEC limit, the Commission wanted to negotiate 'framework agreements' between the Community and the third countries concerned (Commission 1976a, 1–23). These accords, to be made by the Community acting as a whole, would take account of the principles gaining general acceptance in UNCLOS III and contain three main elements:

1 reciprocal fishing rights;
2 access to possible future surpluses;
3 phasing out of existing rights where no reciprocal arrangement is possible.

The Commission envisaged three major types of agreement:

1 with countries where the Community had an interest in fishing their waters, but they had no interest in Community fisheries (for example, the USA and Canada), the Community should seek terms of fishing access that were at least as good as other countries enjoyed;
2 with countries with which the Community had interlinked fishing interests (for example, Norway, Iceland, the Faroes and the USSR), reciprocal access arrangements and joint conservation measures should be established;
3 with countries that fish in the projected 200-mile zone, but in whose waters Community fishermen had no interest (for example, Poland, East Germany, Sweden and Spain) the basic objective would be to phase out their fishing in EEC waters, although there might be some reciprocity.

In trying to achieve such agreements, the Commission urged that the Community 'make use of all the instruments available to it' (Commission 1976b, 9). In particular, it should use its trading strength; access to EEC fish markets could be made dependent on the degree of fishing access granted to Community fishermen by third countries such as Norway and Iceland.

TACS AND OTHER CONSERVATION MEASURES

The Commission (1976a, 1–2) detailed the widespread severity of over-fishing in order to justify its proposals for conservation policies aimed at 'an optimum yield from the resources'. The basic instrument of control was to be the fixing of an annual Total Allowable Catch (TAC) for each stock or group of stocks. The fixing of TACs was to be accompanied by a whole range of measures relating to such things as mesh size, permissible equipment, fishing seasons, closed areas, and so on.

These proposals emphasize how much the Commission's awareness of fishery management problems had evolved since the original formulation of the CFP in the mid-1960s (see Chapter 4). In place of the cursory references to overfishing found in its earlier reports and proposals, knowledge from the fields of fishery economics and fishery science was now being fed into the policy-making process by the Commission. For example, simplistic references to 'optimum' fishing and 'MSY' were now being replaced by much more sophisticated statements of objectives, albeit in typically turgid bureaucratic prose:

> In view of the interdependence of stocks and the complex effects on each of them of exploitation techniques specific to others, seeking the optimum level for stocks as a whole will not necessarily coincide with achieving the optimum level for each individual stock.
>
> It would therefore seem that the aim of a rational conservation policy cannot be the automatically systematic search for the biological optimum for each stock taken separately; on the contrary, the adoption of conservation measures which were not developed in a more general context would lead to contradictions and run counter to the general objectives of such a policy.
>
> The conservation policy must therefore be accompanied by a policy of rational management of resources, with the aim of reconciling in respect of Community resources as a whole biological constraints and economic constraints resulting from the diversity of technical and social structures and the multiplicity of market requirements to be met. (Commission 1977a, 3)

In these new proposals, the Commission also described the institutional structures it thought essential for formulating such policy. National fishery organizations would forward all the necessary information at their disposal to a Community Scientific and Technical Committee for Fisheries. This Committee would consider how each stock, or group of stocks, should be managed and report each year to the Community institutions. Collaboration with third countries was essential for this purpose. On the basis of these reports the Commission would make its annual stock-management proposals to the Council of Ministers which would decide what measures to adopt. Once adopted, the Commission would implement them through a Management Committee for Sea Fisheries.

CATCH QUOTAS

Following the fixing of TACs the Commission (1976a, 8) proposed to 'distribute the permissible catches fairly amongst the fishermen of member states, using a system of quotas'. The volume of these permissible catches would equal:

1 the total of the Community TACs *minus*
2 the total catches allocated, if any, to non-member countries in the Community zone *plus*
3 the total catches by the Community states in the waters of non-member countries.

The sharing of this permissible catch among Community fishermen should be done, argued the Commission, 'primarily on the basis of the member states' fishing performances in the past, related to a reference period to be determined' (Commission 1976a, 12). Nevertheless, it also maintained that the straightforward allocation system based on past performance 'may have particularly serious social and economic repercussions for the northern regions of the UK and Ireland' (Commission 1976a, 12). This would be especially so where the permissible catch for a given species fell below the previous level of exploitation, as would often be the case. It was therefore proposed that a 'Community reserve stock' be established for each of the main species every year according to:

1 the 'vital needs' of fishermen in 'northern Britain' and Ireland; and
2 the extent to which catches have been reduced below their previous level.

This reserve stock would enable an additional quantity to be allocated 'on a priority basis' to those British and Irish fishermen 'who have traditionally fished the stocks in question' (Commission 1976a, 12).

COMMUNITY LICENSING SYSTEM

The Commission proposed a Community system of fisheries control supervising all allocation and conservation measures both at sea and at landing points. This was seen as:

the only way of ensuring that the sacrifices made by fishermen in order to replenish resources are not in vain as a result of the irresponsible behaviour of the other fishermen who are less heedful of the need to comply with the conservation measures and, in particular, catch quotas. (Commission 1976a, 13)

Control of fishing should be based on a Community system of licensing that would require:

1 the registration of vessels and skippers engaged in professional fishing;

2 the systematic recording of information about the position, intensity and results of the fishing activity of each vessel;
3 the compilation at regional, national or Community level of the information concerning fishing activities supplied by skippers operating under the licence system;
4 the establishment of a progressive system of financial or administrative sanctions including: warnings, penalties and licence withdrawal from skippers and/or vessels.

In the first instance such a system would apply only within the 12-mile limit of member states, but the Commission clearly wanted the gradual extension of such control into the proposed 200-mile Community fishing zone. It also stressed that, unlike international fisheries bodies such as the NEAFC and the ICNAF which could only make recommendations (see Chapter 3), the Council of Ministers was able to adopt 'any measures, including binding ones' and 'ensure that they were observed' as Community law (Commission 1976a, 13). It recognized however that such systems were costly and difficult to administer. Consequently, national administrations, which would be mainly responsible for applying Community regulations in their waters, would be required to make an 'appreciably greater effort' in the field of fisheries management. In order to facilitate this complex task, the Commission thought it 'necessary to formulate a list of permitted landing points and to concentrate marketing in officially recognized selling centres' (1976a, 14). Moreover, all species subject to catch limits would have to be publicly sold to ensure that restrictions were being observed.

COMMUNITY AID FOR STRUCTURAL REFORM

The Commission recognized that much of the Community fishing fleet was now obsolete in a world of 200-mile limits and overfishing; it thus argued (1976a, 14):

It will therefore be necessary to effect a major reduction and redirection of fishing capacity to bring it to an optimum level in relation to fishing potential, and also to adapt land-based structures and the other activities closely linked to onshore activities.

More specifically it proposed the following measures:

1 an overall reduction in catch capacity to be achieved by withdrawing surplus distant-water vessels, scrapping older boats

and selling newer vessels to non-Community countries or converting them to non-fishing activities;

2   a progressive conversion of fleets to facilitate a 'rational management' of the resources available to the Community;

3   a significant reduction in the production capacity for fish-meal because of the severe overfishing of pelagic stocks and the need to maintain a natural balance in the marine food chains upon which fishing for direct human consumption depended;

4   an encouragement to POs to cut back their fishing operations in line with the introduction of catch quotas;

5   an encouragement to exploit new species and new areas;

6   a limitation and Community harmonization of national aids for the construction of new fishing boats to prevent further overcapacity.

Aware of the political difficulties involved, the Commission suggested that this structural reform of the fishing industry would have to be effected progressively to avoid serious economic dislocation. But specific measures to deal with the severe difficulties of distant-water fleets ejected from waters off Iceland, Norway and elsewhere were urgently required.

In order to implement a restructuring programme, the Commission (1976a, 16–18) was able to propose another policy instrument not available to international fishery management organizations; namely, financial help to facilitate changes and compensate those harmed as a result. Over a five-year period it provisionally proposed the expenditure of some 400 million EUA (approx. £250 million) from the Community's EAGGF fund to aid the desired remodelling of the industry. This reduction in catching capacity would obviously lead to unemployment. Consequently, the Commission proposed that a range of other Community funds be used in addition to EAGGF. For example, the European Social Fund should assist in the occupational retraining of redundant fishermen, and the European Investment Bank and the Community's Regional Development Fund should also help to create new employment in fishing regions.

COMMUNITY ACTION IN INTERNATIONAL ORGANIZATIONS

The Commission (1976a, 21) repeated its long-held belief that:

The Community role in bringing about international co-operation for the conservation and management of resources must be made by the Community considered as a single coastal state and acting as such.

In other words, the Community should act as a single unit in international bodies like the UNCLOS III and the NEAFC. Clearly, the Commission sought to maximize its own role in this respect, maintaining that within the NEAFC and ICNAF 'it could, in consultation with the representatives of the member states, conduct negotiations on behalf of the Community, while in other cases the member states should negotiate jointly and in consultation with the Commission's representative' (Commission 1976a, 22).

DIRECTORATE-GENERAL FOR FISHERIES

The Commission's comprehensive proposals clearly manifested a desire to maximize the Community's role in the formulation of fishery policy at the expense of the individual member state. This was also reflected in the creation of a distinct Directorate-General for Fisheries within the European Commission in April 1976: in addition, the staff working on fisheries was increased to around 50 persons. Although this was still a small number in relation to the work involved and comparable situations in national civil services, it was a substantial upgrading of what had previously been a poorly staffed section of the Directorate-General for Agriculture.

The 'Hague Resolutions' of 1976

In September 1976, the Commission transmitted its new proposals to the Council (Commission 1976a, 22). They immediately proved unacceptable to the member states as a whole and deadlock ensued on fundamental issues relating to the control, conservation and allocation of fishery resources.

In an effort to reduce these differences, the Foreign Ministers of the Community held an informal meeting in the Hague at the end of October 1976. This did not produce a final settlement, but led to the so-called 'Hague Resolutions' on 3 November 1976, which laid down the following guidelines for the future development of the CFP:

(a) the member states of the Community would, in concert, extend the limits of their national fishing zones to 200 miles, or the median line, around their North Sea and Atlantic coasts from 1 January 1977;

(b) fishing by non-Community (i.e. third country) vessels in these extended fishing zones would be governed by agreements between the Community acting as a single body and the third states concerned;

(c) the Commission be given authority by the Council to open negotiations on behalf of the Community with certain third countries with a view to concluding 'framework agreements' on fishing access;

(d) the Commission be given authority by the Council to negotiate the Community's participation as a single body in international fisheries organizations and conventions;

(e) when conservation measures were needed in the waters of member states, they should be adopted by the Community as a single body but that, pending the agreement of an agreed Community fishery system incorporating such measures, individual member states could take on an interim basis appropriate measures to ensure the protection of the resources situated in the fishing zones off their coasts provided that such measures did not discriminate according to nationality and that member states sought the approval of the Commission before applying them;

(f) the Community's EAGGF would meet part of the cost of inspection and control measures in the fishing zones off Ireland and Greenland where the country's financial resources were limited but the sea areas involved were extensive and rich in marine resources;

(g) Ireland's fishing industry be secured a continued and progressive growth on the basis of the Irish government's Fisheries Development Programme for coastal fisheries which provided for an increase in the national catch from 75,000 tonnes in 1975 to 150,000 tonnes in 1979;

(h) Greenland and 'northern parts' of the UK also had communities 'particularly dependent' upon fishing and related industries and that 'account should be taken of their vital needs' in 'applying the CFP'. (Commission, internal memo, Hague Resolutions, not published in *OJEC*)

In essence the Hague Resolutions – sometimes clear, sometimes vague – reflected a measure of accord with the proposals for a Community *external* fisheries policy, but very serious differences over what sort of *internal* fisheries system should be adopted to conserve and allocate the resources within the 200-mile/median line zones of the member states.

Community action in external fisheries policy

The Hague Resolutions clearly accepted that the Community should act as a single body in external fisheries affairs. Acceptance of this loss of individual sovereignty on the part of member state governments was, in part, a consequence of Community law established in the Treaty of Rome and interpreted by various judgements in the European Court of Justice.

In particular, the so-called Kramer case of July 1976 confirmed the precedence of the Community in international fisheries affairs (Judgement 1976). Dutch fishermen challenged the legality of Dutch national conservation measures, arguing that the Community alone was competent to produce such fisheries legislation. This led to the Court being asked whether or not the Community had authority to conclude international fishery conservation agreements that would be binding on member states. The Court decided that the Community did possess such power, thus reinforcing previous judgements that asserted the primacy of Community authority in dealings with third countries on matters relating to trade and resource management. Simplifying the legal complexities somewhat, it can be said that the Court was upholding the argument that each time the Community adopted a common internal policy with common rules, the member states lost rights to make external agreements with non-Community countries that affected this internal policy. A CFP had been adopted that had regulations related to virtually all aspects of fisheries: fishing rights, conservation, trade, markets, etc. Therefore, the basic logic of the Court's judgement in the Kramer case required that the Community act as a body in dealings with third countries on fishery matters. The Hague Resolutions reflected a general acceptance of this argument.

Member states adopt 200-mile/median line fishing zones

The agreement to deal with third countries in unison was manifested in the Hague Resolution that led all member states to extend their national fishing limits to 200 miles or a median line in concert on 1 January 1977. Given their historical antipathy towards such large exclusive fishing zones, why did the Community countries take this action?

First, by the mid-1970s, the broad consensus among most participants in the ongoing UNCLOS III favoured such zones as part of a new global law of the sea regime. Secondly, the Community states were being increasingly confronted by the political reality that countries with lengthy coastlines adjacent to rich fishing grounds were successfully establishing such 200-mile zones regardless of what UNCLOS III might eventually decide. This meant that member states were suffering a drastic reduction in fishing rights off non-Community countries. Having failed to prevent this development, so deleterious to their distant-water fishing industries, the EEC states moved towards an uneasy consensus whereby they would attempt to minimize their losses by establishing their own 200 mile/median line fishing zones. This would facilitate the elimination or reduction of fishing carried out by non-EEC states in the waters around the Community and, hopefully, provide some new catch potential for member-state fishermen displaced from distant grounds. Linked to this, in some minds, was the idea that 200-mile/median line zones around the EEC would establish unified legal authority over a large sea space around West European shores, thus facilitating the implementation of effective conservation policies that would ultimately increase the fishery potential of the Community.

The change of policy towards wide national fishing zones was most striking in the UK. Britain's defeat in the last of the so-called 'Cod Wars' with Iceland led to the latter successfully implementing a 200-mile limit in October 1975. Norway and others declared their firm intention to follow suit. Confronted with this inexorable trend, the British distant-water fishing industry abandoned its traditional role as arch-defender of international fisheries. By January 1976 the Hull-based British United Trawlers Ltd (1976, 19) was insisting that:

> The UK (and indeed each member state within the EEC) should, as urgently as possible ... establish its jurisdiction over the fishery resources within 200 miles or median of our coasts. (sic)

In September 1976 the UK government responded by announcing its intention to establish such a zone on 1 January 1977. It left no doubt that the new limit would be unilaterally implemented if need be (Hansard 1976a; *The Times* 1976).

This threat of unilateral action arose because the Community's short-coast states, such as West Germany and the Benelux countries, were reluctant to sanction the large-scale partitioning of the seas under national jurisdictions. But they too were having to face the reality of being unable to prevent the enclosure of the seas into exclusive zones and were increasingly conscious that common Community action in this sphere was likely to minimize their losses. They had not forgotten the equal-access provisions they had inserted in the original CFP regulation and the Treaty of Accession. Consequently, they thought more in terms of a single 'Community pond' being created by a 200-mile/median line limit, rather than the minuscule segments of sea-space they would be arbitrarily allocated as a result of their geographical configuration and the geometric logic of marine boundary-making. Thus, they too could envisage the combined strength of the Community successfully reducing third-country fishing in such a 'pond' to their advantage. They too, as Community partners acting in concert with long-coast states like Britain and Ireland, could envisage the wealth of a common 200-mile EEC zone winning reciprocal fishing rights in non-Community waters that would be unobtainable if they only had their own tiny fishing zones to bargain with. For such reasons, the short-coast Community states eventually abandoned their resistance to the Commission's proposal for a concerted introduction of 200-mile/median line zones and all member states established such zones simultaneously on 1 January 1977.

It is important to understand that the so-called 'Community pond' thus created was composed of separate 200-mile/median line zones created by individual member state legislatures and subject to national jurisdiction (in the UK case, the Fishery Limits Act of 1976). However, these zones were also subject to any Community legislation that member states had accepted under the Treaty of Rome and the Treaty of Accession, as well as the common fishery regulations that have stemmed from these. Thus, for example, the equal-access provision and exceptions to it, incorporated in the original CFP, would continue to apply throughout all these member-state zones. It was on this point that profound divergences of interest amongst the Community states revealed themselves. The concerted action of 1 January 1977 had created a vast sea area subject to Community and national laws, but who was to catch what, where and how within it?

7 Equality of access or exclusive national fishing zones?

A common market means a common sea. (Regnier 1977, 5)

Fish are no respecters of territorial waters. (Commission 1979b)

The most effective way of achieving our objectives lies in the establishment (within our 200-mile EEZ) of an exclusive UK 100-mile/median fishing zone. (British United Trawlers Ltd 1976)

Unfortunately, before we went into the common market, the Six decided, with that spirit of cunning greed which they describe as Community feeling, that our fish should be their common resource. (Mitchell, Grimsby MP, 1977)

Following the failure to adopt the Commission's 1976 proposals and the inconclusive Hague Resolutions, the arduous struggle for control of fishery resources within the Community continued for years as annual deadlines for a settlement were set but not met. This conflict assumed a political importance that the relatively minor role of fisheries in national economies scarcely justified, but the image of fishermen fighting for sea space often stimulates nationalistic emotions that militate against compromise. The major issues at the heart of this dispute remained:

1 How much fish was there available to catch? What should the TAC for each species in EEC waters be? Who should decide these TACs? What criteria, conservation or otherwise, should be used to set them?
2 How should these Community TACs be shared among member states and/or regions as quotas? What criteria should be used to determine these quota allocations?
3 By what means should each country and/or region be assured of its allocated quota? Should a Community control and catch-reporting

system in EEC waters free from national access discrimination prevail, or should restricted access to exclusive national and/or regional zones also play an important role in ensuring each country or area its allotted share?

4   How should these TACs and quotas be enforced? Should each member state ensure enforcement in the waters under its jurisdiction, or should there be a system of EEC inspectors enforcing such measures throughout the whole 'Community pond'? Should these conservation and allocation measures be of a purely Community character, or could national measures co-exist with them?

Although, for simplicity's sake, such issues can thus be stated separately, it is crucial to remember that they are interlinked. For example, the British government constantly stressed that it could not agree to a division of TACs into national quotas without simultaneous agreement on access regulations (i.e. one means of taking the quota) and conservation measures (i.e. the means of enforcing the quota). In addition, other aspects of fishery policy inevitably kept weaving themselves into the already complicated conservation–quota–access–enforcement negotiation matrix. For example, the TACs and quotas proposed by the Commission often involved a substantial reduction in fishing effort. This led inexorably into the structural policy issue of how this effort decrease might be achieved? Should there be an all-round reduction in effort, or should certain sectors of the fishing industry – for example, the displaced distant-water fleets – be re-quired to make the biggest sacrifices? Furthermore, should those permanently, or temporarily abandoning fishing in the interests of conservation be compensated in some way? If so, would the Community and/or the individual member states provide the financial resources? Similarly, there was little point in a country getting a generous fish quota if the CFP's market system allowed cheap foreign imports of fish to outsell insufficiently protected domestic production which, in consequence, remained unsold Community 'surplus'. Also, Community negotiations on fishing access rights with third countries were constantly impinging on discussions about the internal system. Countries were understandably reluctant to agree to an internal quota from the 'Community pond' before knowing what fishing oppor-tunities they were going to get in non-EEC waters. In addition, a whole range of non-fishery matters also influenced the attempt to negotiate a new CFP as politicians tried, usually without success, to produce a Community 'package-deal' within which concessions on fisheries would be 'traded-off' against concessions in, say, the agricultural sphere. Clearly, CFP negotiators were confronted with a puzzle of many possible permutations. Nevertheless, some major patterns of converging and diverging interests can be picked out.

The problem of allocation

The basic problem blocking a new CFP agreement concerned the allocation of resources within the so-called 'Community pond' created by the extension of member states' fishing zones to a 200-mile/median line. In broad terms, this conflict initially divided the continental states on one side from those of the British Isles on the other. Whereas the former insisted on the widespread application of the 'equal-access' principle, Britain and Ireland were equally determined to achieve a substantial measure of national preference for their fishermen through the establishment of national fishing zones from which their common market partners would be excluded or enjoy only limited access.

The continental states, broadly supported by the Commission, insisted that fish within the 200-mile/median lines of member states constituted a resource to which Community fishermen, regardless of nationality, should share equal conditions of access (despite British mythology to the contrary, this does not necessarily mean 'free access' for all 'up to the beaches'). With their limited coastal resources, their traditional pattern of fishing around the British Isles and their distant-water fishing severely reduced by the extension of 200-mile limits elsewhere, the continental states were bound to welcome the reaffirmation of the national non-discrimination principle and the protection of historic fishing rights in the Commission's 1976 proposals. Having struggled so hard to maintain such a system of fishing access rights in the Treaty of Accession, these states were unlikely to abandon it at the moment it became most useful to them!

The case for equality of access

THE LEGAL BASIS

Those defending the equal-access concept depended heavily on the 'acquis communautaire' (i.e. the established body of Community law).

They pointed to the legal provisions of the original CFP regulations and the Treaty of Accession. The fact that national fishing zones were now extended to 200 miles made no difference. Article 7 of the Treaty of Rome still stated that 'any discrimination on national grounds shall be prohibited', and Article 2 of the original CFP regulation still unambiguously declared that 'rules applied by each member state in respect of fishing in the maritime waters coming under its jurisdiction shall not lead to differences in treatment of other member states' (see Chapter 4). True, Articles 100 and 101 of the Treaty of Accession (Chapter 5) permitted exceptions to the equality of access provisions within 6 miles of member states' coasts and out to 12 miles in regions where fishing was of particular importance. But these were temporary derogations due to finish at the end of 1982 unless the Council of Ministers decided otherwise.

COUNTERBALANCE OF ACCESS TO MARKET

The so-called equal-access principle was also defended by a range of economic and biological arguments. Was it not basic justice, argued its protagonists, that the free movement of fish products within the EEC be counterbalanced by equal conditions of entry to fishing grounds? Why should Britain and Ireland deny continental fishermen access to waters they had traditionally exploited and then expect to export freely to other member states where there would be an increased demand for imports following decreased landings from domestic fleets cut off from fisheries around the British Isles? The idea of a few member states getting a quasi-monopoly of fish supply was, many argued, contrary to the spirit of the Community: in the words of the editor of *France-Pêche* 'a common market means a common sea' (Regnier 1977, 5).

DEFENCE OF HISTORIC RIGHTS

The will of continental states to maintain access to British and Irish waters was especially strong on the question of historic rights. Such rights in the 6- to 12-mile zone around the British Isles had been formalized in the 1964 European Fisheries Convention and protected in the Treaty of Accession. The French, who enjoyed a considerable number of such rights, were particularly determined on this issue (Appendix Map 1.1 and Appendix Map 1.2). They, and others, argued that the amount of fish they took in these historic right zones was relatively small, thus constituting no threat to the British and Irish fishing industries. A study carried out by the Commission showed that the UK took some 500,000 tonnes in its 12-mile limit compared to some 80,000 tonnes taken by all other member states in the same British zone. Some 50 per cent of the catch within twelve miles of Ireland was taken by fishermen from other Community countries who argued that this was not excessive given the underdeveloped state of the Irish fishing industry. The Head of the 'Internal Resources' division of the Commission's Directorate-General for Fisheries supported the view that the historic rights of continental states around British shores constituted no real threat to local fishermen (Boos 1979). He pointedly referred to a study produced by British United Trawlers Ltd (1976) which was, in fact, designed to put pressure on the UK government to declare an exclusive 200-mile/median line. This study argued that the catch in the British 12-mile zone was potentially higher than the past or present UK total catch in all waters near or far (Table 7.1). If this was the case, why were the British so concerned to eliminate these relatively unimportant historic rights? Why, continued the argument, should continental fishermen be evicted from their traditional fishing grounds to make space for British distant-water vessels expelled from theirs around Iceland and elsewhere? In the legal and economic context of EEC membership this was totally unacceptable. The point was reinforced by comparing the estimated potential catch (3.5 million tonnes) in the British 200-mile/median zone with the actual UK catch

Table 7.1 Potential catches within the UK 200-mile/median line zone

Zone	Catch
Within UK 200-mile/median line	3.5 million tonnes
Within UK 100-mile/median line	2.8 million tonnes
Within UK 50-mile/median line	2.5 million tonnes
Within UK 25-mile/median line	1.9 million tonnes
Within UK 12-mile/median line	1.1 million tonnes
Actual UK total catch within 200-mile/median line, 1973	0.67 million tonnes
Actual UK total catch within all waters, 1973	1.15 million tonnes

Source: British United Trawlers Ltd (1976).

(667,000 tonnes) from this area in 1973 before the expulsion of distant-water vessels from around Iceland and Norway (Commission 1975b).

ALL FISHERMEN DEPEND ON FISHING

Continental states also resisted the argument that the 'dependence' of certain British and Irish regions on fishing justified an abandonment of the national non-discrimination principles underpinning the CFP. They made the obvious, but often missed, point that all fishermen are 'dependent' on fishing. Politicians in all member states are aware of the jobs – and votes – based on this industry. Even the Belgians with a mere 1400 fishermen, were sensitive to this point; in relation to the CFP, the Chief Inspector of Fisheries at Ostend argued:

> However from the point of view of a common policy the size of a national industry should not be of any importance, as a fisherman remains a fisherman whatever country's colours his boat is flying. Moreover from a regional viewpoint this rather small (Belgian) industry is indeed significant: the population of the coastal area amounts to about 185,000 people, of which 45,000 find employment in their own region. With its 6000 jobs (including ancillary activities) the fishing industry is the most important source of employment for the coastal population. (Martens 1977, 12)

In similar vein a Dutch government official wrote:

> As a country lacking minerals and other raw materials Holland has built up a tradition in North Sea fishing over about twenty centuries ... making ... it clear why the Dutch fishing industry with its very mobile fleet tends to advocate free entry to EEC waters. (Smit 1977, 9)

Such sentiments were forcibly expressed in one way or another from Jutland to Sicily.

SHARED COSTS AND BENEFITS

Continental governments also refuted the notion that the CFP created only losses for their British and Irish counterparts. Apart from free access to a vast number of consumers in the common market, it was even suggested that Community membership also brought advantages to all in the field of fishing rights. For example, following the

concerted action by EEC states to declare a 200-mile/median line
fishing limits on 1 January 1977, many East European and other vessels
had to cease catching in West European waters. This, it was argued,
left space to accommodate some of the displaced UK distant-water
effort and allow the Irish industry to grow. A Community official
expressed the opinion, perhaps rather wishfully, that it was 'doubtful
whether the USSR would have respected the 200-mile zones of single
member states' if they had not been 'backed by the Community' (Boos
1979). Furthermore, it was argued that the combined strength of the
EEC, with the powerful bargaining cards afforded by its large
markets, was more likely to win substantial access to the fishing zones
of non-Community countries than single member states alone.

EFFECTIVE CONSERVATION

Another line of argument used to defend the notion of a 'Community pond' free from national discrimination concerned resource
conservation. If all member states, including Britain and Ireland,
would co-operate to develop the immense potential of EEC waters by
enforcing an agreed conservation policy many of the conflicts over
fishing rights would disappear. Nowhere was the arbitrary folly of
state boundaries more apparent than in the field of fishery conservation, insisted those who had been disadvantaged in the nationalistic
partitioning of sea space. The Commission, the most enthusiastic
proponent of this common approach to conservation, argued that:

> when we look at the maps of fish stocks in the waters of
> western Europe ... the areas of spawning, of feeding, of migra-
> tion, and of maturity, none of these fits in with the geometry of
> median lines and of 200-mile limits. Fish are no respectors of terri-
> torial waters. No plan for the management and conservation of these
> fish resources can be framed merely in national terms. (Commission
> 1979b)

In thus rejecting national fishing limits, the Commission emphasized
the Community's capacity to develop and enforce measures to protect
fish stocks; the EEC with its law-making powers was not another
NEAFC. In so doing the Commission rejected the argument – much
favoured in Britain and Ireland – that exclusive national fishing zones
were the only effective way of controlling overfishing, given the
problems of obtaining international co-operation (Gallagher 1977, 2).

THE USE OF QUOTAS

Clearly, the British and Irish desire to allocate and conserve fish stocks through use of wide national fishing zones was not acceptable to the rest of the Community. But this did not mean that a 'free-for-all' was advocated in their place. Instead, the Commission's proposals for a system of allocation and conservation based upon national quotas were broadly supported. The Community principle of national non-discrimination might forbid the use of exclusive national fishing zones but not the application of national quotas. Such was the logic of 'communautaire' thought! Exactly how these national quotas would be decided remained a fundamental problem to be resolved by negotiation in the Council of Ministers (see below), but there was broad agreement that they should reflect historic fishing patterns in what were now EEC waters. West Germany was also concerned that there should be compensation for loss of fishing in third-country waters, and Denmark was concerned to obtain some sort of regional preference for Greenland where fishing was of great importance in development plans.

The case for exclusive national fishing zones

The initial response of the British and Irish governments to the maintenance of the equal-access principle within the Commission's 1976 proposals was one of uncompromising rejection. This reflected the fervent demands of all types of fishermen scattered throughout many politically marginal constituencies around the British Isles. Although there were differences of degree, there was almost total unanimity that wide exclusive national fishing zones for Britain and Ireland should form a permanent part of a revised CFP. This attitude was based on several factors.

DUBIOUS MORALITY OF EQUAL ACCESS

First, many British and Irish considered the moral foundations of the original CFP to be dubious. It was difficult to deny that the legal provisions of this policy and the Treaty of Accession supported equal access. But many in the British Isles were convinced that they had been rushed through for highly suspect motives just before the entry of the UK and Eire into the Community. The Commission might protest its innocence along with the original 'Six' and point out:

1   that the CFP had its beginnings in the early 1960s;
2   that the UK distant-water industry had first favoured equality of access;
3   that no attempt to re-model the access provisions had been made in the Labour government's re-negotiation of EEC membership terms in 1974–5;
4   that Britain, in successive 'Cod Wars' with Iceland, had led resistance to the introduction of 200-mile fishing limits in Europe.

But none of these arguments, if indeed heard, could destroy the widespread conviction that the moral underpinnings of Community law on fishing rights were shaky. Austin Mitchell, Labour MP for Grimsby – a fishing port long attached to the idea of open international access to fisheries – expressed such sentiments as follows:

> Unfortunately, before we went into the common market, the Six decided, with that spirit of cunning greed which they describe as Community feeling, that our fish should be their common resource. (Mitchell 1977)

CHANGED CIRCUMSTANCES

Representatives of Britain's distant-water fishing industry were on rather stronger ground when they argued that circumstances had changed and the CFP's fishing access provisions should change accordingly. The loss of fishing opportunities consequent upon the generalized spread of 200-mile limits produced a dramatic change of attitude in the large and politically influential British distant-water industry after the last 'Cod War' in 1975.

From being a vigorous supporter of international open seas, this sector of the industry now ranged itself alongside inshore fishermen to insist on the need for wide exclusive national fishing zones around the UK. By January 1976 British United Trawlers Ltd (1976) of Hull was urging that:

> The most effective way of achieving our objectives lies in the establishment (within our 200-mile EEZ) of an exclusive UK 100-mile/median fishing zone. This is the most crucial single factor affecting the survival of fish stocks and the UK fishing industry.

In effect, given the configuration of Britain's 200-mile/median line EEZ, this proposal meant that the bulk of UK waters would be closed to foreign fishermen, including those from the rest of the European

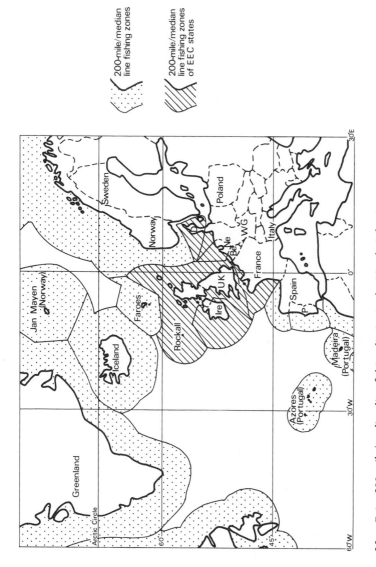

Map 7.1 200-mile/median line fishing limits in the North Atlantic

Source: Map entitled 'Global aspects of marine fisheries', US Department of State (1978), Washington, DC, Office of the Geographer.

Community (Map 7.1). Thus a new resource base would be created at the expense of continental fishermen to give the UK industry what British United Trawlers Ltd termed 'a great and exciting future'.

The drastic nature of this about-face amongst British distant-water fishermen can be understood when the scale of the decline affecting ports like Hull is grasped. In January 1975, 429 vessels were operated by members of the British Fishing Federation, the main representative body of this branch of the industry. By September 1978 this number had fallen to 233, representing, or so it was claimed, the loss of some 3500 jobs at sea (*The Financial Times* 1978) (see also Figure 2.10).

DEVELOPMENT OF IRISH FISHING

Irish motivations for an extension of exclusive fishing rights differed from those in the British deep-sea industry, although they were sometimes similar to those of Scottish and English nearer-water fishermen. Ireland's government saw its underdeveloped, essentially inshore industry ready for expansion, rather than burdened with problems of overcapacity and contraction. Determination to maintain this growth potential hardened as fishermen from neighbouring countries, including Britain, sought to increase their activities in the waters around Ireland to compensate for losses elsewhere. The Irish Fishermen's Organization articulated this determination by insisting on an exclusive national fishing limit of at least 50 miles to be respected by all states whether in or out of the EEC (Heskin 1977, 14–16).

THE BRITISH AND IRISH CONTRIBUTION

In justifying their demand for large exclusive fishing zones with the Community, Britain and Ireland pointed to what they perceived to be their large 'contribution' to EEC fishery resources. The advent of 200-mile limits had radically altered the geographical pattern of sovereignty over sea-space (Map 7.1). Under this new system Britain and Ireland maintained that they contributed around 62 per cent and 8 per cent respectively of the 'Community pond' in the North Atlantic, and that, as a consequence, their share of the catch from this area should reflect these proportions. This was a rather crude argument that ignored the complex geographical distributions of highly mobile fish stocks that varied greatly in value. Nevertheless, it had a strong, simplistic appeal that led to British demands for some 60 per cent of the total EEC catch (*Eurofish Report* 1977a). The Irish tended to be less ambitious, but contrasted their 8 per cent contribution to Community sea-space with the fact that, during the mid-1970s, their fishing industry took just 15 per cent of the total catch within Ireland's 200-mile/median line and 2 per cent of the whole catch from EEC waters (see Table 7.2).

Table 7.2 Comparison of member states' proposed 1978 quota shares (in weight) with their share of the 200-mile/median line zones of the Community in the Atlantic and North Sea (excludes Biscay)

Member state	% share of 1978 EEC internal quota by weight (Col. 1)	% share of EEC 200-mile/median line zones (Col. 2)	Col. 1 as a % of Col. 2
UK	26	62	42
France	8	4	200
Belgium	1	0.3	333
Netherlands	4	5	80
W. Germany	8	4	200
Denmark	47	17	276
Ireland	2	8	25

Source: Eurofish Report (1978d).

REGIONAL DEPENDENCE ON FISHING

A further justification for British and Irish claims referred to an allegedly high degree of 'dependence' on fishing in several regions of the British Isles, where incomes were low, unemployment high and out-migration a persistent problem. The whole of Ireland – especially the west coast – fell into such a peripheral zone of the common market, and fishing ports, large and small, from South West England to Humberside to the Highlands and Islands of Scotland could argue that they existed in a similar depressed regional context. How could one persist with a CFP that, by virtue of its equal-access provisions, threatened to worsen the plight of such poorer areas and increase imbalances that the Community's regional policy was pledged to alleviate? Exclusive fishing zones, continued those developing this argument, constituted the only effective way of ensuring that such regions retained control over one of their few natural advantages.

EFFECTIVE CONSERVATION

The British and Irish also maintained that exclusive national fishing zones were the best way of conserving fisheries. Overfishing had flourished under weak international commissions like the NEAFC and was becoming more acute. Only the adjacent coastal states, according to many British and Irish observers, would have both the political will and the legal enforcement apparatus to protect these resources in their 200-mile/median line zones. Explicitly rejecting the quota system favoured by the European Commission and the continental states, officials of the UK's White Fish Authority enlarged on this point as follows:

> The basis of the UK's claim for a wide coastal belt under national control is that direct effort limitation is more effective than a quota system, both for conservation purposes and for the protection of the vital interests of fishing regions. (Steel and Buchanan 1977, 7)

Within Britain and Ireland there was little confidence in the European Community's ability to provide a more effective international framework for conservation than the NEAFC. In 1978 the Managing Director of a British fishing company gave voice to this widespread scepticism thus:

> The Commission have argued that NEAFC failed because it was a voluntary regime, whereas the Community will have a statutory regime on the basis of agreement reached by majority vote. However, the painful and tortuous wrangling of the Council of Ministers and the Commission over the last two years on some of the basic conservation issues such as the North Sea herring with . . . some countries trying to gain exceptions in a situation where scientific evidence is indisputable, breeds absolutely no confidence that the EEC regime will show any higher ratio of science to politics. (Wood 1978)

Of course, many protagonists of such viewpoints recognized that fish are no respectors of national fishing limits. But it was wrong, they argued, to confuse the issue of resource ownership with that of the need to co-operate to conserve. Obviously, an effective UK conservation policy would depend on working closely with the rest of the Community. But, they added sharply, in the vital North Sea arena, UK co-operation with Norway was more important than with all of Britain's EEC partners together. The fact that Norway had rejected the embrace of the Community did not make such co-operation impossible.

RESOURCE OWNERSHIP

Many of those in Britain and Ireland pressing for exclusive fishing limits were frankly opposed to membership of the EEC. Others, however, defended themselves against the charge of being anti-Community in spirit. Ignorant of, baffled by, or unable to accept the Byzantine complexity of Community legislation in this domain, even pro-marketeers wondered why they should share 'their' fish with other member states when no such 'pooling' of natural resources – for example, North Sea oil and gas – seemed to be required in other sectors; in the words of one representative of the British fishing industry:

> The basic Treaty of Rome quite clearly spells out that 'the Community will not own the natural assets of any of the member states' (sic) and there is no way that Dutch gas, Italian olives, German coal, French uranium, French vineyards or indeed any of the other various natural assets of the member states could ever be exposed to common ownership or exploitation. (Wood 1978)

In fact, the legal situation was considerably more complex than this blunt statement suggested (see Chapters 4 and 5 and Article 36 of the Treaty of Rome). For a start, the Commission and most of the 'Nine' were insisting not on common ownership of fish resources but equal conditions of access to them regardless of nationality. Furthermore, although resources such as oil and agricultural land remained 'national' assets, the 'rights of establishment' enshrined in the Treaty of Rome allowed persons from one member state to settle in another and use those resources; a German farmer could operate in France and so on. Moreover, the lack of a Community approach to resource use in certain fields did not, from the viewpoint of bodies like the Commission, justify its abandonment in fisheries policy, where the highly mobile nature of fish stocks threw doubt on the whole notion of ownership, national or otherwise. However, such legal niceties left British and Irish fishermen unimpressed. Their claim to wide exclusive fishing zones was, in their view, the equivalent of France protecting its agricultural wealth and the Dutch profiting from their natural gas; that was reality as perceived in the fish docks of the British Isles whatever Community lawyers might argue!

A conflict of great complexity

In the interests of simplification, a broad pattern of conflict over fishing rights, aligning Britain and Ireland on one hand against the continental states on the other has been described. In fact, the geographical pattern of conflict was far more complex. For example, the French were particularly determined to protect the 'historic rights' that they had established around the British Isles in international treaties over the years. This reflected the strength of pressures emanating from Breton and Norman fishing communities. The West Germans, however, were more preoccupied with maintaining, or obtaining, access to third-country waters in order to provide opportunities for their severely depleted deep-sea fleet based in ports such as Cuxhaven; consequently, they tended to be more ready to make access concessions to the UK within the 'Community pond' in order to get them. As for the Italians, the securing of fishing rights in Mediterranean and West African waters was their priority. The Italians occasionally hankered after fishing opportunities in the North Atlantic as well, but received no sympathy from their northern partners already locked in a bitter struggle over who should get what of a diminishing resource (Commission 1977b). In contrast, the Italians obviously did not share the concern of the Danes and West Germans to preserve fishing rights in a Baltic Sea divided into 200-mile/median line zones to their marked disadvantage.

These conflicts were, moreover, not always concerned with fishing limits. For example, in defence of their demands for large North Sea quotas, the Danish defended their 'industrial' fishing for reduction purposes with a vigour equalled only by French opposition to it (Christensen 1977). These attitudes are elucidated when it is noted that during the 1970s some 80 per cent of the Danish catch was used to produce fish-meal and fish-oil, whereas 99 per cent of France's much smaller landings went into direct human consumption. Why should our herring fishing for food suffer, argued the French and others, when it is the industrial fisheries of Denmark and Norway that have produced such severe overfishing of these species? In response, the Danes complained of an unjustified antipathy towards industrial fishing which, they argued, utilized species unfit or unwanted for human consumption and provided vital feedstuffs for livestock that produced the meat, milk and eggs people did want to eat.

The habitual statement of fishing interests in 'national' terms simplifies, but frequently distorts, reality. At a regional level within France, for example, one finds certain Bretons determined to preserve access to Norway lobster (nephrops) stocks off South West England and Ireland, Boulogne fishermen concerned with North Sea herring quotas, those operating out of La Rochelle worried about the activities of Spanish fishermen in the Bay of Biscay, and their compatriots in Mediterranean ports preoccupied with sardine prices! Similarly, West Germans fishing with near- and middle-water vessels have been hurt by the loss of Baltic and North Sea fishing, and the large trawler owning companies in Bremen and Cuxhaven have been severely affected by the loss of distant-water grounds.

Even within the UK, the deep-sea sector's switch in favour of exclusive national fishing zones did not mean that all British fishermen were now united on all fronts. The traditional fears of inshore fishermen were reinforced by the prospect of large boats out of ports such as Hull and Aberdeen diverting their substantial surplus capacity towards nearer-water stocks and threatening the livelihood of communities from Lands End to the Shetlands. There was only a limited sense of national solidarity linking the skipper-owners of small inshore vessels with the large companies dominating distant-water fishing. The former tended to see little future for the latter after the last 'Cod War' and welcomed the running down of the deep-sea fleet.

Attitudes within the overwhelmingly inshore and middle-water Irish fishing industry closely paralleled those found among their British counterparts. But, although fishermen within Ireland were of a fairly homogeneous character, there was potential for schism in the formulation of Irish national fishing policy. Mr Brendan O'Kelly, chairman of the Irish Sea Fisheries Board, reminded his compatriots that it was not enough simply to catch more fish in some exclusive national zone, for they also had to be sold. The implication was that demands for an exclusive Irish fishing belt within Community waters must be tempered by a recognition that the growth of Ireland's fishing industry depended on access to the common market's many consumers (*Eurofish*

Report 1980). This cautionary note found echoes in the Irish government. Fisheries still formed part of the overall CAP which was of enormous benefit to Ireland with its large farming population dependent on exports. Furthermore, the Irish were large net beneficiaries of Community regional and social policies (*Economist* 1981). Such factors moderated the Irish government's fishery policy in a way that conflicted sharply with the more nationalistic and narrowly defined demands of Ireland's fishermen.

Ireland's position as a clear net beneficiary of EEC policies, differentiated it from the UK and made the establishment of a united front on the fishing access issue difficult. To many in Britain, the CFP was just one more heavy cost of Community membership among few, if any benefits. The tortured and continuing history of national conflict between Britain and Ireland also made Irish officials wary of being too closely allied with their UK counterparts, despite their obvious concordance on exclusive national fishing rights.

The tangle of converging and diverging interests was complicated still further by the traditional tensions between fish producers, fish merchants and fish processors. For example, fishermen often want to block imports, or secure government guarantees, to push up prices. This conflicts with the desire of merchants and processors to maintain cheap, regular fish supplies regardless of origin.

So although generalizations about 'national interests' can be valid, especially because the political structure of the Community tends to reduce issues to such crude terms, the real complexities must not be forgotten when trying to understand the persistence of conflict over the allocation of fish resources within the Community. The MP for Grimsby, Austin Mitchell, encapsulated this reality in Britain's highly diverse fishing industry:

> The fishing industry comprises a collection of competing interests, united behind a passionate desire for a fifty-mile limit. . . . How long will this unity last? . . . There is a jostling scrum of rival ports, and a clash of area against area, the South West defending its mackerel against Humberside, Humberside criticizing the Scot's indiscriminate scooping up of everything in their purse-seiners. . . . Grimsby sets out its case for being the only fishing port on the Humber. So the arguments go on.
>   Sectional differences cut across geographical. Merchants want fish to keep their staff and distribution networks going. If we can't

catch it, they'll have to import it, even from Iceland. Owners are divided. The big distant-water boys ... (are) preoccupied with the need for a long-term agreement to give them access to distant waters.

Many of the smaller boats, such as the Seine Netters, have been doing well, but are worried by the increasing competition in the North Sea. The really small inshore boats feel discriminated against by the other two ... and really want a 12-mile limit. Then come the unions ... torn between the need to preserve jobs onshore and the threat to the catching side of the industry. (Mitchell 1977)

Such divergences exist in the fishing industries of all member states, reminding us to be wary of the simplifications made by national politicians in search of solutions to complex conflicts and authors trying to synthesize a mass of individual interests and actions!

8 Persistent deadlock in the search for a new CFP

> a 50-mile limit of exclusive control is a *sine qua non* of an acceptable solution. (Leaders of British fishing organizations, *Eurofish Report* 1978a)

> The 50-mile demand responded to nothing that was realizable.... It is not possible to dine 'à la carte' at the Community table. One cannot have the benefits of regional, social and other Community policies and refuse to accept fundamental Treaty requirements concerning discrimination or equal treatment. (European Commissioner for Fisheries, *Eurofish Report* 1978b)

In May 1976, the British government demanded exclusive national fishing zones – varying in width from 12 to 50 miles – that would apply to its Community partners (*Hansard* 1976b). Such zones would, it maintained, provide an effective framework for conserving fish stocks around the UK and ensure that British fishermen obtained a 'fair' share of them. This fell short of the full 50-mile (or more) limit desired by most in the UK fishing industry. Evidently, the British government was seeking a solution that stood some chance of being accepted by other EEC states. It knew that a unilateral declaration of new limits beyond 12 miles limiting the activities of other Community fishermen would break its legal obligations under the existing CFP and the Treaty of Accession (see Chapter 5). Moreover, it might upset the recently renegotiated terms of common market membership in which the CFP had been left untouched. Furthermore, it would be extremely difficult, perhaps impossible, to enforce such limits without the co-operation of other Community states. The Irish government was less inhibited in making a clear demand for a full 50-mile exclusive fishing zone within the 'Community pond' (*Eurofish Report* 1977b).

The 1977 standstill agreement

These British and Irish demands obviously ran counter to the Commission's 1976 proposals and received absolutely no recognition in the Hague Resolutions (see Chapter 6). This, and the fact that other states, while accepting the broad philosophy of the Commission's proposals, were unhappy with the quotas they were being offered led to stalemate. Consequently, the Council uneasily agreed that fishing in 1977 should be maintained at 1976 levels pending a final settlement. This 'standstill' accord depended on the will of individual member states for its enforcement! Thereafter, the struggle for control of fishery resources within EEC waters became ever more complicated as both the Community, acting as a body, and individual member states introduced measures of uncertain legality in attempts to create conservation/allocation systems that conformed to the interests of the initiator. Not surprisingly, it was the British and Irish who were most prominent in taking unilateral action.

The Irish autonomous measures of 1977

The Hague Resolutions permitted individual member states to take autonomous conservation measures, provided that no equivalent Community regulations existed and they did not discriminate on national grounds. In February 1977, Ireland unilaterally introduced what was overtly a purely conservation measure in its EEZ. This banned vessels exceeding 33 m (110 ft) and/or 1100 bhp from fishing in zones extending 50 to 150 miles from the Irish coast (Bourgeois 1979). But this conservation measure also had a marked impact on the allocation of fishery resources. Ireland's EEC partners were quick to point out that this measure discriminated against them in practice, if not according to the strict letter of the law, in that it allowed virtually all Irish vessels to continue fishing in the zone affected, but excluded a large number of other Community vessels that exploited these waters (see Table 8.1).

After attempts to find a compromise had failed, the Commission initiated Treaty infringement proceedings against the Irish government in the Community's Court of Justice. In defence, Ireland claimed that its measures were necessary on conservation grounds, had nothing to do with nationality and had a varying impact on countries simply because of the different structures of the national fleets concerned. The Court, however, decided that the Irish had indeed indulged in a covert form of national discrimination by careful choice of the banning criteria; consequently, in July 1977, it ordered Ireland to suspend its unilateral measures. Conscious of its legal obligations, as

Table 8.1 Community fishing vessels operating in waters around Ireland

Member state	Total powered coastal & deep-sea vessels, 1976 (A)	of which over 33 m & 1,100 BHP (B)	% B of A
Ireland	1,520	2	0.18
France	3,905	160	4.00
Netherlands	544	94	17.20
UK	2,520	276	10.60
	Total fishing vessels normally operating in waters affected by the Irish measures (A)	of which over 33 m & 1,100 BHP (B)	% B of A
Ireland	1,100	1	0.19
France	407	101	24.80
Netherlands	57	57	100.00
UK	26	–	–

Source: Bourgeois (1979).

well as its other Community interests, the Irish government complied with the Court's decision, but maintained its opposition to the Commission's access proposals.

The UK autonomous measures of 1977

Invoking, like the Irish, the clause in the Hague Resolutions permitting autonomous national conservation measures, the British government (SI 1977a, b, c, d) told the Commission in January 1977 that it intended to introduce:

(a) a ban on herring fishing in an attempt to save stocks which had been severely reduced by overfishing in the North Sea and elsewhere;

(b) restrictions on fishing for Norway pout, in an area of the North Sea in UK waters that became known as the 'Norway Pout Box', in order to reduce the amount of industrial fishing by Danes and others for this species, and protect the young haddock and whiting stocks in this 'box' which British fishermen exploited for direct human consumption;

(c)   control of permitted by-catches of protected species (e.g. those fishing for sprats were permitted a 10 per cent by-catch of herring, those fishing for Norway pout a 5 per cent by-catch of herring, and so on) in order to reduce the possibility of the argument that such species were caught accidentally while in the pursuit of other stocks;

(d)   a ban on carrying nets of various sizes on the same voyage in order to prevent the use of prohibited nets when inspection seemed unlikely.

The UK government stressed that it was operating strictly within the Hague Resolutions by ensuring that all these measures applied equally to British fishermen as well as other EEC operators; there was no question of discriminating on national grounds. Moreover, none of these measures appeared to discriminate in practice as much as the abortive Irish autonomous measure discussed above. This lack of discrimination led the Community as a whole to adopt all these measures, except the Pout Box controls, in a conservatory regulation of February 1977 (Council 1977). As regards the Pout Box, the Council was only able to agree on more temporary measures that banned industrial fishing in the area between 21 February 1977 and 31 March 1977 and, later, between 1 September 1977 and 31 October 1977. Although the Commission proposed that this ban be extended until the end of the year, the Council was unable to agree so to do. Whereupon, the UK invoked the Hague Resolutions again and extended the Pout Box ban unilaterally after having sought, and obtained, the approval of the Commission.

The failure of the Council to prolong the Pout Box ban as a Community regulation resulted from Danish objections. Denmark's fishmeal industry obtained about 25 per cent of its massive catch for reduction to fishmeal from Norway pout. It, and the Danish government, felt that such industrial fishing was being unfairly discriminated against in favour of the haddock and whiting fishing carried out by British fishermen and others. Consequently, Denmark, in the Council of Ministers, refused to accept the severity of the ban unilaterally imposed by the British with the support of the Commission (for further discussion of the Pout Box conflict, see Chapter 9).

Other countries were unhappy with other elements of the UK's measures. For example, France challenged the legality of a British

Order of March 1977 which limited to 20 per cent the whitefish by-catch permissible with small mesh nets when fishing for prawns. On 1 October 1977 the French trawler 'Cap Caval' was boarded within British fishery limits by UK inspectors and found to have about 2.9 tonnes of whitefish on board and 1.8 tonnes of prawns (nephrops) in the hold. The master of the trawler was summoned before the Pembroke Magistrates Court, convicted under the British Order for carrying nets of too fine a mesh and sentenced to a fine of £150 plus £50 costs (Bourgeois 1979). The French government, supported by the Commission, referred the case to the European Court of Justice, claiming that the Order was contrary to Community law since it concerned a matter that should be dealt with by EEC institutions rather than individual member states acting unilaterally. Furthermore, the French, and the Commission, claimed that the British had failed to seek the approval of the Commission before introducing this measure as required by the Hague Resolutions (see above). France also maintained that the NEAFC, which Britain referred to in partial justification of its actions, had recommended by-catches of 25 per cent rather than 20 per cent in cases of this sort. The Commission, however, did not challenge the content of the UK measure – in fact it had proposed even more stringent ones – but opposed the unilateral national way in which it had been adopted.

The UK remained firm, insisting that it was following impartial NEAFC recommendations and taking effective, enforceable measures that were not forthcoming from the Community, whatever the Commission might propose. Brushing aside arguments that Britain was the major obstacle preventing the establishment of an effective Community fisheries regime, the UK government insisted that it had to take such autonomous action in the legal vacuum created by the lack of a proper CFP.

From early 1977 until European Court judgements in 1979, 1980 and 1981, the 'Cap Caval', 'Pout Box' and other issues dragged on in a legal situation of immense complexity and related political hostility, particularly between Britain and the rest of its Community partners. In 1977, the UK issued another 30 or more Orders regulating fishing, while the EEC made around 40 regulations concerning conservation of stocks in Community zones, the control of third-country fishing in these zones and so on. In general, the UK Orders implemented, or were subsequently supported by, Community regulations, although this was not always the case. For example, the Order banning herring fishing within Britain's North Sea waters implemented an EEC regulation. But when this regulation expired on 31 January 1978 the UK Order remained in force and thus became a unilateral measure (SI 1977b).

The political reality creating this confused legal situation was the continuing contest to decide who should control fisheries. Britain and Ireland continued to assert that individual member states should exercise a large measure of national authority in the waters under their jurisdiction, whereas the Commission and the other member states sought to increase the legal competence of Community institutions across all 200-mile/median line zones in the EEC. At the heart of this conflict, as always, could be found the related issues of how to protect, enlarge and divide the common market's 'fish cake'!

It cannot be stressed too often how related the issues of conservation and allocation are. Although the measures introduced by the UK, Ireland and the Community were designed to protect fish stocks, they inevitably had allocational effects, as the Irish autonomous action clearly demonstrated. The 'Pout Box' measures also, whether unilaterally maintained by the UK or implemented by the Community as a whole, discriminated against the Danish fishmeal industry in favour of fishermen seeking haddock and whiting for direct human consumption. Similarly, the UK mesh and by-catch regulations at issue in the 'Cap Caval' case can be seen as an allocational measure discriminating in favour of those seeking whitefish rather than prawns. In such cases, it is extremely difficult to determine whether the discrimination involved is 'national' in character or not; the same evidence could produce different judgements on the matter. In the Irish case discussed above, the European Court decided that, in practice, national discrimination had occurred. However, the unilateral UK measures did not so obviously affect vessels from different states in what might be deemed a discriminatory manner.

The UK demand for 'dominant preference'

Initially, the UK government had wanted exclusive national fishing zones varying in width from 12 to 50 miles, but in June 1977 this was changed to 'dominant preference' for British fishermen in the 12- to 50-mile belt. This notion clashed less obviously with the CFP's national non-discrimination principle than the unequivocal demand for exclusive fishing zones. Towards the end of 1977, the UK government had incorporated this new concept into a coherent package that sought to ensure that Britain obtained a 'sea lion's' share of EEC fishery resources in the 'Community pond' as follows:

1 an exclusive 12-mile national fishing zone around the UK within which the historic rights of other member states would be phased out after 1982 when the arrangements of the Treaty of Accession came to an end;
2 dominant preference for British fishermen in the 12- to 50-mile zone beyond, which would be expressed in a share of catch quotas in this area reflecting Britain's '60 per cent contribution' to EEC fish resources;
3 a normal share of EEC catch quotas in areas beyond 50 miles and in third-country waters;
4 a 20 per cent (demersal species) to 25 per cent (pelagic species) share of future increases in Community TACs arising as a result of successful conservation measures;
5 the right of coastal states to enforce conservation measures in their 200-mile/median line zones;
6 the enforcement of Community quotas through effort limitation that would require, among other things, the issuing of licences to a restricted number of vessels specifying the amount of fishing time allowed on particular stocks in particular areas, and so on.

Exactly what 'dominant preference' would mean in quantitative terms was left open to negotiation. Originally some 60 per cent of the total EEC catch had been demanded in line with what was perceived by Britain, but not by other states, as its 60 per cent 'contribution' to Community fish resources. At other times, the UK wanted an arrangement which gave it 95 per cent of the catch within its 200-mile/median line (*Economist* 1978a). However, by December 1977, Mr Silkin had indicated that an allocation giving British fishermen some 44 per cent of the total catch of the most valuable species in EEC waters could form the basis for agreement (*Eurofish Report* 1978a). This was some 40,000 tonnes above Britain's recent historic catch in these waters and 30,000 tonnes more than its total catch in all waters in 1977 (*Eurofish Report* 1977c)! But the UK government thought such demands were justified in order to compensate its distant-water industry for losses of fishing rights in third-country waters.

Not surprisingly, Britain's partners thought otherwise. Even the Irish Fisheries Minister, Mr Lenihan, found the British demands 'totally unrealistic' and revealed the limitations of any Anglo-Irish fishing alliance by making the tart observation that Mr Silkin seemed not to have realized that Britain had lost its Empire (*Eurofish Report* 1977d, 1978c)!

The Commission's proposals for 1978

To break the deepening stalemate, new proposals were presented to the Council as a coherent package in January 1978 (Commission 1978b). Supported by the European Parliament, the Commission maintained the basic structure established in its 1976 proposals and the Hague Resolutions (see Chapter 6). However, changes had been made in an attempt to meet British and Irish objections. In particular, the idea of fishing plans was introduced and greater movement was made towards recognizing lost fishing rights in third-country waters as a criterion for determining national shares of the available Community catch. The overall package of proposals was made up of several distinct, but interrelated elements.

CONSERVATION AND CONTROL

In addition to proposing much reduced TACs for many species, involving an overall cutback of some 10 per cent in the EEC's total catch in 1978 (see below), the Commission wanted to introduce several other conservation measures such as: the phased introduction of a 90-mm mesh-size requirement in certain areas to prevent capture of immature whitefish; a maximum 10 per cent by-catch rule in conjunction with a Norway 'Pout Box' (see above) to protect young haddock and whiting in the North Sea; a variety of restricted fishing zones for certain species; and a continuation of the ban on North Sea herring fishing.

Aware that fishermen have little faith in the effectiveness of control measures in countries other than their own, the Commission pursued its objective of getting a Community system of enforcement involving inspection at sea, checks on landings and fishing effort, compulsory catch reports, vessel licences, and so on.

COMMUNITY FINANCIAL AID

To ease the difficulties of reducing fishing effort and adjusting catching capacity to the realities of a world now dominated by 200-mile fishing limits, the Commission proposed the use of Community funds to reimburse up to 50 per cent of a member state's expenditure on:

redeploying surplus capacity to underexploited species; prospecting new fishery resources; reducing fishing activities while overfished stocks were recovering; breaking-up or converting obsolete vessels. The Commission also suggested EEC aid to encourage: a reduction in the capacity to produce fishmeal and oil; an increase in the consumption of lesser known species; and the early retirement of fishermen between the ages of 50 and 65. It also proposed that Ireland and Greenland receive Community help to cover the costs of enforcing fishery regulations in the vast spaces of the 200-mile/median line zones that surrounded their lowly populated lands.

IMPLEMENT THIRD-COUNTRY AGREEMENTS

Clearly, the implementation of agreements on fishing rights with third countries would facilitate the share-out of the EEC's internal resources by determining what was available to whom outside the 'Community pond'. States were reluctant to commit themselves to some internal EEC quota until they knew what external resources, if any, were available to them.

FISHING PLANS

Fishing plans were designed, in part, to meet British and Irish demands for restricted access to certain zones without infringing the national non-discrimination principle. Such plans could, in the interests of achieving these objectives, extend to areas beyond 12 miles from the baselines and 'would normally relate to endangered stocks or stocks whose exploitation is of special importance to coastal populations'. They 'may not discriminate as between fishermen of the member states of the Community or affect their right of access', but they 'shall take into account that vessels which, due to their limited range of operation, can only exercise their activities close to the coast, should have priority in the coastal areas'. Moreover, 'the activity of other categories of vessels must be harmoniously introduced into the global fishing activity of all the vessels operating in the area and, in particular, undue concentration of long-range vessels in areas closest to the coast should be prevented' (Commission 1978c).

In short, fishing plans were designed to: conserve the fish stocks of a particular area; allocate and manage catch quotas in that area; regulate historic and other fishing rights in that area; ensure priority access to fishermen based in ports adjacent to the fishing plan area (e.g. by making a preferential grant of fishing licences to boats within two hours' steaming time of the fishing grounds in question) (European Parliament 1978). The Commission thought that such plans would protect the so-called 'Hague regions' (i.e. Ireland, Greenland and 'North Britain' cited in the 1976 Hague Resolutions) and meet British, Irish and Danish (i.e. Greenland) demands without sacrificing the national non-discrimination principle. However, fishing plans, structural measures and conservation controls would not in themselves resolve the allocational issue that lay at the heart of the CFP dispute. The crucial element, upon which everything else ultimately depended, still concerned the definition and division of the Community's fishery resources.

AN OVERALL REDUCTION IN COMMUNITY TACS

In October 1977 the Commission had presented the Council with very detailed proposals in which it had calculated TACs for each stock – internal, external, and joint – of each species available to Community fishermen (Commission 1977c). These TACs, which involved some 60 fish stocks, were based closely on ICES and ICNAF recommendations for catch levels in 1978. This underlined the Commission's wish to base its proposals on the most neutral and widely accepted scientific advice available. A group of experts put at the Commission's disposal by the member states helped in this task. The determination to curb overfishing meant that many of the proposed TACs involved serious cutbacks. For example, the proposed North Sea haddock TAC was some 50 per cent below the one adopted by the NEAFC in 1976, whereas the 1977 ban on North Sea herring fishing would continue. Overall, these proposals involved a reduction of some 10 per cent in the EEC's 1978 catch compared with the average total annual catches for the period 1973–6. Such cutbacks intensified the problem of allocating the proposed TACs among the different Community countries.

DIVISION OF TACS INTO QUOTAS

In developing criteria to determine the allocation of these TACs, the Commission 'endeavoured to carry out the operation as transparently as possible' (Commission 1977c). Aware of the acute tensions involved in sharing out dwindling resources, it produced a very detailed document describing the procedure adopted to determine the national quota proposals. Table 8.2 and Figure 8.1 present the Commission's basic check-list of steps taken in the allocation process plus its summary flow chart of what was a very complicated operation. The main criteria used by the Commission were: historical catch performance; preference for regions particularly dependent on fishing; and, somewhat reluctantly, compensation for losses of fishing rights in third-country waters.

Historical catch performance

The Commission's attachment of the criterion of historical catch patterns was based on several factors. First, the idea that countries would go on catching roughly the same proportion of a given stock as in the recent past had an appealing simplicity and, to many, a basic sense of fairness. Secondly, such a principle did least to disrupt existing fishing patterns. Thirdly, most countries of the Community – France, Denmark, Belgium and the Netherlands – had traditionally concentrated their efforts on what were now Community waters and stood to benefit from the adoption of this criterion. None of these had suffered losses in non-Community waters to the same extent as Britain and West Germany (see Chapter 6).

However, the simplicity of this criterion is more apparent than real. A major difficulty arises when trying to decide the reference period according to which the historical catch levels of a particular country may be defined. National governments obviously try to fix reference periods that maximize the size of their historical catch. Denmark, for example, increased its catch from the North Sea enormously in the last two decades and obviously favoured a reference period that corresponded to the time when Danish catches were at their peak. Other countries whose catch of a particular stock has been declining in real or relative terms would favour a reference period stretching back to a time when their catch was high in relation to others. Clearly, the opportunities for statistical manipulation of annual catch levels which rise and fall with rapidity are immense; no one reference period will please all.

Well aware of this problem, the Commission based its calculations of historical catch performance on reference periods adopted by the NEAFC in 1976 when making recommended quotas (Commission 1977c). It declared its motives in adopting these so-called 'NEAFC keys'. Firstly, they were seen as coming from a neutral body that had calculated historical catches on the basis of a balance between short and long reference periods. Secondly, this 1976 NEAFC allocation, although not mandatory, had set catch expectations to which individual member state's fishermen had already made some adjustment. Thirdly, these 'keys' had produced allocations about

Table 8.2 Check-list of steps taken by Commission in deciding allocation of quotas (see Figure 8.1)

Internal stocks
1 Take NEAFC quota or 1976 catch distribution
2 Apply 1978 TAC to give 'expected' 1978 distribution
3 Replace Irish catch where relevant by the raised 1975 catch
4 Reproportion the remainder of the TAC
5 Calculate the special needs for North Britain and obtain from non-reciprocal third-country catches or, where this is insufficient, from other member states. If needs are already met, then, of course, no adjustment is made
6 In certain cases the original NEAFC quotas included an allocation under the title 'others'. For the moment this has been left for redistribution at a later date

Joint stocks
1 Steps 1 and 2 as above
2 Calculate distribution of expected 1976 quota on this basis between EEC zone and Norwegian zone
3 Adjust EEC and Norwegian catch according to the formula likely to flow from the framework agreement
4 Consider the special needs for North Britain. Adjust the UK catch available from exclusion of non-reciprocal third countries, from other member states, and in extreme cases, that likely to be available from the reciprocal waters
5 Where a surplus of available catch remains this is redistributed proportionately to the member states (except North Britain)
6 (a) check the practical capacity of the special needs fleet to take the special needs catch under the biological situation obtaining or
   (b) check that the special needs catch is equivalent to the maintenance of an appropriate level of activity

External stocks
1 Steps 1 and 2 as before
2 Calculate approximate catch possibilities likely to be negotiated by the Community
3 Distribute to the member states in proportion to their previous share of the member states catches in these waters

Source: Commission (1977c).

which some measure of agreement had been achieved in the recent past among the member states of the Community. In sea areas where the NEAFC criteria were inapplicable, the Commission based its proposals upon similar keys produced by the ICNAF and the Baltic Commission.

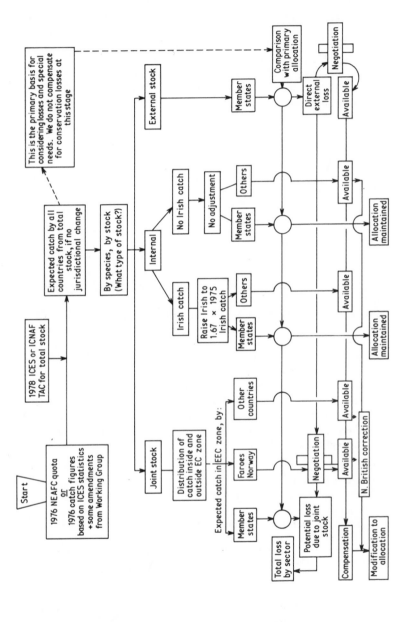

Figure 8.1 Summary flow chart of Commission's quota allocation procedure (see also Table 8.2)
Source: Commission (1977c).

Where no quotas or historical catches had been fixed previously by an international fishery commission, the Commission based its proposals on 1976 catch levels. It recognized that use of a single year reference period to define historical catch was somewhat arbitrary, but argued that 1976, which immediately followed the introduction of 200-mile fishing limits by several important fishing countries, best reflected fishing patterns existing before the upheavals associated with the loss of fishing rights off Iceland, Norway, Canada and elsewhere.

Regions dependent on fishing

The use of the historical catch criterion alone would not have met the requirements of the Hague Resolutions (see above) which afforded preferential treatment to Ireland, Greenland and North Britain where 'local populations' were deemed to be 'particularly dependent on fishing'. In the case of Ireland, the Resolutions had been very specific; the Irish catch should double between 1975 and 1979. In pursuit of this target, the Commission proposed a 1978 quota for Ireland which was 166 per cent of its 1975 catch. This increase came from resources formerly exploited by non-Community countries (now eliminated from EEC waters) or from those previously fished by other member states.

The Hague Resolutions had been much vaguer in dealing with preferential treatment for other regions. For 'North Britain', the Commission proposed to guarantee 'local' fishermen a minimum allocation equal to their catches in 1975. This year was deemed to be representative of a period in which such fishermen had met their 'essential needs' by catches taken from the North Sea and west of Scotland. 'Local' fishermen were defined as those using boats under 80 ft in length and operating out of ports 'dependent mainly on fishing'. In applying these definitions the Commission used statistics provided by Britain. Preference for Greenland was given by proposing a share of stocks adjacent to its shores essential to meet its needs before allocating the rest to other Community fishermen.

Compensation for third-country losses

The importance attached to this criterion in the Commission's initial allocation proposals of October 1977 was much less than Britain or West Germany thought reasonable. The Commission proposed to compensate losses of fishing rights off third countries only to the extent made possible by gains to the Community arising from the elimination or reduction of third-country catches in the fishing zones of member states (Commission 1977c). The reluctance of the Commission to give greater weight to this criterion was based on the belief that losses suffered by one Community country, or sector, could not be compensated by simply transferring them to another. This would revolve rather than solve the problem. Moreover, the Commission argued that such a solution would involve 'intolerable changes in fishing patterns' and provoke political conflict of un-resolvable complexity. Furthermore, from a Community perspective, it made little sense to eject fishermen from grounds they had long exploited in order to make space for displaced distant-water vessels often ill-equipped to exploit different and unknown resources nearer home.

In resisting British and West German pressures on third-country losses, the Commission also emphasized that the resource base of Community fishermen had shrunk in other ways as well. In particular, there were losses due to overfishing and subsequent conservation measures. Those exploiting North Sea herring had suffered as a result of the 1977 ban imposed to stop the destruction of this fishery. Similarly, the 10 per cent overall reduction in proposed TACs for 1978 would harm many fishermen. For these 'conservation losses' the Commission proposed no compensatory allocation at all. Consequently, there were limits on the extent to which nearer-water fishermen should be asked to reduce fishing effort in order to help those evicted from non-Community waters.

In November 1977 the Commission produced a detailed assessment of the lost fishing opportunities in third-country waters (Commission 1977d), but urged caution in interpreting the available figures. To attribute all such losses to the extension of fishing limits would be erroneous; overfishing, biological changes, increased fuel costs, diminishing profit margins and conservation measures had also led to decreased catches in non-Community waters. The reference period chosen against which to measure projected third-country losses for 1978 was 1973–6. These years more-or-less corresponded with the progressive shift in fishing limits from 12 to 200 miles and, according to the Commission, best indicated the impact of these extensions. The British would have preferred a reference period from an earlier time when their activities in distant waters went virtually unchallenged. The main conclusions of the Commission's analysis are summarized in Table 8.3.

Table 8.3 The Commission's calculation of national losses in third-country waters, 1978

Projected 1978 losses	France	W. Germany	UK
Total loss (based on 1973–6 average national catches of main species)			
in tonnes	86,282	226,792	253,778
as % of 1973–6 national average	34%	67%	43%
Third-country losses (based on 1973–6 average national catches of main species)			
in tonnes	52,093	173,458	213,231
as % of 1973–6 national average	20%	52%	36%
Same % loss by main species			
Cod	44%	42%	50%
Haddock	30%	82%	29%
Saithe	7%	30%	23%
Whiting	2%	–	+6%
Plaice	–	–	7%
Redfish	–	93%	98%
Herring	11%	54%	–

Source: Commission (1977d).

In absolute terms, Britain was the largest loser, followed by West Germany. In relative terms the roles were reversed. Britain and West Germany together accounted for nearly 90 per cent of Community losses in third-country waters. France was the only other member state significantly affected.

The Commission thought there were four ways in which such losses could be partially compensated:

1 from stocks in member state zones for which there were, as yet, no TAC and allocation proposals (about 30,000 tonnes);
2 by substituting species not yet fully exploited, such as horse mackerel and blue whiting (about 750,000 tonnes);
3 through structural programmes using Community aid to facilitate adaptation to the new, reduced circumstances;

4   through financing research into the possibilities of exploiting the largely underfished grounds of the Southern Hemisphere.

Clearly, the Commission was still not prepared to propose more substantial compensation for third-country losses by reducing the catch shares of nearer-water fishermen. In the proposals it eventually put before Council in January 1978, the Commission reduced the British and West German claims for third-country losses (213,000 and 170,000 tonnes, respectively) by some 20 per cent and included a higher proportion of lower-valued species in this compensation than the claimants thought desirable.

TAC AND QUOTA PROPOSALS FOR 1978

After weeks of difficult negotiations, the Commission eventually interpreted the various allocational criteria – historical catch, regional preference, and third-country losses – to propose the 1978 share-out described in Table 8.4 These proposals meant that the UK would obtain about 70 per cent of the catch in waters now under its juris- diction and some 31.5 per cent of the TAC within the 'Community pond'. This represented a substantial increase on the originally proposed 21 per cent, which had been about proportional with Britain's historical share of the total EEC catch in all waters. With regard to absolute catches in all waters, the British allocation was a mere 0.5 per cent down on its historical catch (i.e. 1973–6 average). Ireland excepted, this ensured that Britain would suffer a much smaller reduction than its partners in purely quantitative terms and increase its proportional share of the total Community catch. But much of this 'preferential' allocation to Britain was made up of the less valuable pelagic species. These proposals meant that the UK loss on the more valuable demersal species for 1978 (compared to 1973–6) was some 20 per cent (160,000 tonnes), whereas its gain on pelagic species was some 130 per cent (170,000 tonnes). This compared to a total EEC loss over the same period of 20 per cent for demersal species (excluding blue whiting) and a gain of 42 per cent for pelagic fish (excluding herring and horse mackerel) (Boos 1979). Essentially, Britain's loss of distant-water, high-value demersal fisheries was being compensated by a larger share of lower-valued pelagic species found within Community waters.

Ireland was the only country that received an increased quota; this was in line with objectives of the Hague Resolutions (see above). Most

Table 8.4   The Commission's national quota proposals for 1978 (all figures in '000 tonnes)

	1973-6 average catches	% EEC total	Commission's 1978 proposal	% EEC total	% change (1978/1973-6)
EEC catch quota proposals for all waters					
EEC total	4,580.0	(100.0)	4,121.0	(100.0)	− 10.0%
Belgium	48.6	(1.0)	43.0	(1.0)	− 11.0%
Denmark	1,746.0	(38.1)	1,455.0	(35.3)	− 16.6%
France	617.0	(13.5)	576.0	(13.9)	− 6.6%
W. Germany	440.0	(9.6)	388.0	(9.4)	− 11.9%
Ireland	77.0	(1.7)	97.0	(2.4)	+ 26.0%
Italy	388.0	(8.5)	371.0	(9.0)	− 1.0%
Netherlands	222.0	(4.8)	155.0	(3.7)	− 30.0%
UK	1,041.0	(22.7)	1,036.0	(25.1)	− 0.5%
Proposed allocation of TAC within EEC waters					
EEC total	–	–	2,700.0	(100.0)	–
Belgium	–	–	24.7	(0.9)	–
Denmark	–	–	1,147.0	(42.5)	–
France	–	–	242.0	(9.0)	–
W. Germany	–	–	250.0	(9.2)	–
Ireland	–	–	79.0	(2.9)	–
Italy	–	–	–	–	–
Netherlands	–	–	129.0	(4.7)	–
UK	–	–	852.0	(31.5)	–

Source: Eurofish Report (1978a).
Note: Community reserve TAC was 250,000 tonnes of horse mackerel.

states had to accept substantial absolute cutbacks averaging 10 per cent overall. Of course, these reductions varied greatly in detail: for example, the French were asked to accept cuts of 23 per cent for saithe, 18 per cent for cod and 10 per cent for hake, whereas the Netherlands was confronted with a general reduction of 30 per cent in its national catch. To soften the blow, the Dutch were offered 7000 tonnes more herring from these much restricted stocks in order to keep a traditional sector of their industry alive. Similarly, the Belgian cutback was compensated in part by a high proportion of high-value species in the national quota.

The Irish government acceptance

Unlike the British, the Irish government decided to stop pressing for an extended exclusive fishing zone and accepted the 1978 proposals. It embraced the idea of fishing plans as a suitable framework within which to conserve and allocate resources. Fishing plans were based on regional rather than national criteria and thus did not offend the national non-discrimination principle so dear to defenders of the CFP. Ireland's Minister for Fisheries, Mr Lenihan, defended his government's change of policy in these terms:

> It is not in my view a realistic proposition to press the policy of a 50-mile limit at the present time. I am satisfied, however, that substantial advantage can be secured through the adoption of ... fishing plans operating on an interim basis for the year 1978 and designed to offer a special preference for Irish fishermen up to 200 miles from our coast. (*Eurofish Report* 1978b)

Many Irish fishermen disagreed and reacted with hostility to what they saw as a capitulation by their government. The chairman of the Irish Fisherman's Organization protested:

> How can the government now be ready to accept a bureaucratic system of fishing plans which are completely contrary to its stated aims ... (and which) ... would turn fishermen into computers and would need as many patrol boats and aircraft to monitor the situation as there would be boats fishing. (*Eurofish Report* 1978b)

Rejecting protestations that acceptance of the plans was only provisional, he maintained that 'the Minister might as well admit that he has relinquished Ireland's bargaining position and thrown away any case for a 50-mile limit'.

Given the hostility of Irish fishermen to these fishing plans, why did the Irish government accept the idea? Firstly, the European Court ruling on Ireland's autonomous measures (see above) had clearly established the precedence of Community law over national decisions. Secondly, Irish ministers, if not fishermen, were well aware of the benefits Ireland obtained from Community membership in other spheres, such as agricultural policy. Mr Gundelach, the European Commissioner for Agriculture and Fisheries, bluntly told a meeting of Irish fishermen that their government had made an inevitable decision:

> The 50-mile demand responded to nothing that was realizable. . . . It is not possible to dine 'à la carte' at the Community table. One

cannot have the benefits of regional, social and other Community policies and refuse to accept fundamental Treaty requirements concerning discrimination or equal treatment. (*Eurofish Report* 1978b)

Thirdly, there were benefits for the Irish fishing industry in Community membership. The policy of doubling Ireland's catch in four years – which had been accepted by all member states in the Hague Resolutions – depended on finding new markets. If Ireland opted out of the common market, its fish products might lose free access to it. The chairman of the Irish Sea Fisheries Board was aware of this when insisting that 'we must develop our industry on the basis that our home market is Europe' (*Eurofish Report* 1980). Furthermore, Irish fishing was receiving developmental aid from the Community to finance its expansion. Between 1972 and 1977, Ireland obtained about £8 million for 67 fishery projects from the EEC with the promise of more to come. Also, partly as a result of accepting fishing plans, the Commission was proposing that Ireland receive some £30 million over five years in order to increase its fishery protection service. If Ireland were to introduce some 50-mile limit unilaterally, it would not have the resources to carry out an effective policing operation within it. Far better, argued the government, to co-operate with the Community, get preferential treatment for Irish regions within fishing plans and still continue to benefit from common market membership in other ways.

British rejection

Despite receiving what its partners considered to be preferential treatment, Britain refused to accept the 1978 proposals. The other member states endorsed them at an informal meeting of fisheries and agricultural ministers on 29 January 1978 in Berlin that Mr Silkin, the British minister responsible, boycotted. Why did the British government block agreement once again, whereas Ireland now aligned itself with the continental states in declaring its intention of observing the Commission's proposals?

Firstly, the proposed 31 per cent British share of the Community catch still fell far short of the 45 per cent, or thereabouts, demanded. Secondly, much of the UK quota was made up of horse mackerel, an underexploited species that would be difficult to sell. Thirdly, there was still no recognition of Britain's claims to an exclusive 12-mile limit free from historic rights, nor any formal recognition of the UK demand for dominant preference in the 12- to 50-mile zone. Furthermore, the principle of keeping fishing access conditions free from national discrimination persisted, clashing with Britain's national approach to problems of fishery allocation and control (*Hansard* 1978).

There was some speculation at the time that Mr Silkin was close to agreement with his European counterparts (*Economist* 1978b). It seems he once suggested that fishing plans might form the basis for a settlement, but only if they satisfied *de facto*, if not strictly *de jure*, Britain's demands for preferential treatment. However, the British fishing industry, which doggedly pursued the government's every move, remained resolutely opposed to such subtleties. The three leading British fishing organizations united to denounce the Commission's proposals as 'totally unacceptable'. In their view, the UK quota offered was 'hopelessly inadequate' and a '50-mile limit of exclusive control is a *sine qua non* of an acceptable solution' (*Eurofish Report* 1978a).

Persistent stalemate

Following Britain's rejection of the 1978 proposals, fishery affairs within the Community continued to evolve inconclusively in an uncertain legal limbo. Quotas proposed by the Commission were tacitly accepted by all member states except the UK, which accused the others of not enforcing them. Arrangements on quotas with third countries were 'rolled over' for short periods pending an internal settlement. Deadlines for agreement on a new CFP were regularly broken. General declarations of intent emanated from the Council, which continued to fudge the crucial issues. For example, when the Council failed, yet again, to resolve the conflict by the end of the 1979 'deadline', it issued yet another unbinding declaration that set yet another final settlement date (31 March 1980) and asked, yet again, that member states 'conduct their fisheries in such a way that the catches of their vessels during the interim period shall take into account TACs submitted to the Council . . . (by the Commission) . . . and the part of the TACs likely to be made available to third countries under agreements or arrangements made by the Community with them' (Council 1979a, b, c). On conservation, the Council, again seeking the lowest common denominator of agreement, urged that member states apply those measures in force by 3 November 1976 and that any new regulations should be adopted in accordance with the procedures laid down in the 'Hague Resolutions' of the same date (see Chapter 6).

On this last point, the British continued to clash with the rest of the Community. They had been actively introducing unilateral conservation measures since the beginning of 1977. During 1978 this process continued apace: a ban on herring fishing off the west of Scotland was imposed, along with restrictions on Manx and Mourne herring fishing; an extension of the Norway Pout Box 2° eastwards for six months every year from 1 October upset the Danes; the declared intention, later deferred, of introducing a 70-mm mesh for Norway lobster (nephrops) fishing from 1 November 1978 was resisted by the French government sensitive to the interests of its fishermen operating to the south-west of the British Isles. The Commission continued to be more exasperated by the unilateral nature of these measures rather than their content.

National elections hinder negotiations

The difficulties of resolving this stalemate were exacerbated by the frequently recurring prospect of national elections somewhere in the Community. This made governments very sensitive to the charge of 'selling-out' national fishing interests. For example, the UK's determination to maintain its demands during 1978 was stiffened by the possibility of an election in the autumn of that year and the certainty of one by the end of spring 1979. Although fishermen made up a mere 0.1 per cent of the British labour force, fishing is a sensitive political issue capable of generating national passions not associated with other larger industries. In addition, many British fishing communities were located in electorally marginal constituencies at this time. Of the 22 main 'fishing' seats in the latter years of the 1974–9 Labour government, 9 were held with majorities of less than 6 per cent of the total vote; in Aberdeen it was 0.7 per cent and Grimsby 1.2 per cent (*Economist* 1978c). If Mr Silkin's vigorous defence of British objectives in Brussels helped to produce a 3 per cent swing to Labour in such constituencies, his party would gain 5 extra seats. In a period of minuscule parliamentary majorities and subsequent Liberal–Labour pacts such considerations were not insignificant.

Although the British government's stance was reinforced by electoral prospects, other countries were tempted to stall in the hope that a future Conservative government – with a greater overall commitment to Community membership – would be more likely to compromise. Such thoughts formed part of the background to the stalemated negotiations for a lengthy period, in that the British elections widely predicted for autumn 1978 did not take place until May of the following year. In the event, the new Conservative government adopted much the same negotiating stance as the intransigent Mr Silkin, so that hopes of a speedy resolution of the CFP were dashed as the familiar recital of opposing positions continued into the 1980s. This underlines the danger of attributing too much importance to these electoral factors at the expense of interest groups who were able to exert considerable influence on governments of whatever political persuasion.

It was not only in Britain that electoral prospects influenced the progress of the CFP negotiations. The Danes, who had a major interest in fisheries, held a general election in October 1979; this made concessions to Britain on the 'Pout Box' (see above) and other issues virtually impossible. Later, West German general elections in autumn 1980 and a French presidential election in spring 1981 cramped freedom of negotiation in these two national camps where the electoral balance of forces, as elsewhere in Europe, was finely balanced. On national television in the major 'end-of-campaign' debate between the two French presidential candidates, M. Mitterand, the challenger, specifically chastized M. Giscard d'Estaing for failing to defend French fishing interests with sufficient vigour against the British; his opponent indignantly refuted the charge in some detail! Dutch, Irish, Belgian and Italian elections at various intervals, plus referenda on Community membership in Greenland further complicated the decision-making process. Thus, the existence of a *de facto* national veto in the Council of Ministers along with almost constant elections in the offing, combined with vociferous fishing interest groups to form potent decision-blocking mechanisms within the Community's institutions.

A CFP settlement through majority voting?

Attempts to resolve the fisheries problem were thus foundering as the Community's cumbersome policy-making process proved a blunt instrument incapable of cutting through conflict to decision. Britain's adamance that the new common policy must be adopted as a coherent package, rather than built up bit by bit, compounded the problem, as did its insistence that unanimity must be achieved on all proposals related to a new fisheries settlement. Such a 'veto' on matters of 'vital national interest' had been established *de facto*, if not *de jure*, by General de Gaulle's French government in the so-called 'Luxembourg

Compromise' of 1966 (see Chapter 1). Frustrated by the repeated failures to establish a new CFP, some suggested that this assumed 'right' of national veto be challenged in the Council of Ministers and the European Court in an attempt to break the deadlock caused by Britain's refusal to accept the 1978 proposals. The West Germans were particularly irritated by the way in which failure to settle the internal fishery dispute was hindering agreements with third countries, thus preventing their hard-hit distant-water fishermen from getting access to non-Community fish stocks.

During 1978 the clash between those wishing to strengthen majority voting on fishery matters and those insisting on unanimity came to a head. Following its rejection of the January 1978 proposals, the UK government, represented on agriculture and fisheries by the strongly 'anti-market' Mr Silkin, blocked all moves that threatened to lead to the sort of CFP unwanted by Britain. For example, it vetoed the fishing plans sought by Ireland and others. However, in July 1978 the Council was able to agree on two relatively minor internal measures that did not appear to compromise anyone's basic negotiating stance on the overall CFP; these involved the spending of 5 million EUA to improve the Irish inshore fishing industry and Italian fish farming, plus 46 million EUA for Ireland and 10 million EUA for Denmark as a contribution towards the cost of fisheries surveillance in Irish and Greenland waters between 1977 and 1982.

Then, the Council's West German president, Herr Josef Ertl, maintained that this agreement had been made on the basis of majority voting according to Article 43 of the Treaty of Rome. Mr Silkin saw this as an attempt to undermine the UK's 'vital' fishing interests in that it could prove a precedent for adoption of the CFP bit by bit through majority voting in the Council. He therefore refused to accept that the Council had agreed, and tried to have the standard reference to Article 43 eliminated from the surveillance regulation. However, Herr Ertl refused to budge and an eventual compromise was reached whereby a note was written in the Council minutes that read, 'in agreeing to the recital of Article 43 in this regulation the UK states that it insists on the right concerning this and other fishery regulations to invoke its fundamental national interests' (*Eurofish Report* 1978d). In effect, Mr Silkin, quietly supported by the French, had reiterated the political reality of the 'Luxembourg Compromise' and blocked once again the possibility of reaching a fisheries agreement through majority voting.

9 Step-by-step towards a revised CFP

> These decisions, we now see, are the decisions typical of ordinary political life – even if they rarely solve problems but merely stave them off or nibble at them, often making headway but sometimes retrogressing. . . . It is decision-making through small or incremental moves on particular problems rather than through a comprehensive reform program. (Braybrooke and Lindblom 1963, 71)

The deadlock over Community fishery policy began to ease towards the end of the 1970s. One contributory factor was the election in May 1979 of a Conservative government in Britain resolved to demonstrate a more positive UK commitment to the Community after years in which Labour's attitude to membership had been lukewarm or, as in the case of Mr Silkin, the former Minister responsible for fisheries, frankly opposed. This new flexibility in the British approach was manifested in a relaxation of the previous insistence that a new CFP be adopted as a comprehensive package rather than built up in stages. Consequently, the 1980s saw a gradual step-by-step piecing together of various elements in a new policy, although none of the governmental participants lost sight of the final goal of creating a complete system of Community fisheries management. Although the new Conservative administration facilitated this change of strategy, it would be wrong to exaggerate the degree to which it differed from its Labour predecessors; it continued a vigorous pursuit of fishery objectives similar to those advocated by Mr Silkin. Factors other than the British change of government were also involved in facilitating the laborious steps along the route towards a reformed CFP.

Decisions in the European Court of Justice

One possible key to releasing the deadlock lay in the European Court of Justice (see Chapter 1). The intervention of the Court had terminated Irish unilateral action in mid-1977, thus contributing to

Ireland's acceptance of the Commission's 1978 proposals. Perhaps the Court would find the UK's independent national position contrary to Community law, so compelling a more conciliatory attitude.

One legal strategy lay in attacking the UK's unilateral conservation measures. However, the Commission was reluctant to start Court proceedings. The British claim that their unilateral conservation measures conformed to EEC law by applying equally to all Community fishermen was not without foundation. However, some states argued that certain measures did, in fact, discriminate on national grounds, despite their apparent legal neutrality. For example, the Danes were particularly unhappy about the Norway Pout Box measures and the French about the proposed 70-mm mesh for Norwegian lobster (nephrops) fishing (see Chapter 8).

The 'Norway Pout Box' issue

The aim of the Pout Box – an area of the North Sea off North East Scotland – is to protect juvenile stocks of haddock and whiting from industrial fishing for Norway pout. Massive exploitation of the latter with small-mesh nets inevitably produces a by-catch of young whitefish, thus reducing the potential of those fishing for direct human consumption (Commission 1978a).

The Pout Box originated in 1977 as a Community measure following pressure from Britain (Council 1977). At that time it covered the area between 56°N and 60°N, and 4°W to 0° (Map 9.1). But, owing to Danish objections, the Council proved unable to agree on a continuation of the measure at the end of 1977. The Danes obtained up to 30 per cent of their massive catch for fishmeal and fish-oil (1.5 million tonnes in 1974) from Norway pout. They felt that their industrial fishing was being unfairly discriminated against in favour of UK fishermen seeking haddock and whiting.

The Danish veto led Britain, with the approval of the Commission, to maintain the Pout Box restriction as an autonomous national measure. However, in mid-1978 the UK decided, unilaterally, to extend the box 2° eastwards from 1 October to 31 March each year, on the grounds that by-catches of young whitefish were generally much higher during this peak of the industrial fishing season. This angered the Danish government, which put great pressure on the Commissioner for Agriculture and Fisheries, Mr Gundelach, himself a Dane, to resist the extension. This time Denmark's case received a

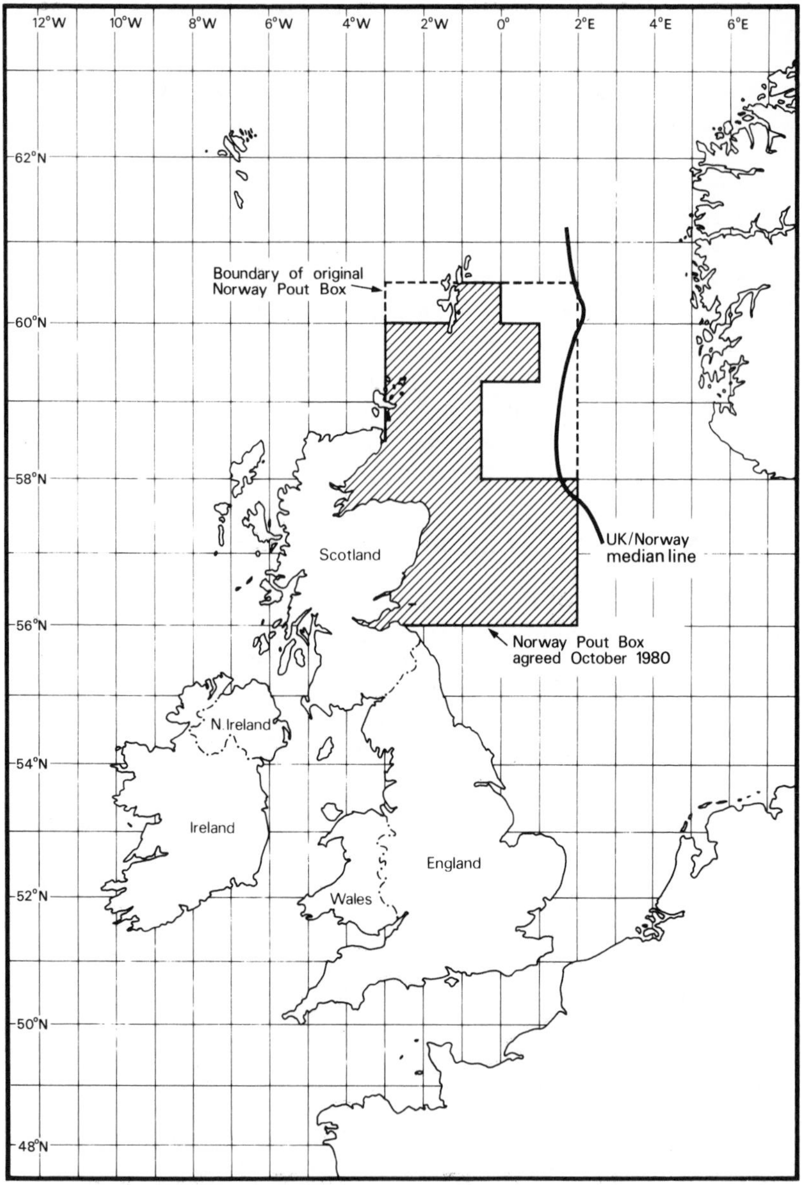
12°W
10°W
8°W
6°W
4°W
2°W
0°
2°E
4°E
6°E
62°N
60°N
58°N
56°N
54°N
52°N
50°N
48°N
Boundary of original Norway Pout Box
UK/Norway median line
Scotland
Norway Pout Box agreed October 1980
N.Ireland
Ireland
England
Wales

Map 9.1 The Norway Pout Box
Sources: Council (1980a); ICES (1979).

more sympathetic hearing, because the Commission and other member states – which normally shared Britain's hostility to large-scale industrial fishing – objected to the unilateral manner in which the measure had been introduced. Furthermore, the Commission now suspected that the new measure went beyond what was strictly necessary to conserve stocks and constituted a *de facto* national discrimination against Danish industrial fishing.

The Commission therefore produced an alternative to the spatial extension of the Pout Box each winter. It proposed a smaller area extended 1° eastwards along with a 10 per cent by-catch limit on small-mesh industrial fishing directed at Norway pout and other species. It argued, along with the Danes, that this would adequately protect young haddock and whiting as well as striking a fair balance between the different fisheries. The British rejected this approach on several grounds. Firstly, the belief that such controls could not work because the stocks involved were so intermixed geographically during the critical fishing seasons that large by-catches were inevitable. The enforcement of a 10 per cent by-catch rule would simply lead to great amounts of excess dead whitefish being dumped at sea by fishermen anxious to avoid prosecution. A partial closure of the fishery was therefore essential. Secondly, the British thought that such by-catch limits would prove costly, perhaps even impossible, to enforce effectively. No one could hope to distinguish species with any precision after they had been mixed in a hold for a fortnight before being pumped onto the quayside. Finally, even if the by-catch could be recorded accurately, and the measures enforced, it would still consist of immature whitefish lost to the breeding stock.

All sides cited ICES evidence to support their cases. However, although such international scientific bodies can clarify, with greater or lesser certitude, a variety of conservation options, they cannot choose between them. In this case, ICES could not 'scientifically' decide what the 'right' balance between industrial and human consumption fishing should be. The final decision inevitably remained a question of political economy. For example, the 2° extension implemented by the British would reduce the Norway pout catch by about 220,000 tonnes, thus permitting a long-term annual gain to the human consumption fishery of about 26,000 tonnes of haddock and 37,000 tonnes of whiting. If the box was extended by only 1°E, as proposed by the Commission, the Norway pout catch would be reduced by some 190,000 tonnes, but the whitefish gains would not drop greatly; to 23,000 and 34,000 tonnes of haddock and whiting, respectively. Various further options are shown in Table 9.1, demonstrating that there was no simple 'conservation' option; a political choice had to be made. Britain made this choice unilaterally in a way which, according to its opponents, went beyond the basic needs of stock conservation to produce a discriminatory allocation in favour of British fishermen, thus breaching the 'Hague Resolutions'.

THE COURT RULES AGAINST THE UK

In early 1979 the Commission initiated proceedings against the UK government, motivated as much by a desire to clarify the larger issue of sovereignty over fisheries within the Community as to settle the Pout Box conflict. In July 1980, the Court ruled that Britain's extension of the box was indeed contrary to Community law and required that a common solution be found (Judgement 1980). This judgement was based on the unilateral nature of the measure as well as the belief that it was not purely conservational in character. It confirmed an earlier Court ruling of October 1979 (Judgement 1979) in the 'Cap Caval' case which had been initiated by the French following arrest of one of their trawlers for contravening a unilateral British measure (see Chapter 8). Here again, the Court passed judgement against Britain for acting without adequately consulting the Commission. It did not contest the content of the UK measure in this case.

These judgements, which supported the Community's claims to overriding authority on fishery matters, helped to unblock the negotiating impasse that had been reached on conservation policy. The Pout Box judgement was accepted by the British Conservative government and paved the way for resolution of the dispute by the Council in September 1980 (Council 1980a). This compromise agreement produced a Pout Box that was more irregular in shape than before, as well as being smaller (see Map 9.1). The Danes would be allowed to pursue industrial fishing for Norway pout in the deepest waters of what had previously been the extended 'Winter Box'. Here the whitefish by-catch problem was less severe. Some 80 to 90 per cent of the young haddock and whiting stocks covered by the old system would still be protected by the new box which would exist all-year-round, not only in winter. This settlement received a hostile reception in the UK, especially in Scotland, but the British government argued that effective conservation of these international stocks required the co-operation of Denmark and other countries.

Table 9.1 Various fishing-effort options in the Norway Pout Box

Options	Total loss in industrial fishery as a % of 1976 total	% long-term gain in human consumption fisheries in yield per recruit	
		Haddock	Whiting
Closure box 1 in winter (Oct.–Mar.): i.e. 56°N to 60°N & 4°W to °0	−1	+3	+7
Closure box 2 all year round: i.e. 56°N to 60°N & 4°W to 1°E	−25	+11	+38
Closure box 3 all year round: i.e. 56°N to 60°N & 4°W to 2°E	−28	+17	+47
Reduction in industrial fishing of:			
20%	−20	+10	+25
30%	−30	+20	+50
40%	−40	+22	+58
60%	−60	+35	+100
80%	−80	+49	+156
100%	−100	+65	+228

Source: ICES (1979).

Community agreement on conservation measures

The Pout Box settlement was part of a package of conservation measures agreed in September 1980, involving restrictions on mesh sizes, types of gear, by-catches, closed seasons and areas (Council 1980a). One of the other major disputes resolved within it concerned fishing for nephrops in the Celtic and Irish Seas; disagreement between Britain and France over permitted mesh sizes and whitefish by-catch levels in these fisheries had led to the 'Cap Caval' case, which produced a Court ruling against unilateral measures imposed by Britain (see above). Following the Court's judgement, Britain and France agreed that the minimum mesh size in the Irish Sea would be 70 mm (as the UK had long wanted), but only 60 mm in the Celtic Sea (where politically powerful Breton fishermen were very active). However, the Irish protested that this 'two-size' compromise between the British and the French was impracticable. Consequently, the final decision in the Council decreed that the minimum size should be 60 mm for both areas. But regional variations were permitted elsewhere; for example, the minimum size for whitefish meshes was 80 mm in the North Sea, 75 mm in the English Channel, and 70 mm (single twine) or 75 mm (double twine) in the Irish Sea.

Another incremental step towards a Community system of resource conservation was taken in March 1980 when the Council decided that member state fishermen must adopt a common method of reporting their catches to the Commission (Council 1980b). This would provide information for the Scientific and Technical Committee for Fisheries – set up by the Commission in June 1979 – in carrying out its task of providing advice on fishery management. Such information would also facilitate the Commission's task of controlling national quotas when the member states eventually went beyond their 'gentlemen's agreement' on the share-out of TACs – which were being fixed annually by Council regulations – and laid down legal allocations of the stocks available.

These limited conservation agreements marked a British retreat from a previous insistence that the reformed CFP be adopted as a comprehensive package rather than implemented bit by bit. The rulings of the European Court contributed to this change. However, evidence that many obstacles remained to be overcome, even in the conservational sphere, was soon forthcoming.

CONSERVATION DEPENDS UPON ALLOCATION

Pending the introduction of a comprehensive new CFP, the conservation measures outlined above were extended on a temporary basis until the end of October 1981. Thereafter, individual member states applied similar temporary measures. This failure to put these conservation measures on a permanent Community legal basis was due to Danish reservations about their proposed quotas in the revised CFP (see below). Denmark's dissatisfaction on this allocational issue soon manifested itself on a conservational matter. In early 1982 the Commission asked all member states to stop herring fishing in the southern North Sea following evidence that the agreed 20,000 tonnes TAC for the stock had been surpassed (Commission 1982a). It pointed to the Danes as the principal cause of this, suggesting that they had exceeded their proposed quota by 10,500 tonnes. In reply, the Danes argued that they had only agreed to respect the overall Community TAC for the stock, not the national quota proposals which had never been formally adopted by the Council; therefore their alleged catch of some 11,500 tonnes had not broken any Community regulation. This was small comfort for states such as West Germany, Britain and France which were obliged to accept closure of this fishery before taking their proposed quotas under the ineffectual arrangements then operating (*Eurofish Report* 1982).

This incident underlined the inability of the Commission to take effective action in the absence of Council regulations. In July 1981 the Commission maintained that, given the failure of the Council to establish a system for conserving fishery resources by the end of 1978 as required by Article 102 of the Treaty of Accession (see Chapter 5), it had the duty and right under Article 155 of the Rome Treaty to require that member states pursue their fishing activities in accordance with what the Commission proposed (Commission 1981a, 1). In other words, the Council's failure to adopt a new CFP had created a vacuum the Commission was obliged to fill. Whatever the lawyers might make of the Commission's case – and there was ample scope for argument – its inability to prevent the overfishing of the proposed quotas made clear the need to resolve the basic allocational issues underlying the CFP conflict before there was a hope of applying a really effective system of conservation.

Reform of the CFP's market system

Although most attention had been focused on fishing rights during the 1970s the CFP's marketing system, set up as part of the overall policy in 1971, also came under mounting pressure for reform. This original system operated price-support and import-control mechanisms similar to those found in the rest of the overall CAP (see Chapter 4). The basic objectives were to prevent prices for internally produced fish falling too low and to control cheap imports, so that fishermen's incomes would be maintained at a 'reasonable' level. However, for several reasons, market policy was not working satisfactorily.

During the 1970s the Community became increasingly dependent upon fish imports following the loss of distant-water rights, the spread of overfishing and resultant catch controls. Between 1975 and 1980 imports of all categories rose by around 100 per cent in value (OECD 1975–82). This increase was composed largely of valuable fresh, chilled and frozen fish from Iceland, Norway, the Faroes, Sweden, Canada, the USA and South Africa. The reference price system, designed to raise the cost of imports to a level where internal producers were not undercut, proved to be rather unresponsive. Large quantities of fish imports often penetrated the common market below the reference price for months before the Commission took action to stem the flow. Such sluggishness displeased neither the Community's fish processors nor its individual consumers, who obviously welcomed regular supplies of cheap, good quality fish from whatever source. But many Community fishermen protested about this failure to control imports.

However, these same fishermen needed to be aware of another broad trend. During the first 10 years of the CFP's existence, fish consumption per capita within the Community had been steadily falling as this foodstuff changed from being a relatively cheap form of protein into a relatively expensive one. Clearly, any amendments to the system would have to avoid making fish even less attractive in comparison to other foodstuffs. Furthermore, no government was keen to reproduce the costly problems of 'surpluses' seen in some other CAP sectors.

A reformed market policy was agreed in principle in September 1981 and implemented, albeit with difficulty, in mid-1982 (Council 1981a). This marked another step by Britain away from its insistence on simultaneous agreement of a reformed CFP as a whole and another success for its partners who had been striving for a progressive step-by-step construction of a new policy. It could be argued that the UK was thus throwing away potential bargaining counters in the continuing struggle over quotas and access. But British Ministers were also under pressure from their fishermen to control the flow of cheap imports and tighten up the price-support system. Moreover, the Conservative government, more than its Labour predecessor, was keen to demonstrate a positive approach on Community issues in order to counter the oft-made accusation that the British were systematically anti-EEC. Thus, Britain pressed hard for this market agreement, supported strongly by the French who were similarly concerned to check imports, support incomes and maintain employment in their unsettled fishing communities.

Clearly, the CFP conflict could no longer be simplified to a case of Britain versus the rest. In fact, it was the Danes, anxious to maintain cheap, regular supplies to their processing industries (and keen to obtain a bargaining lever in their quest for a larger EEC fish quota) who put up most resistance to this new accord. The West Germans had similar interests to the Danes, but in the complex bargaining leading up to the agreement the British had lifted their 'reserve' on a new fishing rights arrangement with Canada in exchange for the more protectionist trade system they wanted. West Germany had long been frustrated by Britain's refusal to permit EEC ratification of the Canadian deal which provided some desperately needed fishing opportunities for German distant-water vessels, but provoked British fears that cheap imported Canadian cod would depress domestic prices. West German satisfaction over this Canadian accord helps explain another element of the mini-package deal underpinning the new market agreement; some 25 million ECU of infra-structural aids, largely beneficial to the inshore industries of Ireland, Italy and the UK, were also released, despite the habitual budgetary reserve of the West Germans (Council 1981b).

Under the reformed system, the ability to enforce import reference prices was strengthened and speeded up to protect fishermen's incomes. However, to allay fears that automatic application of reference prices would hinder the flow of supplies to processors and consumers, a measure of discretion was left to the Commission. If import prices remain below the reference price for three consecutive days, a member state can require the Commission to decide within a further six days whether to: suspend tariff concessions; raise the import price to the reference price by applying an appropriate duty; ban further imports.

In addition, a more flexible system of withdrawal prices was introduced to stabilize markets. POs continue to be responsible for compensating their members following withdrawals of fish from the market when prices are low. They would be able to withdraw fish from within a range of −10 per cent to +5 per cent of the official EEC withdrawal price and receive reimbursement from the Community's EAGGF guarantee fund. This represented a rather higher level of price support than hitherto. However, a determination to prevent the accumulation of large 'surpluses' in storage ensured that the new system would not provide open-ended support. Firstly, EAGGF guarantee payments to POs were limited to 20 per cent of the annual catch. Secondly, a degressive system of EEC reimbursement for withdrawn fish was set up whereby refunding would be reduced as the amount of fish withdrawn increased. The Community would reimburse 85 per cent of the withdrawal price on the first 5 per cent of the annual catch of a given species; 70 per cent on 5–10 per cent of the annual catch; 55 per cent on 10–15 per cent; and 40 per cent on 15–20 per cent. Beyond that point POs would have to finance any withdrawals from their own funds.

Another basic element of the new system was the 'carryover premium', available for up to 15 per cent of the total sales of any given product, by which the Community would partially finance the costs of short-term storage and/or basic processing of valuable top-quality food fish in times of temporary glut in order to prevent its reduction into fishmeal. The Commission calculated that the total cost of these measures to the Community budget would be about 10–15 per cent above the previous amounts (about 30 million ECU p.a.) spent on supporting fish prices in the early 1980s.

The new market regime also permitted, but did not oblige, member states to extend market discipline to those fishermen not belonging to POs. In the early 1980s some 70 per cent of the Community's production of fresh or chilled whole fish and fillets was being marketed through the 71 POs recognized by the EEC. The original CFP regulation had not made the membership of such organizations obligatory; consequently sales by non-members not bound by EEC marketing regulations could disrupt the incomes of those operating within the Community system. The new agreement allowed member states to require that non-members obey the marketing rules laid down by the Community and the PO governing the area where they landed their catches. However, for a PO to be able to extend market discipline in this way its production and marketing activities would have to be of significant importance in the market for one or more of the products concerned. In effect, member states were given the discretion to respond to pressures from POs in their own countries as circumstances required.

Towards a new structural policy

Structural policy is concerned with adapting the Community's fishing industries to resources, to markets and to socio-economic conditions. Following adoption of the original regulation in 1971, the Council produced measures to modernize out-dated salt-cod fleets (mainly French) as part of the package-deal whereby the original CFP had been agreed (see Chapter 4). Later, in November 1975, the Commission, again in the context of the original agreement, proposed a regulation for the restructuring of the inshore fishing industry (Commission 1976c) but progress was slow owing to the reluctance of some member states – notably West Germany – to increase Community expenditure.

In the mid-1970s a major new impetus to structural reform was provided by the need to adapt to the radically reduced fishing opportunities resulting from the extension of 200-mile fishing limits and extensive overfishing. In broad terms the Commission thought this required a cutting down of surplus fishing capacity along with a remodelling of the industry to exploit available resources efficiently and face up to international competition. It would entail a large reduction in the number of distant-water vessels, plus a modernization of the inshore and middle-water fleets most suitable for operation in EEC waters. The development of the inshore industry obviously tied in with the Community objective of using the fishing industry as a source of regional economic development and employment (Commission 1980a, b). The Commission articulated such aims clearly in its 1976 proposals (see Chapter 6), but, yet again, financial reservations and failure to agree on other elements of CFP reform made progress extremely slow. Structural policy only tended to emerge on front stage following accusations of 'unfair' national subsidies distorting common market competition. Nevertheless, the Community was able to adopt some interim structural measures pending a full reform of fishery policy. In pursuit of the long established aim of rejuvenating inshore fishing, a Council regulation of July 1978 authorized the EAGGF to provide subsidies for the construction of vessels in the 12 to 24 m class (Council 1978). The scheme evoked a strong response and was extended in later years with its scope being enlarged to include vessel modernization and aquaculture as well. By mid-1981 some 60 million EUA had been allocated to the scheme and in June 1982 a further 25 million EUA were approved by the Council to finance some 295 projects. Usually EAGGF aid was limited to 25 per cent of the total investment, but in certain economically deprived areas – Ireland, Northern Ireland, Southern Italy, Greece and Greenland – this ceiling could be lifted to 50 per cent. This bias in favour of economically weak peripheral areas with substantial fishing communities can be measured by noting the geographical distribution of these inshore development funds up to March 1981: Ireland 31 per cent, Northern Ireland 10 per cent, Scotland 12 per cent, Mezzogiorno 27 per cent, Brittany 7 per cent, Greenland 3 per cent, others 10 per cent (Commission 1981b).

THE PROBLEM OF EXCESS CAPACITY

The success of this interim measure was clearly related to the fact that it was allocating benefits rather than costs. It did nothing to reduce the excessive capacity of Community fleets. Here structural policy struck right upon the sensitive political issue of which states and regions should have what fishing industries and employment. In the painful business of allocating reductions and unemployment, no Fisheries Minister wanted to be a loser. Perceptions of national interest were inevitably more potent determinants of behaviour than any wider sense of 'European' community! The scale of the problem can be judged by examining the situation in Britain. A British analysis (Mackay 1981) concluded that the UK's 1979 catch could have been achieved with 33 per cent fewer vessels (measured in GRT). It also concluded that Britain's proposed quota – 36 per cent of major species from the 1981 Community TAC – could be taken efficiently by only 71 per cent of the existing fleet tonnage. In terms of 'days of fishing effort' the excess of British capacity was put at 30 per cent. To use British catching potential to the full, it was estimated that the UK would require 54 per cent of the total Community TAC. To many British fishermen an augmentation of the UK quota in this way was an obvious solution to 'their' surplus capacity problem; after all did not Britain 'contribute' something like 60 per cent of the 'Community pond'? But such an increase would intensify the problems of excess capacity in other member states. Once again the CFP negotiations foundered as they hit against the problem of distributing losses in a situation of diminished resources.

The Commission (1980a, b, c; 1981b) proposed to overcome this problem of surplus capacity by using scrapping grants and temporary laying-up premiums. All vessels over 12 m or 25 GRT would qualify for scrapping premiums of some 300 ECU per GRT. States worried about the growth of Community expenditure were wary of such a generalized proposal, fearing that funds would be wasted on numerous vessels that would soon be withdrawn from the industry without such incentives. West Germany, the largest 'net contributor' to the EEC budget, was especially sensitive on this point having made a substantial national effort to trim its fleet to match new circumstances. Consequently, the amount proposed by the Commission for this purpose was progressively reduced, from 130 million ECU in mid-1980 to a mere 70 million ECU one year later. Some observers thought these sums were far too low to have an appreciable impact. For example, a British study estimated that the proposed scrapping premium would have to be three times greater to produce a substantial withdrawal of the more modern vessels (Mackay 1981). The objective of laying-up premiums, rather than scrapping, was to maintain a reserve capacity in case fishing opportunities increased in the future as a result of successful conservation measures, increased access to third-country waters or whatever.

Those in favour of a limited financial effort by the Community wanted member states to assume primary responsibility for cutting down capacity. But the Commission feared that, left to themselves, individual states would not encourage reduction of fleets to a point where fish could be produced more efficiently. To the sharp disapproval of many of its partners, Denmark had actually increased its capacity in the difficult years of diminishing fishing opportunities, 1972 to 1978, whereas the Netherlands had remained essentially stable (see Figure 2.6). Countries such as West Germany, the UK and France, which had shed considerable capacity (largely as a result of losing distant-water fishing) did not want to see their relative share of the 'Community fleet' fall any more. Indeed, as we have seen, the British fishing industry wanted to increase its share of Community TACs in order to use more fully its excess capacity.

Another element complicating the restructuring debate was that of trade protection. One way to maintain 'surplus' capacity, and thus avoid politically invidious decisions, is to protect the fishing industry against cheaper imports from outside the Community. The British, under pressure from a well-organized fishing lobby, increasingly aligned themselves with the French in advocating this approach (see above).

So structural reform was fraught with conflicting approaches. Despite endeavours in the Commission to produce a model of an efficient 'European' fleet, there is no single 'ideal' set of structures to be aimed at. Inevitably, value judgements have to be made. No technician can produce 'objective' solutions to relieve politicians of their decision-making task.

NEW FISHING OPPORTUNITIES

As part of its effort to solve the problem of surplus capacity, the Commission (1980b) proposed that Community funds could be used to promote exploratory voyages to seek new species both within and outside Community waters as well as joint-venture fishing operations between Community and non-member countries. It was proposed that some 9 million EUA be made available to grant up to 50 per cent of the costs of exploratory voyages to test the potential of species such as blue whiting. These grants would be restricted to vessels over 33 m according to the original proposals. This would effectively give preference to British and West German distant-water boats laid up or facing the scrapyard. However, Denmark, supported by France and the Netherlands, wanted a lower limit of some 24 m so that many more of their vessels would qualify. Again fears of a burgeoning budgetary expenditure producing no very precise effect were raised!

An increasing number of countries insisted that the resources off their shores should be exploited in some joint-venture involving both Community fishermen and local populations. Such ventures could take various forms. The coastal state could provide crew for an EEC vessel or charter it. It could insist that all, or part, of the catch by such vessels be landed in local ports for processing or sale. Several private and government-supported initiatives had produced such agreements during the latter 1970s. However, it was often a costly, high-risk business. Consequently, in its 1980 proposals, the Commission proposed that some 6 million EUA be made available to assist those seeking to use their fishing capacity in this way. These proposals were of greatest interest to the French and Italians who already participated in joint-ventures off West Africa and elsewhere in search of tuna, hake, shrimps, squid, and so on.

The Commission maintained that Community aid to aquaculture – already initiated under the interim inshore measures discussed above – was 'vital'. Eager to be associated with an area of growth rather than retrenchment, it argued that fish farming had great potential, particularly in regions where remoteness from markets had discouraged development. A sum of some 40 million ECU over five years was being mooted by the Commission in the early 1980s (Commission 1980b).

HARMONIZATION OF NATIONAL AIDS

While the Commission struggled to obtain relatively meagre funds for a common structural policy, individual member states, often expending larger sums from their national exchequers, pursued their separate policies in this sphere with little regard for overall Community objectives. The aids given by individual EEC countries to their fishing industries were many, varied and often difficult to detect. The Commission argued that such aids distorted competition and should be harmonized. Periodic accusations by one member state that another was giving 'unfair' aid reinforced the Commission's view (Commission 1980b).

In attempts to elucidate the problem, the Commission had frequently requested states to furnish details of national aids given; Article 93.1 of the Rome Treaty required that they so do. Nevertheless, in mid-1980, the Commission had to report that only three countries – Denmark, West Germany and Belgium – had reported full details of the years 1974–8. However, it was able to conclude that aids varied greatly from country to country and had been steadily increasing in recent years as difficulties in the fishing industry grew. Obviously, this lack of clarity and mutual trust did nothing to help the tortuous search for a reformed CFP. In effect, governments often gave fuel subsidies, investment grants, etc., in an attempt to maintain the 'status quo' in their particular national fishing industry. It was easier for Fisheries Ministers to direct financial aid towards their compatriots (and electors) than to advocate job losses in the context of some Community programme.

Despite the strong evidence it had at its disposal, the Commission refrained from taking states to the European Court for breaking EEC competition law by giving some of these aids. Such financial help stemmed from strong pressures put upon national governments by fishermen. An attack on such help might make the emotional climate associated with the CFP imbroglio even more uncongenial for agreement. Thus, it seemed more realistic to promote Community structural aid as a carrot that might help overcome the fundamental conflicts on fishing rights (as it eventually did) rather than attempt to beat member states with a legalistic stick in this particularly sensitive area.

A fisheries settlement as part of a larger package-deal?

In addition to the conflict over fisheries, Britain was in dispute with its partners over what it considered to be its excessively large 'net contribution' to the Community budget. During the first months of 1980 Britain also found itself in the habitual position of resisting the proposed farm price increases within the CAP to the irritation of other member states. Some saw the possibilities of linking these issues in a single negotiating framework so that they might be resolved in the sort of large 'package deal' that had facilitated Community agreements in the past. For example, concessions to the British on the budget question might be offered in exchange for a reduction of their demands on farm prices and fisheries. In May 1980, joint Council sessions of Agricultural, Fisheries, Finance and Foreign Ministers did attempt to reach simultaneous agreement on these various problems. However, although short-term budgetary and farm price deals were struck, a Council declaration, which formally established the general guidelines within which a new CFP should be formulated by the end of 1980, was the more meagre fruit of the fisheries deliberations; it read as follows:

1   The Council agrees that the completion of the CFP is a concomitant part in the solution of the problems with which the Community is confronted at present. To this end the Council undertakes to adopt, in parallel with the application of the decisions which will be taken in other areas, the decisions necessary to ensure that a common overall fisheries policy is put into effect at the latest on 1 January 1981.
2   In compliance with the Treaties and in conformity with the Council Resolution of 3 November 1976 (i.e. the Hague Resolution) this policy should be based on the following guidelines:
    (a) rational and non-discriminatory Community measures for the management of resources and conservation and reconstruction of stocks so as to ensure their exploitation on a lasting basis in appropriate social and economic conditions;
    (b) fair distribution of catches having regard, most particularly,

to traditional fishing activities, to the special needs of regions where the local populations are particularly dependent upon fishing and the industries allied thereto, and the loss of catch potential in third-country waters;

(c) effective controls on the conditions applying to fisheries;

(d) adoption of structural measures that include a financial contribution by the Community;

(e) establishment of securely based fisheries relations with third countries and implementation of agreements already negotiated. In addition, endeavours should be made to conclude further agreements on fishing possibilities, in which the Community – subject to the maintenance of stability on the Community market – could also offer trade concessions.

3 Furthermore, Article 103 of the Act of Accession (i.e. the Article laying down the manner in which any new provisions to follow the expiration of derogations to equal access in December 1982 should be made) shall be applied in conformity with the objectives and provisions of the Treaty establishing the EEC, with the Act of Accession, *inter alia* Articles 100–2 and with the Council Resolution of 3 November 1976, in particular Annex VII (i.e. the Hague Resolution). (Council 1980c)

The unresolved conflicts underlying this declaration were immediately apparent as different delegations published their various versions of what it meant! The French and Germans, for example, stated that the first section of this declaration established a clear link between the new budgetary arrangements won by Britain and the successful completion of the CFP by 1982. If Britain continued to block a fisheries agreement by insisting on its 'excessive' quota/access demands, then other member states would be justified in blocking the UK's hard-won budgetary rebate. The British government, sensitive to accusations of 'horse-trading' at fishermen's expense, denied that any such definite linkage existed. Continental states also pointed to clauses in the declaration concerning the 'objectives and provisions' of the Rome Treaty and 'traditional fishing activities' as evidence that British demands for national preferential access had finally been nullified. Clearly, the British government had retreated significantly from the original UK demands of the latter 1970s, but it continued to emphasize those parts of the declaration referring to the 'special needs of regions ... particularly dependent on fishing' and the 'loss of catch potential in third-country waters' in pursuance of its claim for a very large share of the fishery resources available to the Community.

The budgetary and farm-price conflicts were defused, albeit temporarily, in this large Council session because failure to do so would have created extremely serious and immediate tensions in the Community. But the fisheries dispute, while continuing to consume considerable political energies, did not directly concern so many people as these other issues with which it was being linked. Moreover, negotiators were aware that the ten-year transitional agreement on fishing rights did not run out until the end of 1982. However much people might want a new CFP before this date, this was the ultimate deadline at the back of their minds. The incentive to settle for a less than satisfactory agreement before this crucial date was thus reduced, as the failure to settle before the 1 January 1981 deadline fixed in the Council's May Declaration demonstrated yet again. Despite ministerial denials, the linkage of fisheries to the budgetary and agricultural problems doubtless played a role in getting Britain to reduce its fishing access and quota demands, thus permitting another step towards a final agreement. But the CFP dispute was not ready for resolution in the multi-issue compromise envisaged by some of Britain's partners.

10 Agreement on access and quotas in a new CFP

From a British point of view, it is a superb agreement. (P. Walker, UK Fisheries Minister, *The Times* 1983)

But although I am broadly satisfied that the deal is the best that could be achieved in the circumstances, there is little cause for rejoicing. I fear the CFP is too rigid, too full of unnecessary rules and regulations. It is the inefficient fishermen, not the efficient ones, who stand to gain most. (K. Hjortnaes, Danish MP, *The Times* 1983)

I cannot greet this agreement with jubilation. But what we are presented with is something better than a dangerous free-for-all. (J. Quinn, British MEP, *Eurofish Report* 1983a)

Although the Community had been building up bits of an overall fishery policy, agreement on fishing access and quotas – the crucial allocational issues upon which the ultimate success of a new CFP depended – remained elusive. However, as the legal deadline posed by the termination of the existing arrangements on 31 December 1982 approached, progress towards resolution of this basic conflict over who should catch what fish in what areas was made.

Towards solution of the access problem

Britain had rejected the 1978 proposals because, among other things, it would not accept the fishing access arrangements favoured by its partners (see Chapters 7 and 8). Thereafter, it continued to press for an exclusive 12-mile zone free from historic rights plus some form of preferential access out to 50 miles as a means of ensuring that British fishermen would be able to catch a 'fair' share of the Community's TACs. Britain was gradually able to augment its proposed catch quotas towards an 'acceptable' level (see below), but on the interrelated issue of fishing access the UK Conservative government gradually retreated from early positions. Nevertheless, it continued to insist on arrangements that would give British fishermen a greater measure of exclusive use to the waters around their shores than they had enjoyed in the past.

In broad terms, the access issue separated the islands of Britain, Ireland, and Greenland from the continental states, but it came into sharpest focus as a Franco-British conflict. Whereas the British wanted to extend the derogations to equal access incorporated in the Treaty of Accession, the French strove, at the very least, to maintain the status quo. Thus, whereas the British desired a completely exclusive national 12-mile zone, the French were determined to maintain their legally established historic rights in various parts of the 6- to 12-mile belt. The French also talked of all derogations to equality of access being eliminated at the end of the transition period in December 1982. But defence of their traditional fishing in British waters was doubtless the essential objective behind these more extreme demands.

The particular adamance of France's defence of traditional rights (see Chapter 7) can be explained by the relatively high number of their compatriots fishing in waters around the British Isles (Maps 2.4 and 10.1). The French take a far greater proportion of their national catch from within the UK 12-mile zone than any other member state. During the period 1971–5, French catches inside this belt averaged some 50,000 tonnes p.a; that is some 6 per cent of national average catch. In addition, it took some 22,000 tonnes per annum in the equivalent Irish zone. By 1980, the French estimated that these amounts had been reduced to some 45,000 tonnes in the British zone and a mere 9000 within 12 miles of Ireland. However, the value of these catches to particular fishermen, especially Bretons, remained substantial. The French suggested that if Britain succeeded in eliminating these historic rights, its EEC quotas would almost certainly be cut elsewhere and British fishermen would lose access to valuable species in other member states' coastal zones (Commission 1979a).

France also led opposition to Britain's efforts to create preferential access for its near-water fishermen beyond 12 miles. The British hoped to do this by limiting larger vessels in certain zones around the UK. This was designed to restrict the number of distant- and middle-water boats (often non-British) in these zones to the benefit of local inshore and near-water fishermen using smaller vessels out of adjacent British ports. In December 1980, the UK proposed that two such preferential 'boxes' be established for fishermen exploiting whitefish; one off the

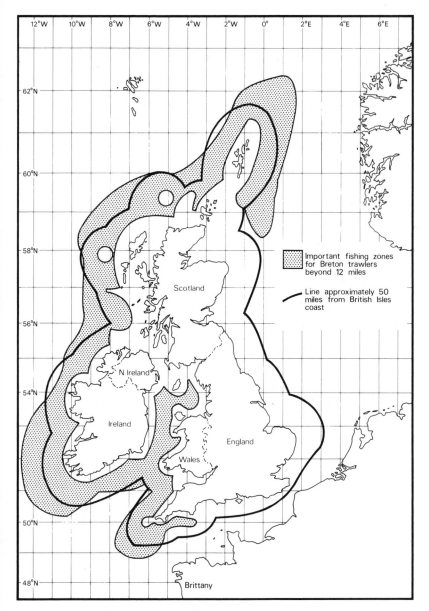

Map 10.1 Fishing zones exploited by Breton trawlers around the British Isles

Source: Commission (1979a).

Orkneys and Shetlands, one in the Irish Sea (Map 10.2). Only vessels under 25 m (80 ft) would, according to the original British proposal, be allowed to operate in these areas (*The Times* 1981; *Eurofish Report* 1981). Some of Britain's partners seemed prepared to accept such an arrangement which carefully avoided discrimination in overt national terms and thus presented no direct challenge to the principle of equal access. However, the introduction of such boxes would, *de facto*, reduce France's traditional activities in these fishing zones, in that the French boats in question were mainly in excess of the 25-m limit proposed. Consequently, the French rejected this British initiative, reminding those involved of the European Court judgement against somewhat similar Irish measures in 1976 (see Chapter 8). The British reiterated that they were not breaking any CFP principle; indeed they were attempting to give concrete expression to the May 1980 Declaration (see above) which reaffirmed the need to protect 'the special needs of regions where local populations are particularly dependent on fishing'.

In its original proposals for a reformed CFP in 1976, the Commission had advocated the permanent establishment of 12-mile belts beyond 1982 to protect inshore fishermen, although its initial ideas of phasing out historic rights were quickly abandoned (see Chapter 6). Later in its 1978 'package' the Commission had urged the use of fishing plans to sort out details of access and fishing rights in particular areas (Chapter 8). It stuck to this general approach over the years as it manipulated details in search of common accord. In mid-1980 it was, for example, still proposing that the limited-access arrangements incorporated in the Treaty of Accession be prolonged to ensure that inshore fishermen in 'dependent' regions had 'a definite advantage over their competitors fishing in the same stocks, shared only by certain fishermen in other member states (i.e. those with historic rights) to most of whom the same socio-economic conditions apply'. This would ensure that the preferential quotas allocated to these 'Hague Regions' could 'actually be fished in practice'. Moreover, the Commission accepted the British argument for controls beyond 12 miles to guarantee 'the full use of these priority quotas', but still felt that these should be elaborated within Community fishing plans that respected genuine historic rights (Commission 1980d). By March 1981, the Commission had clarified its criteria for defining such areas of controlled access as follows:

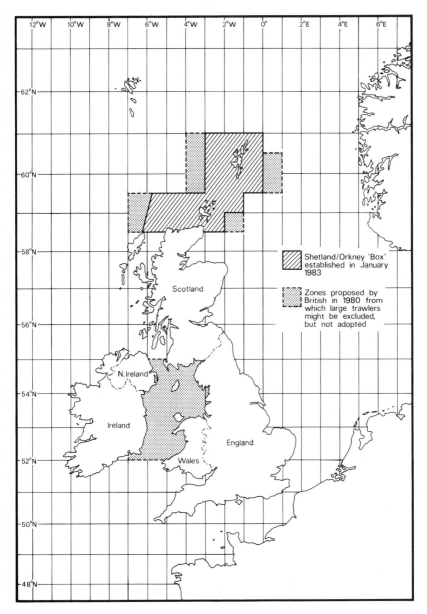

Map 10.2 Proposed and agreed protected fishing zones around the UK
Source: The Times (1981); *Eurofish Report* (1981); Council (1983b).

Such arrangements presuppose that the fishing activity involved is related to a zone that may be considered sensitive ... concerns species on which an overly concentrated fishing effort is of a nature to threaten fishing activities using less sophisticated catching gear and that the absence of special rules could compromise the maintenance or the development of coastal fishing. (Commission 1981c)

Effort in such zones could, in the Commission's view, be controlled to protect regional fishing communities but 'the means used may not have as their intention or as their consequence the introduction of discrimination in favour of national interests, nor may they serve to support a structural policy meant to favour the adaptation or the development of the fishing activities of nationals of a particular member state'. In other words, Britain could not introduce preferential fishing zones for the benefit of its displaced distant-water fishermen to the cost of other Community citizens. Access restrictions could be based on criteria relating to particular regions or sectors but not on nationality.

In the middle of 1982, after a series of bilateral discussions – notably between British and French governments conveniently free from immediate electoral pressures – a compromise emerged on the fishing access issue. In essence, Britain conceded that total elimination of historic rights within the 12-mile limit was politically impossible in a Community context, whereas the French and other member states accepted that the British government needed to achieve a greater degree of exclusive access protection for its fishermen than permitted under existing arrangements. This basic bargain was translated into a new proposed regulation as follows (Commission 1982b; Council 1983a).

The new regulation would maintain the principle of access to fishing grounds free from discrimination on national criteria. However, the exceptions to this principle permitted by Article 100 of the Treaty of Accession (Chapter 5) would be extended both in space and time (Article 6). In spatial terms the 6-mile limit that member states had been allowed to establish for their 'vessels which fish traditionally in those waters and which operate from ports in that geographical coastal area' (notice the regional rather than national definition) could now be pushed out to 12 miles. However, within sections of the 6- to 12-mile belt the clearly specified traditional rights of other member states would be preserved (see Appendix 2).

This new accord involved the virtual elimination of generalized Community access to large sections of Britain's 6- to 12-mile zone to be replaced with more limited rights for particular countries with long established rights in this belt (compare Appendix Maps 1.1, 1.2 and 1.3). To a large degree this meant that the UK had been able to eliminate the freer access won by the continental states in the Treaty of Accession in 1972 and achieve a reversion to the geography of fishing rights laid down in the European Fisheries Convention of 1964 (see Chapter 3). However, Britain also won some reduction in these historic rights established in 1964, before UK membership of the Community. For example, French, Belgian, German and Irish rights were eliminated between the Butt of Lewis and Cape Wrath. The French also lost some access rights off the west coast of Scotland and Wales, and the Belgians could no longer fish in zones off North and North East Scotland. Britain also obtained rights to fish in parts of the 6- to 12-mile belts around eastern and southern Ireland, West Germany (Heligoland), the northern Netherlands and France (Nord/ Pas-de-Calais).

Beyond 12 miles Britain did not obtain the large measure of 'preferential access' it had sought for so long. Instead, it now effectively accepted the Community regional fishing plan idea the Labour government had rejected in January 1978 (Chapter 8). Thus, particularly strict control of fishing effort in 'certain sensitive regions' was to be introduced. In reality, this meant that the so-called Shetland/ Orkney 'Box' was established (Article 7), although demands for a similar zone in the Irish Sea were dropped (Map 10.2). Within this 'Box' a degree of preferential access was accorded to local fishermen by allocating a restricted number of licences to vessels over 26 m in length wishing to fish for demersal species (except Norway pout and blue whiting, which were subject to other Community control measures). Britain was granted 62 of these licences, France 52, Germany 12 and Belgium 2. Boats under 26 m could fish in the 'Box' without such a licence. The fixing of this length criterion followed a negotiation in which the British view ultimately prevailed. After analysis of fishing patterns in the area, the Commission (1981c) had originally proposed that licences should be required for any vessel over 17 m in length and making voyages longer than 24 hours. In its view these criteria separated 'local inshore fishermen' (who could thus be protected without infringing the national non-discrimination principle) from those moving into the area from beyond the Shetlands and Orkneys.

However, such criteria would have prevented British middle-water vessels from mainland Scotland and elsewhere operating in the 'Box'. Given that the bulk of the UK catch in this zone (some 83 per cent in 1978/9) was made by such boats, the British rejected them and the 26-m length was eventually agreed. This allowed a considerable number of British vessels from ports outside of the Shetlands and Orkneys to fish in the area without a licence, but effectively reduced the number of boats from other member states, in that few were under this limit. There were suggestions from France that vessels under 26 m should be subject to licensing as well, but again Britain was able to resist what would have been a further restriction on British fishermen already accusing government of a 'sell-out' of their interests. However, Britain had to concede that this 'Box' was based on 'Community' rather than 'national' criteria and therefore accept that the licensing system controlling fishing within it was managed by the Commission on behalf of the Community; this was a 'Community' fishing zone, not a 'national' one. Again, a delicate balancing of national and regional interests had taken place within a legal framework that tried not to lose sight of basic Community principle.

In temporal terms these new access arrangements were extended over two 10-year periods. At the end of the first period the Commission was required to 'present a report on the fisheries situation in the Community, the economic and social development of the coastal areas and on the state of the stocks as well as their likely evolution' (Article 8). On the basis of this report and the need to ensure 'a relative stability' in the distribution of catches among member states (Article 4), the Council, by qualified majority vote, would decide what 'adjustments' are required to the access system laid down by Articles 6 and 7 (see above). Towards the end of the second 10-year period the Commission would have to submit another 'report on the economic and social situation of the coastal regions' on the basis of which the Council, again by qualified majority voting, would decide what 'provisions' could follow the access arrangements established in the new regulation. In effect, no fundamental changes to the new regime could take place for at least 20 years, so the British government could claim that it had attained its objective of a firm long-term agreement.

By the early autumn of 1982 most member states were ready to accept a reformed CFP including these new access arrangements. However, the Danes continued to resist, partly because of dis-satisfaction over the proposed new fishing rights (which meant, for example, that they would lose access to much of Britain's 6- to 12-mile zone), but more importantly because they were extremely unhappy with the Community quotas being offered to them. The following section examines how this final question of 'who should fish what, where' was resolved.

New proposals on quotas

Although agreements on a range of fishery measures had gradually been built up, consensus on how fishery resources should be shared remained elusive. Britain had refused to accept the 1978 proposals for CFP reform essentially because it felt that its proposed 31.5 per cent share of the total Community TAC – along with the envisaged access arrangements – was utterly inadequate (Chapter 8). Confronted with this refusal, the other member states decided to apply the quotas proposed by the Commission, but there was little effective way of enforcing this 'gentleman's agreement'. Complaints about fishermen exceeding these quotas continued to flourish. In such conditions of mutual distrust, there was little chance that the Community's agreed conservation measures could develop into effective instruments of resource management.

It will be recalled that the basic criteria used by the Commission to define national quotas in the 1978 proposals were: historic catch performance in the reference years 1973–6; preferential regional allocations to Ireland, 'North Britain' and Greenland; and a measure of compensation for lost fishing opportunities in third-country waters (see Chapter 8). The Council Declaration of May 1980 formally accepted these criteria, reinforcing the one concerned with third-country losses (Chapter 9; Council 1980c). These 'jurisdictional losses' due to fishing limit extensions – but not overfishing – were still being calculated for the reference period 1973–6; that is the period immediately before the widespread adoption of 200-mile zones (Chapter 8). But by 1980 the calculation of 'traditional fishing activities' was being based on the reference period 1973–8 in an effort to overcome the criticism that the 1973–6 period disadvantaged those who had historically taken a larger proportion of their national catches from distant waters before the fishing zone extensions of the mid-1970s. However, the catch figure for 1978 used in this calculation was to be that of the national quota proposed by the Commission rather than any actual amount caught in excess of this figure. Obviously the

Commission was trying to counter any effort to build up a 'traditional catch' in the hope of increasing a quota in the final settlement (Commission 1980a).

In the 1980 proposals the definition of 'North Britain' had also been clarified to include the North East English coast from Bridlington to Berwick as well as Scotland, Northern Ireland and the Isle of Man. But attempts by those in South West England to have their region defined as one especially dependent on fishing had failed (Commission 1980e). Moreover, there had been no change in the way preferences for 'Hague Regions' – or 'Hague transfers' – were to be calculated: Ireland was to obtain double its 1975 catch; boats of less than 24 m operating out of 'local ports' in North Britain would be assured quotas equalling their 1975 catches in that region; and Greenland would be guaranteed adequate quantities to meet its needs.

FROM GENERAL CRITERIA TO A SPECIFIC SHARE-OUT

Although the new proposals clarified the allocational criteria in a manner advantageous to Britain, there was still ample scope for conflict over how these general criteria should be applied in precise practice. Thus, a great variety of quota proposals – all based on the above guidelines – were made and subsequently rejected as unsatisfactory by one or more parties. The variables producing these different allocational outcomes were numerous. For example, what level of compensation should be accorded for third-country losses? In the teeth of Dutch and Danish opposition, Britain and West Germany obviously wanted something approaching 100 per cent compensation, whereas the Commission (1980e) favoured the somewhat arbitrary compromise figure of 50 per cent in its proposals. Similarly, the patterns of quota distribution varied according to what types of fish were included in the calculations. In its first attempts to apply the May 1980 criteria, the Commission based its calculations on six 'major species': cod, haddock, saithe, whiting, plaice and redfish. This removed direct industrial fishing from the calculations to the disadvantage of the Danes (see Table 10.1). Later, the growth of mackerel fishing made it imperative to add this species to the calculations, thus producing a different set of figures (see Table 10.2). Subsequent proposals became ever more sophisticated as other species were incorporated to take account of all the interests involved. By 1981, the Commission's proposals referred to four categories of fish defined

Table 10.1 Proposed quota allocation in tonnes of cod equivalent produced by applying criteria of May 1980 Declaration to six major species (cod, haddock, saithe, whiting, plaice, redfish)

	EEC	W. Germany	France	Netherlands	Belgium	UK	Denmark	Ireland
1 Internal catch possibilities for 1980 based on 1973–8 average (levelled) plus external catch possibilities for 1980	988,795	124,623	144,041	89,989	24,644	273,479	316,295	15,728
	100%	12.60%	14.57%	9.10%	2.49%	27.66%	31.99%	1.59%
2 Internal catch possibilities for 1980 with 'Hague Region' transfers (in brackets) plus external catch possibilities for 1980	988,795 (±28,639)	114,485 (−10,138)	130,536 (−13,505)	88,337 (−1,652)	23,306 (−1,338)	284,950 (+11,471)	314,291 (−2,004)	32,890 (+17,162)
	100%	11.58%	13.20%	8.93%	2.36%	28.82%	31.79%	3.33%
3 Compensation transfers for third-country jurisdictional losses based on 1973–6 average catches	–	+21,171	−19,505	−6,621	14,610	+48,168	−38,601	–
4 Commission's proposal for 1980 (i.e. 50% of line 3)	–	+10,585	−9,752	−3,311	−2,305	+24,084	−19,301	–
5 Final total catch possibilities (i.e. line 2 + line 4)	988,795	125,070	120,783	85,026	21,001	309,034	294,991	32,890
% of EEC total	100%	12.65%	12.22%	8.60%	2.12%	31.25%	29.83%	3.33%

Source: Commission (1980g).

Table 10.2 Proposed quota allocation in tonnes of cod equivalent produced by applying the criteria of May 1980 Declaration to seven major species (mackerel added to six listed in Table 10.1)

	EEC	W. Germany	France	Netherlands	Belgium	UK North*	UK South	Denmark Mainland	Greenland*	Ireland*
1 Internal catch possibilities for 1981 based on 1973–8 average catches (levelled) plus external catch possibilities for 1981	1,120,643	156,767	159,636	99,827	26,525	204,879	139,569	268,650	43,151	21,639
						(30.73%)		(27.82%)		
	100%	13.99%	14.25%	8.91%	2.37%	18.28%	12.45%	23.97%	3.85%	1.93%
2 Internal catch possibilities for 1981 after 'Hague Region' transfers** (in brackets) plus external catch possibilities for 1981	1,120,643 (±44,224)	148,577 (−8,190)	151,589 (−8,047)	94,612 (−5,215)	25,139 (−1,386)	215,460 (+10,581)	132,277 (−7,292)	254,614 (−14,036)	54,915 (+11,764)	43,460 (+21,821)
	100%	13.26%	13.53%	8.44%	2.24%	19.23%	11.80%	22.72%	4.9%	3.88%
3 Compensation transfers*** for third-country jurisdictional losses based on 1973–6 average catches	–	+36,220	−25,749	−19,780	−5,049	–	+75,789	−61,430	–	–
4 Final total catch possibilities (ie: line 2 + line 3)	1,120,643	184,797	125,840	74,832	20,090	215,460	208,066	193,184	54,915	43,460
						(37.80%)		(22.14%)		
% of EEC total	100%	16.49%	11.23%	6.68%	1.79%	19.23%	18.57%	17.24%	4.9%	3.88%

Sources: Commission (1981e); (1982a).

* 'Hague Regions' deemed to be especially dependent upon fishing (see Hague Resolutions).
** negative values equalized so that member states contribute to 'Hague Region' transfers in proportion to their total catch possibilities for 1981.
*** compensation transfers equalized among member states in proportion to their 1973–6 average catches.

according to value, use and other factors (Table 10.3). In an effort to equalize the value of the tonnage allocations of these very different species the notion of 'cod equivalent' was employed in formulating national quotas: examples of such equivalents were: cod (1.0), haddock (1.0), plaice (1.0), redfish (0.87), whiting (0.36), saithe (0.77), mackerel (0.3). Again the scope for conflict is clear.

Another variable influencing quota permutations was the size of the overall TACs. Fishermen and their governments were not just interested in their percentage share of these TACs; they were also concerned with the absolute tonnages they represented for particular species in particular areas. By increasing the proposed TAC for a stock, the Commission could sometimes satisfy demands made by a specific group without substantially changing the politically sensitive overall percentage allocation. Indeed, the Commission was often under pressure to increase TACs against scientific advice in order to produce the tonnages required.

Yet another complicating factor was whether or not by-catches (e.g. haddock caught when fishing for industrial species such as Norway pout) should be included in the quota allocations. By June 1982, to the displeasure of the Danes, the Commission (1982c) was insisting that, in general, such catches should indeed form part of the quota of a particular species allocated to a particular state.

The fact that quotas were geographically allocated zone by zone added another element of complexity to the process of sharing out the Community's fish resources. Fishermen could not take their allocations wherever they liked. Appendix 2, Annex II shows how, strictly speaking, there were no overall 'national' quotas; rather, particular species were allocated to particular countries in particular fishing zones on the basis of traditional fishing patterns, adjusted by application of preferences for the 'Hague Regions' and compensation for third-country losses. The Commission was determined to enforce this geographical share-out of quotas and prevent the allocation process becoming a crude national division of the stocks available. After all, non-discrimination on national grounds was a basic Community principle, although it was severely compromised in this allocational process! The Commission's desire to maintain sight of a Community perspective amid all the nationally motivated bartering also led it to encourage states to exchange their quotas of particular species in particular areas if it facilitated the activities of particular fishermen.

Table 10.3 The Commission's July 1981 quota proposals in cod equivalents by categories

	EEC	W. Germany	France	Netherlands	Belgium	UK	Denmark	Ireland
Category 1 7 major species: cod, haddock, plaice, saithe, whiting, redfish, mackerel	1,202,800 100.00%	167,700 13.94%	157,000 13.05%	86,000 7.15%	23,000 1.90%	433,000 36.00%	290,000 24.11%	46,100 3.83%
Category 2 Other species for human consumption (exc. herring)	431,500 100.00%	32,100 7.44%	120,000 27.81%	78,000 18.08%	23,000 5.33%	37,000 8.57%	136,000 31.52%	5,400 1.25%
Category 3 Herring	116,010 100.00%	14,920 12.86%	5,000 4.31%	9,600 8.28%	800 0.69%	35,280 30.41%	32,120 27.69%	18,290 15.77%
Category 4 Industrial fish: Norway pout, sprat, horse mackerel, blue whiting	182,240 100.00%	12,165 6.68%	11,635 6.38%	4,630 2.54%	55 0.03%	21,255 11.66%	131,110 71.94%	1,390 0.76%
Total in cod equivalent	1,932,550 100.00%	226,885 11.74%	293,635 15.19%	178,230 9.22%	46,855 2.42%	526,535 27.25%	589,230 30.49%	71,180 3.68%

Source: Commission (1981d).

A REFERENCE ALLOCATION

In an effort to prevent a recurring annual conflict over fishery resources, the Commission proposed that the 1982 share-out of quotas be 'a reference allocation' according to which fishery resources would be distributed in the future (Commission 1982b). However, this idea of establishing a kind of template to determine quotas year after year is undermined by the reality that fish stocks periodically wax and wane. What would happen in the future, for example, if a stock that made up a vital part of Britain's 1982 allocation declined? Would Britain then be justified in demanding compensation from stocks upon which one or more of its partners were dependent in order to keep up their quota percentages achieved in 1982? The new regulation proposed to cope with this problem by developing 'the notion of relative stability'. If the aim of achieving a 'greater stability of fishing activities' based on the 1982 reference allocation was compromised by 'the temporary biological situation of stocks' (i.e. stock fluctuations), then subsequent quota proposals 'must safeguard the particular needs of regions where local populations are especially dependent on fisheries and related industries as decided by the Council in its resolution of 3 November 1976'. In other words, quotas would have to give priority to protecting the activities of fishermen in North Britain, Ireland and Greenland. Despite this clarification about how the concept of relative stability would be applied, an element of uncertainty about future quota allocations remains inevitable. Laying down a fixed long-term plan for sharing out fishery resources is politically attractive to many, but the fluctuating nature of fish stocks will always require flexible attitudes from those seeking to exploit them if serious conflict is to be avoided.

Agreement among all member states except Denmark

Following complex bargaining, quota allocations acceptable to all governments, Denmark's excepted, had been worked out by the early autumn of 1982 (Table 10.4). It is impossible to quantify the allocational shifts of quotas among member states in simple quantitative terms given the large number of stocks, areas, fishermen and conditions involved (see Appendix 2). However, one important trend showed how Britain had gradually improved its proposed share of the most valuable species, whereas Denmark saw its portion deteriorating (compare Tables 10.1 and 10.2). This reflected a growing

238 THE COMMON FISHERIES POLICY OF THE EC

Table 10.4 Allocations of seven major species (cod, haddock, saithe, whiting, redfish, plaice, mackerel) compared to 1973–8 reference period (in tonnes of cod equivalent)

	Average 1973–8		Proposals of late 1982		Finally agreed 1982 quotas*	
Belgium	28,800	(1.9%)	28,900	(2.1%)	28,900	(2.0%)
Denmark	360,900	(23.6%)	330,500	(23.5%)	344,000	(24.2%)
France	211,000	(13.8%)	182,700	(13.0%)	183,000	(12.9%)
W. Germany	250,500	(16.4%)	192,100	(13.8%)	182,000	(12.8%)
Ireland	22,800	(1.5%)	60,700	(4.3%)	60,700	(4.3%)
Netherlands	106,500	(7.0%)	100,700	(7.2%)	100,800	(7.0%)
UK	550,800	(36.0%)	509,600	(36.3%)	500,500	(35.8%)
Totals	1,531,500	(100.0%)	1,405,300	(100.0%)	1,424,000	(100.0%)

Sources: The Financial Times (1982); Eurofish Report (1983a); Council (1983d).
*Different interpretations of the complex arrangements led to slightly varying calculations of the 1982 quota share-out. For example, the British government calculated that it had obtained some 37 per cent of these major species.

awareness that Britain would not settle for less and a continuing general antipathy to the rapid growth of Danish industrial fishing which was held responsible for much overfishing in European waters. Obviously, this alteration of the allocational pattern helps to explain why Denmark came to supplant Britain as the major opponent of the Commission's quota proposals and the envisaged new CFP package in general.

The emergence of Danish objections as a final obstacle in the CFP struggle was not surprising. Fishing interests in Denmark are extremely influential, being organized by two large bodies: the Danish Fisheries Association (Dansk Fiskeri Forening) and the Danish Sea Fisheries Association (Danmarks Havfiskeriforening) (Commission 1980f). The influence of the fishing lobby was all the greater in that the quota/access negotiations of 1982 were occurring when a minority government was clinging precariously to power confronted, among other things, with significant anti-common market groups ready to seize upon issues that served their cause. Following a general election, a Conservative–Liberal coalition government took over in September 1982. With a very fragile hold on power, it depended just as heavily as its Social Democratic–Liberal predecessor on the many fishing constituencies scattered around the Jutland coast.

But Danish objections to the proposed quotas were also provoked by factors other than the familiar ones relating to internal national political power balances. Fundamental differences on fishery management strategy also separated them from many of their partners. Most member states had a strong antipathy towards industrial fishing, which they saw as a major cause of overfishing to the detriment of direct fishing for food. Danes, however, defended this type of fishing against what they regarded as ill-informed attacks (see Chapter 2, pp. 62–3).

Many Danes were also unhappy about the attempt to establish a fixed long-term allocation pattern based on 1982 quotas. In recent years, Denmark's catches had grown very substantially (Chapter 2). Although many outside of Denmark saw this as a major contributory factor to overfishing, Danes tended to regard it as evidence of hard-working initiative. To them, the proposal to share out fishery resources according to the 1982 pattern for the foreseeable future smacked of a protectionism that would discriminate against 'efficient' Danish fishermen and allow less enterprising producers to operate free from competitive stimulus. Most Danes own, or have a share in, the boats they use; consequently, the spirit of individual enterprise remains strongly opposed to efforts restricting it to some allocational 'status quo'.

The isolation of Denmark became acute at the Fisheries Council of 25–6 October 1982, when the Ministers of all other member states agreed to adopt the package of CFP proposals described above. The determination to stick to this new comprehensive accord and implement a reformed policy by the end of the 1982 deadline was underlined by giving Denmark's Minister ten days to obtain approval for the deal from his government. If the Danes continued to reject the new package thereafter, the other Community countries would implement the new policy by basing it on individual national measures approved by the Commission rather than Council regulations. This approach neatly side-stepped the vexed issue of majority voting in the Council, making it impossible for the Danes to invoke the 'Luxembourg Compromise' and enforce a de facto veto on a matter of 'vital national interest' (see Chapters 1 and 8). However, the Danes remained unruffled by this tactic, which they knew to be fraught with legal difficulties, and drew the other countries back into further negotiations that extended beyond the 'final' deadline set by the expiry of the 10-year transitional arrangements established when Britain, Ireland and Denmark entered the Community (Chapter 5).

The actual amounts of fish at stake in these final negotiations were small. Denmark's government essentially wanted: 20,000 tonnes of mackerel from the North West Scotland fishery for their boats supplying the processing industry in North Jutland; some 7 boat licences to catch whitefish in the Shetland/Orkney 'Box' (this had been reduced from an original request for 135 such licences); a few thousand tonnes added to its cod quotas in the North Sea. Why did it take three months of meetings – including a European Council of heads of government – to close this tiny tonnage gap and win Danish accord for a new CFP?

The national political pressures on Ministers remained strong. Although several elements in the minority Danish government seemed ready to agree before the year-end deadline, the Fisheries Minister, responding to the opposition of the powerful Common Market Affairs Committee in Denmark's Parliament, refused to concede. Before the government could accept the CFP proposals it needed the approval of this Committee. Given that the opposition Social Democrats had a majority upon it, the ruling Conservative–Liberal coalition had to demonstrate that the maximum possible had been achieved. With some Danes forecasting job losses of up to 10,000 (doubtless exaggerated) in Denmark if the proposed deal was accepted, the dilemma faced by the government was real. Moreover, Danes not directly concerned with fishing were sensitive to the argument that 'tiny' Denmark was being bullied by the 'big' states into a settlement that threatened one of its 'vital national interests'. In the past, Britain had invoked the 'Luxembourg Compromise' to block an agreement (see Chapter 8), so why should Denmark not do likewise, particularly as the fishing industry was of greater relative national importance to it (Chapter 2).

The UK government also had little room for manoeuvre. Although the British Minister responsible, Mr Walker, insisted that he had obtained the support of the leaders of Britain's three main fishing organizations before accepting the new policy,he was not spared severe criticism in the House of Commons from politicians voicing opinions common on many fishing quays. The Labour opposition spokesman on fishing, Mr Buchan, caught the mood of others by alluding to 'bribery and corruption' (a reference to the £15 million in extra national aid to the UK fishing industry announced by Mr Walker at the same time as the CFP agreement) (*The Guardian* 1982). Moreover, the leaders of the fishing organizations made it clear that their acceptance of the new deal was based more on resignation than enthusiasm; the agreement was seen to be better than a 'free-for-all' (*The Times* 1982). Some British fishing bodies continued to protest about the new deal, nowhere more than in the Shetlands. Despite the existence of the large Shetland/Orkneys preference 'Box' (Map 10.2) within which fishing by large vessels from outside the region would be limited (see above), Shetlanders continued to complain that too many such boats, including those from mainland Scotland, had licences. Assurances from both the Scottish Secretary of State and local Liberal MP, Jo Grimond, failed to appease men who sometimes compared their fate with that of the Faroese who had used their political autonomy to withdraw from the CFP framework. Clearly, the British government was in no position to concede any more to the Danes.

The Commission also felt that the scope for further concessions was extremely limited. In the effort to forge the new CFP accord, it had been forced to raise TACs ever higher – sometimes against the counsel of its scientific advisers – and had reached a point where further increases to accommodate the Danes would jeopardize the attempt to establish a credible conservation policy (Commission 1982c). Furthermore, it was feared that an increase in access and quota concessions to Denmark could undermine one of the basic principles upon which the share-out of fish was based, namely traditional fishing patterns. Danish demands for whitefish and mackerel in zones where there was little evidence of them having a history of fishing could, if granted, unravel an essential knot holding together the new CFP package.

DENMARK FINALLY AGREES TO A NEW CFP

As on previous occasions in the CFP saga (Chapter 5) the fate of comparatively few fishermen became a matter of foreign policy as negotiations continued beyond the year-end deadline. More particularly, Herr Genscher, the Foreign Affairs Minister of West Germany (which was due to take over Presidency of the Council of Ministers in the New Year) assumed a prominent role along with his Danish counterpart, Mr Elleman-Jensen, in the effort to take pressure off the beleaguered Fisheries Ministers. Discussions focused on ways of satisfying Denmark's demand for more mackerel without upsetting the arrangements already made; for example, obtaining a larger quota of mackerel from Norway's sector of the North Sea that could be allocated to Denmark. However, such a concession from the Norwegians, who were extremely keen to see a new CFP settlement creating more stable fishing conditions for their fishermen as well, would probably mean that EEC quotas for cod and saithe off Norway's North Cape would be reduced to the detriment of Britain, France and Germany. These intricate moves to mesh together quota allocations to everyone's satisfaction both inside and outside the 'Europond' failed to resolve the affair by the New Year deadline. On 30 December 1982 the Common Market Affairs Committee of the Danish Parliament again rejected a slightly amended deal that apparently had the reluctant support of its government. Thereupon, Britain and the other states (with the support of the Commission) introduced individual national measures which, in effect, implemented the agreement reached by the 'Nine'. The Danish government, caught between its desire to settle and the need to appease its unhappy fishermen, advised its citizens not to challenge this action while also announcing its intention to refer the matter to the European Court.

However, Kent Kirk, a prominent Danish Conservative member of the European Parliament thought this an inadequate response and set off in a blaze of publicity to challenge the legality of Britain's national measures by fishing for sprats within the newly declared 12-mile limit off North East England (Appendix Map 1.3). He was duly arrested, fined £30,000 by British magistrates and declared his intention to appeal to the European Court on the grounds that the British limit discriminated according to nationality, thus contravening the Treaty of Rome and the CFP's equality of access conditions stemming from it.

However, although Captain Kirk clearly felt the legal foundations for his action were strong, it became evident that those of a political character were less so. Talk of a mass invasion of British waters by angry Danish fishermen was not translated into action: Captain Kirk's boat sailed alone. The advice of the Danish government not to contravene Britain's new fishing regulations was heeded. Clearly, most Danes now recognized the political weakness of their isolated position and were accommodating themselves to the new realities. Consequently, following a series of meetings in which the West German and Danish Foreign Ministers figured prominently, a new CFP acceptable to all member states was agreed in Council on 25 January 1983. As in 1971 (Chapter 5) this accord was not achieved without a dose of ambiguity allowing opposing sides somewhat different interpretations.

Denmark's main demand for some 20,000 tonnes of mackerel was met in the following way. Danish fishermen would receive a special temporary quota of 7000 tonnes of mackerel from off the west coast of Scotland until March 1983 in addition to a more permanent allocation of 6400 tonnes in the North Sea. Outside of the Community 'pond', a further 5000 tonnes would come from Norwegian waters and 3500 from the Faroes, thus producing a total of 21,900 tonnes for 1983. For future years the Danes obtained an 'understanding' that the Community would strive to ensure a minimum mackerel quota for Denmark of 20,000 tonnes based essentially on availabilities in third-country waters, but this fell short of being a precise guarantee. If the amounts available in non-Community waters exceeded 20,000 tonnes in the future, then Denmark would receive a priority allocation up to 25,000 tonnes. However, there was some uncertainty as to what would happen if insufficient amounts of mackerel made it impossible to satisfy Denmark's minimum demand in the future. The Danes intimated that they should be allowed back into the West Scotland fishery if that happened, but the British rejected this idea. There was no ambiguity, however, about the refusal to allow Denmark any licences in the Shetland/Orkney 'Box'. Nevertheless, the Danes did succeed in getting the size of this protected zone reduced by a further 20 per cent on its eastern side in the final agreement (Map 10.2). Other minor adjustments, largely involving the transfer of cod and haddock quotas from West Germany to Denmark, helped construct a package that all Ministers could accept.

There was no official publication showing what percentage of the total fish available went to each member state. This was because such crude analyses give a misleadingly simple impression of how the various quotas are allocated. Quotas are shared out on a zonal basis as well as by species and member state (Appendix 2). Although such geographical complexities tend to be ignored by those seeking to present a simple, and favourable, package to their compatriots, they were an important part of the agreed 1982 'reference allocation'. This must be remembered when examining the national breakdown of quotas shown in Table 10.4, as should the fact that varying interpretations of the complex allocational arrangements produce slightly varying figures.

Factors facilitating final agreement

At the same time as the new agreement on access and quotas was announced, the Council also resolved to spend 250 million ECU (approx. £140 million) over three years 'on measures to adjust capacity and improve productivity in the fisheries sector' (Council 1983e). The division of this money between different types of project is shown in Table 10.5. The Community's financial contribution to any approved project was generally limited to 50 per cent of its total cost. British fishing leaders made it clear that they expected their government to match, at the very least, any contribution forthcoming from the Community. Although the Council resolution of 25 January 1983 did not divide this money among member states – these are Community funds for which EEC residents can apply irrespective of nationality – there is no doubt its availability, albeit limited, helped Ministers sell the whole CFP package to their respective national groupings. Given that a substantial proportion of these funds was designed to help fleets adjust to nearer-water fishing following the loss of rights in far-off grounds, Britain could expect to continue as a major recipient of EEC structural aid following a pattern established over the previous 10 years (see Table 10.6).

As shown, the overall CFP package had been built up bit by bit over a period of years. Various factors, such as judgements in the European Court, changes of national governments and availability of Community funds facilitated these incremental steps. The approach of the crucial end-of-1982 deadline, when the 10-year transitional period established in the Treaty of Accession ran out, provided a stimulus to settle the final issues and pull the various strands into a comprehensive new policy. Many of those giving their reluctant accord in Britain felt that the new CFP fell short of their demands, but that it was preferable to the 'free-for-all' they feared if no new Community regulations were implemented to replace those about to expire (*The Times* 1982; *Eurofish Report* 1983a). This spectre of fishing chaos in a legal situation of great uncertainty strengthened the general will to settle. Most governments had become increasingly preoccupied with achieving a more stable framework within which their fishermen could plan with confidence. Moreover, the Community needed to sort out its internal fishing system in order to negotiate solid agreements with third countries of particular interest to West Germany, Britain, France and Denmark. Norway, for example, had become increasingly frustrated by the uncertainties involved in dealing with a Community that had

Table 10.5 Community funds to adjust capacity and improve productivity in the fisheries sector 1983–6, provided for in the CFP agreement of January 1983

Measures proposed	Total expenditure (million ECU)
1 Directive on adjusting capacity:	
(a) temporary withdrawal	44
(b) permanent withdrawal	32
2 Regulation on exploratory fishing and joint ventures:	
(a) exploratory fishing	11
(b) joint ventures	7
3 Regulation on a common measure for restructuring, etc.:	
(a) construction and modernization of fishing vessels	118
(b) aquaculture	34
(c) artificial structures intended for restocking	4
Total expenditure over three years	250

Source: Council (1983e).

Table 10.6 Community funds (EAGGF) for construction and modernization of vessels, 1973–82

Member state	Amount ('000 ECU)	% of total
UK	40,747	35.8
Ireland	21,671	19.1
France	16,488	14.5
Italy	13,279	11.7
Netherlands	7,582	6.6
W. Germany	7,257	6.4
Denmark	4,214	3.7
Greenland	1,247	1.1
Belgium	1,239	1.1
Total	113,724	100.0

Source: Eurofish Report (1983b).

not resolved how much of what stocks should be fished by which countries, nor set up an effective fisheries control system.

Furthermore, the final provisions were intricately balanced in a way that allowed most governments to claim some 'victories' as they faced up to the unenviable task of 'selling' the new CFP to their fishermen and parliaments. The British had not attained the aims first enunciated by the Labour government in the mid-1970s, but they had substantially improved on the conditions offered in the 1978 package (Chapter 8), as well as those associated with the 'status quo'. Britain's 36 per cent or so share of the major species in the new accord was considerably above the proportion it took in nearer waters during the heyday of its distant-water activities when a large part of the industry was sustained by catches from grounds off Iceland, Norway and Newfoundland. In 1973, before the loss of access to these far-off fisheries, Britain was taking about 22 per cent of the total Community catch in what was to become the 200-mile/median line zones of member states (Tables 6.1 and 8.4). In the new CFP it had succeeded in pushing this proportion up to around a third of the EEC total. Moreover, North Britain, which now provided the larger part of UK landings, remained defined as one of the 'especially dependent' fishing regions of the Community, along with Ireland and Greenland, thus ensuring that its quota allocations would be preferentially protected in the future. In addition, the British government had, for twenty years at least, obtained a more restrictive access regime around its shores than that allowed for in the 1972 Treaty of Accession or even the 1964 European Convention.

Britain's antagonists in the CFP saga could also maintain that they had achieved a satisfactory outcome despite a retreat from some of their original demands. The French, while accepting a slight drop in their proportion of catches in Community waters, had protected the bulk of their long-established historic rights around the British Isles. The Netherlands, Belgium and West Germany had done likewise, although they, like France, had to accept a considerable reduction of entry rights to parts of the British 12-mile belt which had been opened up to generalized Community access in the Treaty of Accession. The West Germans faced a 3 per cent cutback in the share they had built up of the seven main species over the period 1973–8 (Table 10.4), but had been allocated a larger proportion of the total catch in Community waters than they had enjoyed in this area before the expulsion of their vessels from distant waters following 1973 (Tables 6.1, 8.4, and

10.1–10.4). Although the Irish had not been able to impose the wide national fishing limit they originally demanded, they had obtained preferential regional status and a very substantial increase, both in absolute and percentage terms, in their share of the Community's available fish resources (Table 10.4). Moreover, Ireland benefited from the more restricted access system incorporated in the new agreement, although the long-established traditional rights of Britain, France, West Germany, Belgium and the Netherlands were protected. Italy and Greece, largely peripheral to quota and access issues concerning the North Atlantic states, could feel satisfied that the new CFP deal held out the continuing prospect of Community spending on structural reform in their often antiquated fishing industries.

As their 'last-ditch' resistance suggests, only the Danes felt that they had not achieved a satisfactory balance of gains and losses in the reformed CFP. They had lost access to large parts of the British 6–12 mile zone gained in 1972 (Appendix Maps 1.2 and 1.3) and had been forced to accept some reduction in the high share of the total Community catch they had built up in recent years. However, one suspects that many Danes perceived their greatest loss in the 'status quo' characteristics of the new regulation that allocated quotas among states on a relatively fixed long-term basis. The freedom that had allowed them to catch progressively more than any other Community country during the 1960s and 1970s had given way to restrictive structures threatening the liberal attitude to fishing prevalent in many sectors of the Danish industry. Nevertheless, the Danes eventually judged that continued resistance to the combined resolve of the other states to implement a settlement would entail substantial costs with little hope of future benefits.

The prospect of Spanish entry into the Community

A major catalytic factor galvanizing the 'Six' into agreement about the original CFP in 1970 had been the prospect of Community enlargement (Chapter 4). A more minor element encouraging movement towards reform of the policy in 1983 was the problem posed by the projected entry of Spain into the Community. The thought of its enormous fishing fleet (Chapter 2) within the EEC led to much colourful talk of a new 'Spanish Armada' invading British and other shores! Would it not be in the common interest of existing Community members to resolve their fishing access and quota problems in a manner that would prevent such a threat-laden eventuality?

Following the extension of 200-mile limits, Spain had striven to maintain as much of its distant-water fishing as possible through bilateral agreements, including one with the EEC. Nevertheless, Spanish rights in EEC waters had been severely reduced in recent years. In the early 1970s over 600 Spanish boats fished grounds in what was to become the 'EEC pond', but by 1982 the Community was granting a mere 130 licences to Spain. Furthermore, many of these licensed vessels could not operate full-time because of the quota cutbacks imposed by the EEC. All this compounded the problems posed by the eviction of Spanish boats from waters off Africa, North America and the vast Portuguese 200-mile zone. Given that Spain had no substantial, well-stocked continental shelf upon which to fall back, it faced acute problems of surplus capacity and unemployment in the fishing industry as it approached Community membership.

In negotiations to enter the EEC the Spaniards could point to elements of the CFP – access free of national discrimination and respect for historic rights – and press for a restoration, even improvement, of its previous position. It was this possibility that led to suggestions that Britain and France – long at loggerheads over access rights – had a common interest to fix a CFP settlement before enlargement in order to prevent an influx of Spanish fishermen into their waters. Such considerations probably made it easier for the French to give ground to British demands for larger quotas and more restricted access. They would thus be able to claim similar preferential treatment for their fishermen competing with Spaniards in the Bay of Biscay. Conflict with Spain had already occurred in this area, with the Spanish challenging the legality of French and EEC restrictions on their activities and sending gunboats to accompany unlicensed vessels exploiting grounds in France's offshore waters.

British and Irish fishermen were also concerned about Spanish fishing in their waters. Supported by local MPs and MEPs, they complained about joint ventures with Spain, whereby Spanish vessels without an EEC licence could register in a Community country, take on a token crew member from the new home port and carry on fishing the same grounds as before. To most local fishermen, this was simply a 'Spanish fiddle' to get round the reductions in fishing effort imposed on Spain's fleet. They rejected the argument that this was a reasonable way for Spanish fishermen to go on exploiting grounds (often far offshore) and species (hake, megrim, anglefish, conger) of little interest to local fishermen and consumers. Moreover, they were not attracted by a potentially attractive aspect of Spanish membership, namely free access to an immense national market for fish; per capita fish consumption in Spain was over twice the EEC average in the early 1980s and imports were growing. Protection of 'their' fishing grounds usually has a higher priority among fishermen than access to consumers. Consequently, the concern of many in Britain, France and Ireland was to establish a new CFP fishing rights system that would protect them from any future threat by Spanish fishermen aware of the principle of national non-discrimination! This was doubtless one motivation, albeit a minor one, helping those within the Community to overcome their differences and set up the new CFP. Whether the entry of Spain would upset this policy and produce substantial changes, as the enlargement of the early 1970s had done, remains to be seen.

11 Conclusion

A comprehensive policy

The reformed CFP adopted in January 1983 as a coherent package had been pieced together incremental step by incremental step over a period of years as Community policy-makers negotiated compromises between conflicting demands vigorously articulated by diverse fishing interests in different countries and regions. Although this process was lengthy and disjointed, the Commission never lost sight of the comprehensive fisheries management structure it was trying to set up. In fact, the new policy completed at the beginning of 1983 was very similar to the Commission's original proposals for a reformed CFP in 1976 (Chapter 6). Six years of deadlocks, disregarded deadlines and intricate bargaining had not destroyed this vision of an integrated policy, the main elements of which are summarized below.

The above cartoon is by Calman (1983).

THE FIXING OF TACS

Article 3 of the new regulation (Council 1983a) (see Appendix 2) legally established the Community practice of setting annual TACs. The Commission will formulate its TAC proposals 'in the light of available scientific advice' marshalled by the advisory Scientific and Technical Committee for Fisheries set up by Article 12. TACs for joint stocks extending beyond EEC waters will be established by the Community acting as a single body and the third countries concerned.

THE FIXING OF QUOTAS

The TACs are to be divided into quotas on the basis of three criteria: traditional fishing patterns; the needs of regions especially dependent on fishing; and loss of catch potential in third-country waters. In an effort to avoid a recurring conflict over the share-out of stocks, Article 4 of the new regulation requires that 'the volume of catches available to the Community . . . shall be distributed in a manner which assures each member state relative stability of fishing activities for each of the stocks considered'. The distribution of quotas in 1982 is to be the 'reference allocation' upon which this 'relative stability' will be based. If stock fluctuations make the maintenance of this 'status quo' arrangement difficult (as they surely will) then priority must be given to safeguarding the needs of regions 'especially dependent' on fishing; namely North Britain, Ireland and, while it remained in the Community, Greenland.

ACCESS RESTRICTIONS

The new regulation does not abandon the principle of national non-discrimination in determining conditions of access to fishing grounds, but in practice has moved further away from it. First of all, quotas are allocated on a member state (i.e. national) basis (Appendix 2). These national allocations cannot be taken anywhere in Community waters; they have to be caught in clearly specified fishing zones (Council 1983b). Further geographical constraints on the movements of national fishermen are laid down in the 12-mile belt around member states. The temporary exceptions to access free of national discrimination permitted by Article 100 of the Treaty of Accession (Chapter 5) are extended by Articles 6–8 of the new regulation in both spatial and temporal terms. First, the 6-mile limit set up around member states in 1972 is now extended to 12 miles. Historic rights within 6 to 12 miles must be respected, but they are defined in spatially more restrictive terms than 1972. Insofar as these historic rights are granted on a national basis, they also constitute an exception to the receding national non-discrimination principle. These exceptions to the concept of a 'Community fisherman' have been extended over twenty years, although the possibility of 'adjustments' being made after ten years to ensure 'relative stability' in the share-outs of quotas is incorporated in Article 8. The perceived need to maintain this stability in catch shares among member states is a primary justification for the persistence of these national access restrictions, although others also see them as an essential element of the conservation measures set up by the Community. The establishment of the Shetland/Orkney 'Box' is also justified on conservation grounds, as well as the desire to protect a regional fishing community especially dependent on fishing. However, the licensing system introduced to control the activities of boats over 26 m in this zone is to be administered by the Community in a move away from national notions of management. Nevertheless, the licences permitting fishing in the 'Box' have been allocated on a national basis. Once again a compromise between Community and national concepts is apparent.

CONSERVATION AND CONTROL

Several agreements on conservation measures had built up slowly in the Community during the 1970s, with a particularly important package being adopted by the Council in September 1980 (Chapter 9). The new CFP confirmed these measures within a 'Community system for the conservation and management of fishery resources' (Appendix 2). The advisory Scientific and Technical Committee for Fisheries set up under the auspices of the Commission is required to 'draw up an annual report on the situation with regard to fishery resources (and) on the ways and means of conserving fishing grounds and stocks' (Article 12). Conservation measures will be formulated 'in the light' of this report (Article 2). A Management Committee for Fishery Resources consisting of representatives from the member states under the chairmanship of the Commission has also been set up (Article 13). Acting by the same weighted majority procedure used in the Council, this Committee is required to adopt an opinion on any measure the Commission introduces. If a majority on this Committee disagrees with any such measure, then the matter must be referred to the Council which 'acting by a qualified majority, may take a different decision within one month' and override the action of the Commission (Article 14).

The essentials of the Community control system are as follows. Regulations adopted by the Council have binding legal force in all member states and are thus enforceable through national courts. Each member state remains basically responsible for the enforcement of Community measures in the waters under its jurisdiction. For example, any Community fisherman operating in the UK zone is subject to control by British inspectors and prosecution in British courts. Skippers from all EEC countries are obliged to maintain a standardized log-book in which to record details of their catching activities. When checks reveal that a quota has been exhausted, the member state concerned is obliged to stop further fishing of that stock. In order to ensure that all member states implement these regulations correctly a multi-national team of thirteen Community fisheries inspectors is to be set up during the course of 1983.

National conservation measures could exist along with those of a Community nature 'provided that they are compatible with Community law and are in conformity with the CFP' (Council 1983c). This means that such measures must not discriminate on national grounds, must be approved by the Commission and must ultimately be subject to the majority decision of Council in the event of disputes. It is envisaged that they would be justified in circumstances such as the following: where delay in introducing a conservation control would be seriously damaging; where strictly local stocks of concern only to fishermen in one member state are at stake; where a member state judges that better fisheries management would be achieved by applying measures to its national fishermen which exceeded the minimum requirements of a Community regulation.

THIRD-COUNTRY AGREEMENTS

The Community has been acting as a body in fishery dealings with non-EEC countries since the Hague Resolution of 1976 (Chapter 6). Consequently, framework agreements about access, quotas and conservation of joint stocks have been concluded with such countries as Norway, Sweden, the Faroes, Spain, USA, Canada, Senegal and Guinea-Bissau, and negotiations with many others have begun

(Council 1983d). The new CFP agreement promises to provide a more sure foundation upon which to base these external arrangements. For example, the Community should find it easier to decide what fishing opportunities it can offer third countries in exchange for external rights now that an internal reference allocation has been established. The Community also participates as a body in international fisheries conventions.

STRUCTURAL REFORM

This part of the CFP developed in a piecemeal fashion after the implementation of the original structural regulation in 1971. For example, action to modernize out-dated salt-cod fleets has been followed by interim measures to develop the inshore sector and aquaculture (see Chapters 4 and 9). The new CFP laid down the basis for a more comprehensive approach to structural reform, although the initial sum of 250 million ECU from Community funds over three years fell short of the Commission's original proposals (Council 1983e). However, it is evident that member states will continue to finance structural projects as well; the degree to which this is harmonized in pursuit of Community, as opposed to purely national goals, remains to be seen.

COMMON ORGANIZATION OF FISH MARKETS

A new common market regulation for fish was agreed in September 1981 and implemented in June 1982 (Chapter 9; Council 1981a); it was not changed in the January 1983 agreement. Thus the whole of the original CFP had now been reformed. Although the marketing system has tended to evolve separately from the more prominent issues of quotas and access, these various parts of the whole fisheries policy are interrelated. For example, it is hoped that the relative stability promised by the new management system of catch controls would make market organization easier. Again, the future will show whether such optimism is well founded.

Future challenges

In January 1983, Community leaders celebrated the resolution of the fisheries conflict after seven years of much publicized, and often acrimonious, negotiations. But would their sense of success last for long? Potential for conflict remains strong among the many diverse elements of the Community's fishing industries, particularly insofar as the new CFP is designed to impose a relatively fixed allocational pattern on an especially fluctuating resource base. The human yearning for a stable, secure, long-term settlement will inevitably be frustrated by the fact that fish stocks will continue to wax and wane through time and migrate large distances through sea space. For example, soon after the triumphant announcement of the 'final' CFP agreement, EEC Ministers had to tackle the problem of re-opening and re-allocating rejuvenated North Sea herring fisheries after years of over-fished decline and eventual closure. In mid-December 1983 they finally produced an interim agreement on this issue after a fractious dispute which also blocked the division of all the other major species into quotas. Thus, a decision determining the share-out of stocks during 1983 was not made until the year was virtually over! However, following this fiasco, the Council of Ministers agreed to the 1984 quotas in January of that year, again raising hopes that the CFP will eventually develop into an effective instrument of fishery management. Nevertheless, the aim of stability will be thwarted, in part at least, as fishing technology continues to develop, affecting some sectors and regions more than others. Moreover, certain fishermen in certain regions will doubtless prove more enterprising than others, despite the 'status quo' allocational elements of the new CFP. Kent Kirk, the Danish fisherman-cum-Conservative MEP, was already predicting in March 1983 that the policy would soon need re-negotiating when it became clear that part of the unexploited British quota would have to be transferred to more efficient operators from Denmark. Only time will tell if Kirk was right, but his attitude underlines the sort of strains to which the new structure will inevitably be subjected in the years ahead.

Fishermen, as Kirk exemplifies, tend to be highly individualistic and rarely fit into large organized systems with ease. The coherence of the overall policy conceived by those in government is not always perceived by those who work under it at sea or on the quayside. The perspectives of those producing fish are focused, understandably, on their individual economic survival. Whether the Community's new system for enforcing common conservation measures proves able to cope with this reality more effectively than in the past remains in question. Some scepticism about the effectiveness of a thirteen-man

Community inspectorate checking national enforcement procedures across ten countries, innumerable ports and many thousands of fishermen is justified however energetically it pursues its task. Despite talk of the new CFP being 'too full of unnecessary rules and regulations' (Chapter 10), it must be remembered that fishing in the EEC is still largely an activity where individual producers with surplus catching capacity at their disposal compete for a share of a common property resource. Many of the classic problems associated with this situation – for example, the lack of any individual incentive to conserve – have not been 'regulated' away, although there are some grounds for hope that they might be better contained in the new CFP system. Similar observations can be made of the regulations concerning market organization. The degree to which they co-ordinate the activities of thousands of producers and merchants in a coherent common market system, albeit regionalized, is a matter of future uncertainty.

Furthermore, fishery policy will obviously continue to involve many governments in a Community structure that, in the well-publicized but poorly understood decision-making centre formed by the Council of Ministers, tends to sharpen definitions of 'national interest' rather than diminish them in some supranational perspective. Consequently, relatively small matters that would receive little public attention in a purely domestic political setting, will doubtless continue to develop into media-stimulated 'crises' at a Community level where Fishery Ministers, and indeed Foreign Ministers, will find it difficult to agree for fear of upsetting some national interest group or electorate. Thus demands emanating out of any one of the member states could easily upset the balance of costs and benefits underpinning the 1983 accord. What would happen, for example, if the Community decided to grasp the thorny problem of reducing surplus fleet capacity in a really determined way? It is easy to imagine the difficulties of national politicians in the Council of Ministers trying to allocate the inevitable costs of such a policy.

Forces threatening the future stability of the 1983 settlement could also come from beyond Community borders. The problem of integrating the large Spanish fishing fleet into the CFP grows ever more immediate and is bound to prove difficult. The Norwegians, who will inevitably stay an important fisheries partner for the EEC states, remain wary of Community overfishing in their waters and could retaliate by reducing EEC fishing opportunities, thus upsetting the allocational pattern at the base of the 1983 agreement. Already in March 1983 another third country, Canada, was refusing to issue the licences needed by EEC fishermen (mainly German) to take the remainder of their agreed quota in Canadian waters. The official reason for this was the limitation on Canadian fish exports to the British sector of the common market, but the Community's decision to ban imports of baby seal skins – of which Canada is a major producer – clearly influenced the attitude of the government in Ottawa. This was a reminder, not only of the importance of non-Community countries in fishery policy, but of the fact that the fate of fishermen sometimes depends on issues originating beyond the narrow confines of their industry.

Obviously it would be naive to think that the new CFP settles EEC fishery problems for the next twenty years. But, at the very least, it does lay down a framework within which management systems can be developed and conflicts contained. An individual's political preferences will determine whether or not he judges this structure more appropriate than others. Those who support the European Community in general will doubtless support the CFP in particular, emphasizing its achievements compared with those of international fishery organizations such as the NEAFC and the way in which it resolved disputes without resort to the kind of 'gun-boat' diplomacy seen in successive Anglo-Icelandic 'Cod Wars'. But those hostile to the Community will tend to point to the lengthy, often acrimonious, wrangling over fisheries, the persistence of 'national' (as opposed to 'Community') ways of thought in the formulation of policy and the fact that the EEC does not include all the fishing countries of Europe. In their view, a simple national partitioning of fishing rights allied to traditional inter-state negotiations on trans-frontier fishery problems would be a preferable political–geographical framework within which to manage Europe's offshore fisheries. However, protagonists on both sides can be sure that conflict over fisheries would have occurred among the states of western Europe over the past two decades whether there had been a CFP or not. The EEC has not been the basic cause of the struggles over who should have what fishing rights in what areas of the North East Atlantic; it is rather one of the political arenas within which these inevitable conflicts have taken place.

Appendix I: Fishing rights within British coastal zone, 1964–83

Appendix Map 1.1 Fishing rights within British coastal zone following European Convention of 1964
Source: Final Act (1964).

Appendix Map 1.2 Fishing rights in 6–12-mile zone around UK, 1972–82, following Treaty of Accession
Source: Treaties Establishing the European Communities (1973).

Appendix Map 1.3 Fishing rights within British coastal zone after 1 January 1983
Source: Council (1983b).

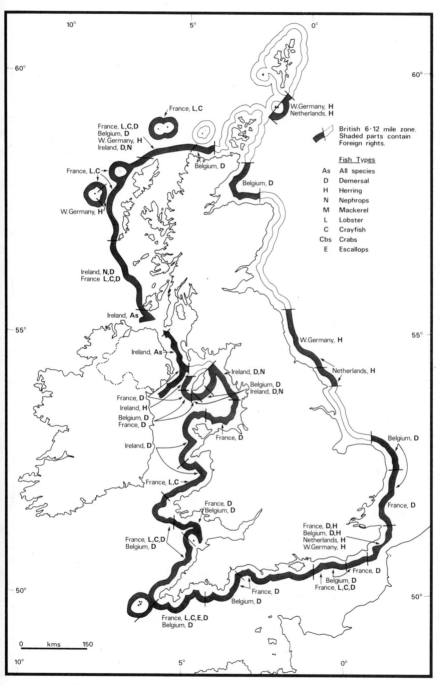

Appendix Map 1.1

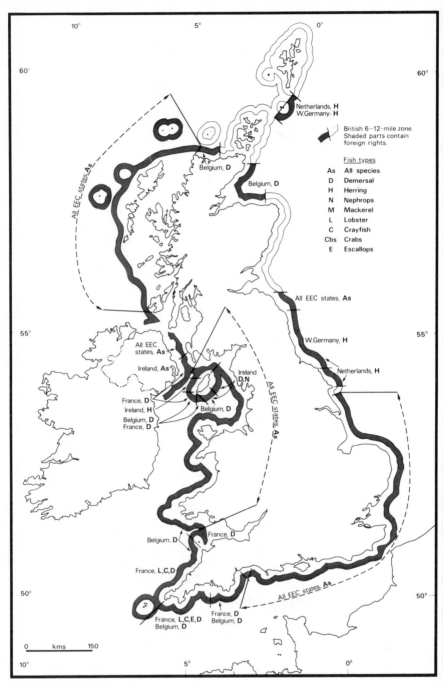

Netherlands, **H**
W.Germany, **H**

British 6–12-mile zone.
Shaded parts contain
foreign rights.

Fish types
As   All species
D   Demersal
H   Herring
N   Nephrops
M   Mackerel
L   Lobster
C   Crayfish
Cbs Crabs
E   Escallops

Belgium, **D**

Belgium, **D**

All EEC states, **As**

All EEC states, **As**

W.Germany, **H**

All EEC
states, **As**

Ireland, **As**

Ireland
D,N

Netherlands, **H**

France, **D**
Ireland, **H**
Belgium, **D**
France, **D**

Belgium, **D**

All EEC states, **As**

Belgium, **D**

France, **D**

France, **L,C,D**

All EEC states, **As**

France, **D**
Belgium, **D**

France, **L,C,E,D**
Belgium, **D**

0   kms   150

Appendix Map 1.2

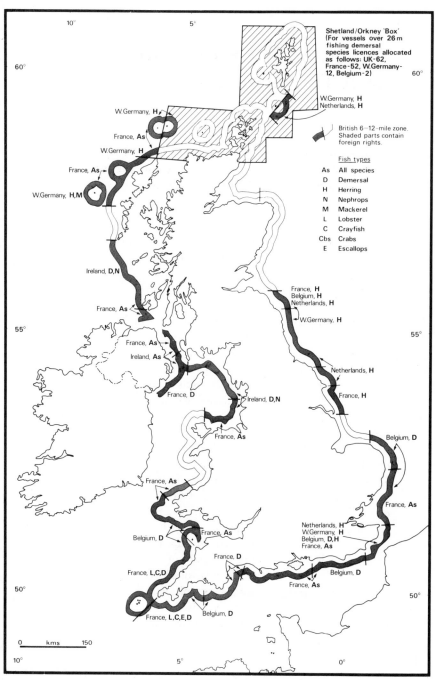

Shetland/Orkney `Box`
(For vessels over 26m
fishing demersal
species licences allocated
as follows: UK-62,
France-52, W.Germany-
12, Belgium-2)

W.Germany, **H**
Netherlands, **H**

British 6−12-mile zone.
Shaded parts contain
foreign rights.

<u>Fish types</u>

As   All species
D   Demersal
H   Herring
N   Nephrops
M   Mackerel
L   Lobster
C   Crayfish
Cbs   Crabs
E   Escallops

W.Germany, **H**

France, **As**

W.Germany, **H**

France, **As**

W.Germany, **H,M**

Ireland, **D,N**

France, **As**

France, **As**
Ireland, **As**

France, **D**

Ireland, **D,N**

France, **As**

France, **As**

Belgium, **D**

France, **As**

France, **D**

France, **L,C,D**

Belgium, **D**

France, **L,C,E,D**

France, **H**
Belgium, **H**
Netherlands, **H**

W.Germany, **H**

Netherlands, **H**

France, **H**

Belgium, **D**

France, **As**

Netherlands, **H**
W.Germany, **H**
Belgium, **D,H**
France, **As**

Belgium, **D**

France, **As**

0   kms   150

Appendix Map 1.3

Appendix 2: Extracts of basic CFP legislation*

Council Regulation (EEC) No. 170/83 of 25 January 1983 establishing a Community system for the conservation and management of fishery resources

THE COUNCIL OF THE EUROPEAN COMMUNITIES

Having regard to the Treaty establishing the European Economic Community, and in particular Article 43 thereof,

Having regard to the proposal from the Commission,[1]

Having regard to the opinion of the European Parliament,[2]

Whereas the Council of the European Communities has agreed that the Member States should act in concert to extend their fishing zones to 200 nautical miles with effect from 1 January 1977 along their North Sea and North Atlantic coastlines, without prejudice to action of the same kind in respect of other fishing zones within their jurisdiction, in particular in the Mediterranean; whereas, since that time and on this basis, the Member States concerned have also extended their fishing limits in certain areas of the West Atlantic, the Skagerrak and the Kattegat and the Baltic Sea; whereas, in this context, in view of the over-fishing of stocks of the main species, it is essential that the Community, in the interests of both fishermen and consumers, ensure by an appropriate policy for the protection of fishing grounds that stocks are conserved and reconstituted; whereas it is therefore desirable that the provisions of Council Regulation (EEC) No. 101/76 of 19 January 1976 laying down a common structural policy for the fishing industry[3] be supplemented by the establishment of a Community system for the conservation and management of fishery resources that will ensure balanced exploitation;

*Taken from OJEC (Official Journal of the European Communities) (1983) L24, 27 January, 1–13, 30–41.

Whereas this system should in particular include conservation measures which may involve, by appropriate means, limitations of the fishing effort, rules for the use of resources, special provisions for inshore fishing and supervisory measures;

Whereas measures regulating fishing effort may include restrictions, established by species or group of species, on catches, with overall catches being limited by reference to a stock or group of stocks;

Whereas the overall catch should be distributed among the Member States;

Whereas conservation and management of resources must contribute to a greater stability of fishing activities and must be appraised on the basis of a reference allocation reflecting the orientations given by the Council;

Whereas, in other respects, that stability, given the temporary biological situation of stocks, must safeguard the particular needs of regions where local populations are especially dependent on fisheries and related industries as decided by the Council in its resolution of 3 November 1976, and in particular Annex VII thereto;

Whereas, therefore, it is this sense that the notion of relative stability aimed at must be understood;

Whereas there should be special provisions for inshore fishing to enable this sector to cope with the new fishing conditions resulting from the institution of 200-mile fishing zones; whereas, to this end, Member States should be authorized to maintain in an initial stage until 31 December 1992 the derogation regime defined in Article 100 of the 1972 Act of Accession and to generalize up to 12 miles the limit of six miles prescribed in that Article; whereas, pursuant to the Act of Accession, these measures constitute the arrangements succeeding those provided for up to 31 December 1982; whereas this regime, after possible adjustments, will be applicable for a further period of 10 years and after this period the Council will be asked to decide upon the provisions which could follow;

Whereas it is necessary to specify the rights which each Member State may enjoy during this period in accordance with this regime;

Whereas specific arrangements of fishing effort should be agreed for certain sensitive regions, taking into consideration the problem of certain coastal fisheries as well as the need to regulate fishing activity in a coastal band;

Whereas, to that end, there is need, among other things, to institute a licensing system;

Whereas the creation of a Community system for the conservation and management of fishery resources should be accompanied by the institution of an effective system of supervision of activities in the fishing grounds and on landing;

Whereas, with a view to the preparation of the scientific and technical information to be used to assess the situation regarding the biological resources of the sea as well as the conditions for ensuring the conservation of stocks, a Scientific and Technical Committee of an advisory nature should be set up under the auspices of the Commission;

Whereas, to facilitate implementation of this Regulation, a procedure should be laid down for close cooperation between the Member States and the Commission within a Management Committee,

HAS ADOPTED THIS REGULATION:

Article 1

In order to ensure the protection of fishing grounds, the conservation of the biological resources of the sea and their balanced exploitation on a lasting basis and in appropriate economic and social conditions, a Community system for the conservation and management of fishery resources is hereby established.

For these purposes, the system will consist, in particular, of conservation measures, rules for the use and distribution of resources, special provisions for coastal fishing and supervisory measures.

Article 2

1   The conservation measures necessary to achieve the aims set out in Article 1 shall be formulated in the light of the available scientific

advice and, in particular, of the report prepared by the Scientific and Technical Committee for Fisheries provided for in Article 12.

2   The measures referred to in paragraph 1 may include, in particular, for each species or group of species:

    (a) the establishment of zones where fishing is prohibited or restricted to certain periods, types of vessel, fishing gear or certain end-uses;

    (b) the setting of standards as regards fishing gear;

    (c) the setting of a minimum fish size or weight per species;

    (d) the restriction of fishing effort, in particular by limits on catches.

Article 3

Where, in the case of one species or a group of related species, it becomes necessary to limit the catch, the total allowable catch for each stock or group of stocks, the shares available to the Community as well as, where applicable, the total catch allocated to third countries, and the specific conditions for taking these catches, shall be fixed each year.

The shares available referred to in the first subparagraph shall be increased by the total of Community catches outside the waters under the jurisdiction or sovereignty of the Member States.

Article 4

1   The volume of the catches available to the Community referred to in Article 3 shall be distributed between the Member States in a manner which assures each Member State relative stability of fishing activities for each of the stocks considered.

2   On the basis of the contents of the report referred to in Article 8, the Council, acting in accordance with the procedure laid down in Article 43 of the Treaty, shall enact provisions effecting the adjustments that it may prove necessary to make to the distribution of the resources among Member States in consequence of the application of paragraph 1.

Article 5

1   Member States may exchange all or part of the quotas in respect of a species or group of species allocated to them under Article 4 provided that prior notice is given to the Commission.

2   Member States shall determine, in accordance with the applicable

Community provisions, the detailed rules for the utilization of the quotas allocated to them. Detailed rules for the application of this paragraph shall be adopted, if necessary, in accordance with the procedure laid down in Article 14.

Article 6

1 As from 1 January 1983 and until 31 December 1992, Member States shall be authorized to retain the arrangements defined in Article 100 of the 1972 Act of Accession and to generalize up to 12 nautical miles for all waters under their sovereignty or jurisdiction the limit of six miles laid down in that Article.

2 In addition to the activities pursued under existing neighbourhood relations between Member States, the fishing activities under the arrangements established in paragraph 1 of this Article shall be pursued in accordance with the arrangements contained in Annex 1, fixing for each Member State the geographical zones within the coastal bands of other Member States where these activities are pursued and the species concerned.

Article 7

1 For species of special importance in the region referred to in Annex II (A) which are biologically sensitive because of their exploitation characteristics, fishing activities will be governed by a licensing system managed by the Commission on behalf of the Community.

2 Vessels which comply with the minimum characteristics laid down in Annex II (C) and which exercise their activity on the species specified in Annex II (B) shall be subject to the system referred to in paragraph 1.

Where the fishing effort of vessels which do not comply with the minimum characteristics provided for in the first subparagraph is likely to jeopardize the satisfactory development of the stocks concerned as a result of a significant increase in such activity as compared with that carried out on the date of entry into force of this Regulation, the minimum characteristics specified in Annex II (C) may be reduced or specific measures adopted to monitor such activity.

3 For each Member State, the number of vessels referred to in the first subparagraph of paragraph 2 which may exercise their activity simultaneously is specified in Annex II (D). The activity of these vessels within the meaning of paragraphs 1 and 2 is subject to a

radio communication procedure designed to inform the competent monitoring authorities of their movements on entering and leaving the aforementioned region.

4   The specific monitoring measures referred to in the footnote to Annex II shall be adopted without prejudice to the provisions of Article 11 of Council Regulation (EEC) No. 2057/82 of 29 June 1982 establishing certain supervisory measures for fishing activities by vessels of the Member States[4] and of Article 8 (2) of Council Regulation (EEC) No. 171/83 of 25 January 1983 laying down certain technical measures for the conservation of fishery resources.

5   The detailed rules for the application and the procedure for the establishment of licences and the communication of the movements of vessels shall be determined in accordance with the procedure laid down in Article 14.

Article 8

1   Before 31 December 1991, the Commission shall submit to the Council a report on the fisheries situation in the Community, the economic and social development of the coastal areas and the state of the stocks and their likely evolution.

2   On the basis of this report and taking account of the objectives set out in Article 4 (1), the Council, acting in accordance with the procedure laid down in Article 43 of the Treaty, shall decide on the adjustments to be made to the arrangements referred to in Articles 6 and 7.

3   The Commission shall submit to the Council, during the 10th year following 31 December 1992, a report on the economic and social situation of coastal regions, on the basis of which the Council, acting in accordance with the procedure laid down in Article 43 of the Treaty, shall decide on the provisions which, once the 10-year-period mentioned in this paragraph has expired, could follow the arrangements referred to in Articles 6 and 7.

Article 9

1   Member States shall supply the Commission, at its request, with all the information relevant to the implementation of this Regulation.

2   The Commission shall each year forward to the European Parliament and the Council a report on the application of measures taken pursuant to this Regulation.

Article 10

Supervisory measures shall be adopted to ensure compliance with this Regulation and with the measures adopted in implementation thereof.

Article 11

The measures referred to in Articles 2, 3, 4 (1), the second subparagraph of Article 7 (2), Articles 7 (4) and 10 shall be adopted by the Council acting by a qualified majority on a proposal from the Commission.

Article 12

The Commission shall set up under its auspices a Scientific and Technical Committee for Fisheries. The Committee shall be consulted at regular intervals and shall draw up an annual report on the situation with regard to fishery resources, on the ways and means of conserving fishing grounds and stocks and on the scientific and technical facilities available within the Community.

Article 13

1   A Management Committee for Fishery Resources, hereinafter called 'the Committee', is hereby established, consisting of representatives of the Member States, under the chairmanship of a representative of the Commission.
2   Within the Committee the votes of the Member States shall be weighted in accordance with Article 148 (2) of the Treaty. The chairman shall not vote.

Article 14

1   Where the procedure laid down in this Article is to be followed, the chairman shall refer the matter to the Committee either on his own initiative or at the request of the representative of a Member State.
2   The representative of the Commission shall submit a draft of the measures to be taken. The Committee shall deliver its opinion on such measures within a time limit which the chairman may fix on the basis of the urgency of the questions under consideration. An opinion shall be adopted by a majority of 45 votes.
3   The Commission shall adopt measures which shall be immediately applicable. However, if these measures are not in accordance with

the Committee's opinion, they shall forthwith be communicated by the Commission to the Council. In that event the Commission may defer application of the measures on which it has decided for not more than one month from the date of such communication.

The Council, acting by a qualified majority, may take a different decision within one month.

Article 15

The Committee may examine any other question referred to it by its chairman either on his own initiative or at the request of the representative of a Member State.

Article 16

This Regulation shall enter into force on the day of its publication in the *Official Journal of the European Communities.*

This Regulation shall be binding in its entirety and directly applicable in all Member States.

Done at Brussels, 25 January 1983.

For the Council
The President
J. ERTL

Notes

1 *OJEC* (1982) C 228, 1 September, 1.
2 *OJEC* (1977) C 57, 7 March, 44.
3 *OJEC* (1976) L 20, 19 January, 19.
4 *OJEC* (1982) L 220, 29 July, 1.

Annex I

COASTAL WATERS OF THE UNITED KINGDOM

France

Geographical area	Species	Importance or particular characteristics
UK coast six to 12 miles		
1 Berwick upon Tweed East Coquet Island East	Herring	Unlimited
2 Flamborough Head East Spurn Head East	Herring	Unlimited
3 Lowestoft East Lyme Regis South	All species	Unlimited
4 Lyme Regis South Eddystone South	Demersal	Unlimited
5 Eddystone South Longships South West	Demersal Scallops Lobster Crawfish	Unlimited
6 Longships South West Hartland Point North West	Demersal Crawfish Lobster	Unlimited
7 Hartland Point to a line from the north of Lundy Island	Demersal	Unlimited
8 From the line due west Lundy Island to Cardigan harbour	All species	Unlimited
9 Point Lynas North Morecambe Light Vessel East	All species	Unlimited
10 County Down	Demersal	Unlimited
11 New Island North East Sanda Island South West	All species	Unlimited
12 Port Stewart North Barra Head West	All species	Unlimited
13 Latitude 57°40′N Butt of Lewis West	All species except shellfish	Unlimited
14 St Kilda, Flannan Islands	All species	Unlimited
15 West of the line joining Butt of Lewis lighthouse to the point 50°30′N–5°45′W	All species	Unlimited

Ireland

Geographical area	Species	Importance or particular characteristics
UK coast six to 12 miles		
1 Point Lynas North Mull of Galloway South	Demersal ⎱ Nephrops ⎰	Unlimited
2 Mull of Oa West Barra Head West	Demersal ⎱ Nephrops ⎰	Unlimited

Germany

Geographical area	Species	Importance or particular characteristics
UK coast six to 12 miles		
1 East of Shetlands and Fair Isle between lines drawn due south east from Sumburgh Head lighthouse due north east from Skroo lighthouse and due south west from Skadan lighthouse	Herring	Unlimited
2 Berwick upon Tweed East Whitby High Lighthouse East	Herring	Unlimited
3 North Foreland Lighthouse East Dungeness New Lighthouse South	Herring	Unlimited
4 Zone around St Kilda	Herring ⎱ Mackerel ⎰	Unlimited
5 Butt of Lewis Lighthouse West to the line joining Butt of Lewis lighthouse and the point 59°30′ N, 5°45′ W	Herring	Unlimited
6 Zone around North Rona and Sulisker (SulaSgeir)	Herring	Unlimited

Netherlands

Geographical area	Species	Importance or particular characteristics
UK coast six to 12 miles		
1 East of Shetlands and Fair Isle between lines drawn due south east from Sumburgh Head lighthouse due north east from Skroo lighthouse and due south west from Skadan lighthouse	Herring	Unlimited
2 Berwick upon Tweed East Flamborough Head East	Herring	Unlimited
3 North Foreland East Dungeness New Lighthouse South	Herring	Unlimited

Belgium

Geographical area	Species	Importance or particular characteristics
UK coast six to 12 miles		
1 Berwick upon Tweed East Coquet Island East	Herring	Unlimited
2 Cromer North North Foreland East	Demersal	Unlimited
3 North Foreland East Dungeness New Lighthouse South	Demersal Herring	Unlimited
4 Dungeness New Lighthouse South Selsey Bill South	Demersal	Unlimited
5 Straight Point South East South Bishop North West	Demersal	Unlimited

---

COASTAL WATERS OF IRELAND

France

Geographical area	Species	Importance or particular characteristics
Irish coast six to 12 miles		
1 Erris Head North West Sybil Point West	Demersal Nephrops	Unlimited
2 Mizen Head South Stags South	Demersal Nephrops Mackerel	Unlimited
3 Stags South Cork South	Demersal Nephrops Mackerel Herring	Unlimited
4 Cork South Carnsore Point South	All species	Unlimited
5 Carnsore Point South Haulbowline South East	All species except shellfish	Unlimited

United Kingdom

Geographical area	Species	Importance or particular characteristics
Irish coast six to 12 miles		
1 Mine Head South Hook Point	Demersal Herring Mackerel	Unlimited
2 Hook Point Carlingford Lough	Demersal Herring Mackerel Nephrops Scallops	Unlimited

Netherlands

Geographical area	Species	Importance or particular characteristics
Irish coast six to 12 miles		
1 Stags South Carnsore Point South	Herring Mackerel }	Unlimited

Germany

Geographical area	Species	Importance or particular characteristics
Irish coast six to 12 miles		
1 Old Head of Kinsale South Carnsore Point South	Herring	Unlimited
2 Cork South Carnsore Point South	Mackerel	Unlimited

Belgium

Geographical area	Species	Importance or particular characteristics
Irish coast six to 12 miles		
1 Cork South Carnsore Point South	Demersal	Unlimited
2 Wicklow Head East Carlingford Lough South East	Demersal	Unlimited

COASTAL WATERS OF BELGIUM

Geographical area	Member state	Species	Importance or particular characteristics
Six to 12 miles	Netherlands	All species	Unlimited
	France	Herring	Unlimited

COASTAL WATERS OF DENMARK

Geographical area	Member state	Species	Importance or particular characteristics
North Sea coast (Danish/German frontier to Hanstholm)			
Six to 12 miles Danish/German frontier to Blaavand Huk	Germany	Flatfish Shrimps and prawns }	Unlimited
	Netherlands	Flatfish Roundfish }	Unlimited
Blaavand Huk to Bovbjerg	Belgium	Cod Haddock }	Unlimited, only during June and July
	Germany	Flatfish	Unlimited
	Netherlands	Plaice Sole }	Unlimited
Thyborón to Hanstholm	Belgium	Whiting Plaice }	Unlimited, only during June and July
	Germany	Flatfish Sprat Cod Saithe Haddock Mackerel Herring Whiting }	Unlimited
	Netherlands	Cod Plaice Sole }	Unlimited

Geographical area	Member state	Species	Importance or particular characteristics
Skagerrak (Hanstholm to Skagen) **Four to 12 miles**	Belgium	Plaice	Unlimited, only during June and July
	Germany	Flatfish Sprat Cod Saithe Haddock Mackerel Herring Whiting	Unlimited
	Netherlands	Cod Plaice Sole	Unlimited
Kattegat **Three to 12 miles**	Germany	Cod Flatfish Nephrops Herring	Unlimited
North of Zeeland to the parallel of the latitude passing through Fornaes lighthouse	Germany	Sprat	Unlimited
Baltic Sea (including Belts, Sound, Bornholm) **Three to 12 miles**	Germany	Flatfish Cod Herring Sprat Eel Salmon Whiting Mackerel	Unlimited

COASTAL WATERS OF GERMANY

Geographical area	Member state	Species	Importance or particular characteristics
North Sea coast **Three to six miles** All coasts	Denmark	Demersal Sprat Sand-eel	Unlimited
	Netherlands	Demersal Shrimps and prawns	Unlimited
Six to 12 miles All coasts	Denmark	Demersal Sprat Sand-eel	Unlimited
	Netherlands	Demersal Shrimps and prawns	Unlimited
Danish/German frontier to the northern part of Amrum at 54°43′ N	Denmark	Shrimps and prawns	Unlimited
Zone around Heligoland	United Kingdom	Cod Plaice	Unlimited
Baltic coast **Three to 12 miles**	Denmark	Cod Plaice Herring Sprat Eel Whiting Mackerel	Unlimited

COASTAL WATERS OF FRANCE AND THE OVERSEAS DEPARTMENTS

Geographical area	Member state	Species	Importance or particular characteristics
North East Atlantic coast Six to 12 miles			
Belgian/French frontier to east of Departement Manche (Vire-Grandcamp les Bains estuary 49°23′ 30″N, 1°2′ WNNE)	Belgium	Demersal Scallops }	Unlimited
	Netherlands	All species	Unlimited
Dunkerque (2°20′ E) to Cap d'Antifer (0°10′ E)	Germany	Herring	Unlimited, only during October to December
Belgian/French frontier to Cap d'Alprech West (50°42′ 30″N, 1°33′ 30″E)	United Kingdom	All species	Unlimited

COASTAL WATERS OF THE NETHERLANDS

Geographical area	Member state	Species	Importance or particular characteristics
Three to 12 miles Whole coast	Belgium	All species	Unlimited
	Denmark	Demersal Sprat Sand-eel Horse mackerel	Unlimited
	Germany	Cod Shrimps and prawns	Unlimited
Six to 12 miles Whole coast	Belgium	All species	Unlimited
	Denmark	Demersal Sprat Sand-eel Horse mackerel	Unlimited
	Germany	Cod Shrimps and prawns	Unlimited
	France	All species	Unlimited
Texel south point, west to the Netherlands/ German frontier	United Kingdom	Demersal	Unlimited

Annex II

Shetland area

A Geographical limits
From the point on the
west coast of Scotland in
latitude 58°30′ N   to 58°30′ N–6°15′ W
From 58°30′ N–6°15′ W   to 59°30′ N–5°45′ W
From 59°30′ N–5°45′ W   to 59°30′ N–3°00′ W along the
                                              12-mile line north of the Orkneys
From 59°30′ N–3°00′ W   to 61°00′ N–3°00′ W
From 61°00′ N–3°00′ W   to 61°00′ N–0°00′ along the 12-mile
                                              line north of the Shetlands
From 61°00′ N–0°00   to 59°30′ N–0°00
From 59°30′ N–0°00   to 59°30′ N–1°00′ W
From 59°30′ N–1°00′ W   to 59°00′ N–1°00′ W
From 59°00′ N–1°00′ W   to 59°00′ N–2°00′ W
From 59°00′ N–2°00′ W   to 58°30′ N–2°00′ W
From 58°30′ N–2°00′ W   to 58°30′ N–3°00′ W
From 58°30′ N–3°00′ W   to the east coast of Scotland in latitude
                                              58°30′ N

B Species
Demersal except Norway pout and blue whiting[1]

C Minimum characteristics
Vessels of a length between perpendiculars of at least 26 metres[2]

D Fishing activity
Maximum number of vessels
France: 52
United Kingdom: 62
Germany: 12
Belgium: 2

Notes

1 Vessels engaged in fishing for Norway pout and blue whiting may be subject to specific monitoring measures concerning the keeping on board of fishing gear and species other than those referred to above.
2 Length between perpendiculars shall be regarded as the distance on the summer load water-line from the force side of the stem to the after side of the rudder post, or to the centre of the rudder stock if there is no rudder post.

Extract from Council Regulation (EEC) No.172/83 of 25 January 1983 fixing for certain fish stocks and groups of fish stocks occurring in the Community's fishing zone, total allowable catches for 1982, the share of these catches available to the Community, the allocation of that share between the Member States and the conditions under which the total allowable catches may be fished

THE COUNCIL OF THE EUROPEAN COMMUNITIES

Having regard to the Treaty establishing the European Economic Community,

Having regard to Council Regulation (EEC) No. 170/83 of 25 January 1983 establishing a Community system for the conservation and management of fishery resources,[1] and in particular Article 11 thereof,

Having regard to the proposal from the Commission,[2]

Whereas, in order to ensure the protection of fishing grounds and fish stocks and the balanced exploitation of the resources of the sea, in the interests of both fishermen and consumers, there should be fixed, each year for the different species, catches of which must be restricted, a total allowable catch (TAC) per stock or group of stocks and the share of these catches available to the Community taking into account its commitments to third countries;

Whereas, in order to ensure effective management of these TACs, conditions on fishing operations should be established;

Whereas, in order to ensure effective management, the TACs available for the Community in 1982 should be fairly allocated among the Member States;

Whereas, in order to make a fair allocation of available resources, particular account must be taken of traditional fishing activities, the specific needs of areas particularly dependent on fishing and its dependent industries and the loss of fishing potential in the waters of third countries;

Whereas, in the case of stocks for which the fisheries are still developing and for which little, if any, scientific data are available, such as horse-mackerel, blue whiting and Norway pout, it does not appear necessary to make quota allocations;

Whereas, with regard to herring stocks, quota proposals for 1983 must necessarily have an *ad hoc* basis and cannot form a basis for future years;

Whereas the allocation of the TAC for shrimp in the zone of French Guyana has been established by Council Regulation (EEC) No. 1177/82 of 11 May 1982 laying down certain measures for the conservation and management of fishery resources applicable to vessels flying the flag of certain non-member countries in the 200-nautical-mile zone off the coast of the French department of Guyana,[3]

HAS ADOPTED THIS REGULATION:

Article 1

1   This Regulation shall fix, for 1982, for certain fish stocks and groups of fish stocks occurring in the Community's fishing zone, total allowable catches per stock or group of stocks, the share of these catches available to the Community, the allocation of that share among Member States and the specific conditions under which these stocks may be fished.

2   The sub-areas, divisions or subdivisions of the NAFO referred to in this Regulation are described in Annex III to Council Regulation (EEC) No. 3179/78 of 28 December 1978 concerning the conclusion by the European Economic Community of the

Convention on Future Multilateral Cooperation in the Northwest Atlantic Fisheries,[4] as last amended by Regulation (EEC) No. 654/81.[5] The definition of the ICES areas referred to in this Regulation is given in a Commission communication.[6]

3   Within the meaning of this Regulation: The Skagerrak is limited on the west by a line drawn from the Hanstholm lighthouse to the Lindesnes lighthouse and on the south by a line drawn from the Skagen lighthouse to the Tistlarna lighthouse and from this point to the nearest point on the Swedish coast.

Within the meaning of this Regulation: The Kattegat is delimited on the north by a line drawn from the Skagen lighthouse to the Tistlarna lighthouse and from this point to the nearest point on the Swedish coast and on the south by a line drawn from Hasenøre to Gnibens Spids, from Korshage to Spodsbjerg and from Gilbjerg Hoved to Kullen.

Article 2

The total allowable catches (TACs) for stocks or groups of stocks to which Community rules apply occurring in waters falling under the sovereignty or jurisdiction of the Member States and the share of these catches available to the Community are fixed for 1982 in Annex I.

Article 3

The allocation among the Member States for 1982 of the share available to the Community of total allowable catches of stocks or groups of stocks occurring in the Community's fishing zone is shown in Annex II.

Article 4

Notwithstanding the provisions laid down in the footnotes to Annex I and in Articles 5, 6 and 8 (1), (2) (a) and (b) (i), all catches of species for which quotas are fixed for 1982 may be retained on board or landed only within the quotas allocated to the Member State concerned.

Article 5

When a positive quota of cod in sub-areas ICES XIV and/or NAFO I has not been allocated to a Member State, the following provisions shall apply with regard to that Member State:
- by-catches of cod in these areas must not exceed 10 per cent by weight of redfish catches by vessels which are trawling, 10 per cent

by weight of halibut and Greenland halibut catches by vessels which are long-lining and 3 per cent by weight of other species. By-catches shall be measured according to the provisions of Article 10 of Council Regulation (EEC) No. 171/83 of 25 January 1983 laying down certain technical measures for the conservation of fishery resources, but may not be measured until a vessel has been fishing in Greenland waters for at least 48 hours. By-catches shall not be counted against total allowable catches,

– fishing for redfish shall be prohibited in that part of NAFO sub-area I bounded by a line running due west from the West Greenland baselines along parallel 64°30′ N to longitude 55°00′ W, south to latitude 61°30′ N and longitude 50°30′ W and due east to the West Greenland baselines.

Article 6

When a positive quota of halibut in sub-areas ICES XIV and/or NAFO I has not been allocated to a Member State, by-catches of halibut of this Member State must not exceed 3 per cent by weight of catches of other species.

By-catches shall be measured according to the provisions of Article 10 of Council Regulation (EEC) No. 171/83 but may not be measured until a vessel has been fishing in Greenland waters for at least 48 hours. By-catches shall not be counted against total allowable catches.

Article 7

For the protection of the 'Eastern' stock of mackerel, fishing for mackerel shall be prohibited in ICES division VI a) north of parallel 58°N from 1 March to 30 April and from 1 November to 31 December.

Article 8

1 When the TAC for herring is nil, by-catches of herring may not be landed unless inextricably mixed with catches of other species. In such cases the maximum allowable by-catch shall be 10 per cent in the case of sprat and 5 per cent in the case of other species.

   Inextricably mixed herring by-catches may not be sorted either on board a vessel or on landing.

2 When there is a positive TAC for herring the following rules shall be observed:

   (a) Skagerrak/Kattegat:

    (i)   the maximum allowable by-catch of herring inextricably mixed with other species shall be 10 per cent for sprat and 5 per cent for other species when using nets with a mesh size smaller than 32 mm;

    (ii) these percentages shall apply to the weight of herring in catches on the deck, in landings or in any representative sample weighing more than 100 kilograms.

  (b) Other zones except Baltic Sea–ICES divisions IIIb), c) and d)

    (i)   the maximum allowable by-catch of herring inextricably mixed with other species shall be 10 per cent for sprat and 5 per cent for all other species;

          Inextricably mixed herring by-catches may not be sorted either on board a vessel or on landing;

    (ii) the use of grading equipment on board fishing vessels is prohibited for herring unless such vessels use, for the fishing of herring, a net, irrespective of the type used, with a mesh the size of which is not smaller than 32 mm.

3 Sorted by-catches of herring shall not be landed once the quota has been exhausted.

4 Directed fishing for herring shall be prohibited in the Skagerrak from 1 January to 31 March and from 1 October to 31 December. This provision shall not apply to fishing within two nautical miles of the baselines by vessels not exceeding 90 feet and using other types of gear than trawl.

5 ....

6 Fishing for herring shall be prohibited throughout the year in those waters between latitudes 53°00′ N and 55°00′ N which are situated between the east coasts of Ireland and Northern Ireland and a line drawn 12 miles from the baselines.

7 Fishing for herring in the Irish Sea (ICES division VII a)) shall be prohibited throughout the year between latitude 53°20′ N and a line drawn between the Mull of Galloway in Scotland and the Point of Ayre on the Isle of Man in those waters which are situated between the west coasts of Scotland, England and Wales and a line drawn 12 miles from the baselines, and from 20 September to 15 November in the part of the Irish Sea (ICES division VII a)) north of latitude 53°30′ N. Logan Bay shall, however, be closed to herring fishing throughout the year.

8 Notwithstanding the provisions of paragraphs 6 and 7, only vessels based in ports adjacent to ICES division VII a) (Mourne stock) may

fish for herring in that division and the only method of fishing authorized shall be drift netting with nets of minimum mesh size 54 mm, stretched mesh. The definition of the relevant vessels must have been submitted for Commission approval.

Article 9

1 ....

2 Fishing for sprat shall be prohibited in ICES statistical rectangles 42F7 and 41F7 from 1 July to 31 October and ICES statistical rectangles 41E6 and 39E8 and in the inner waters of the Moray Firth west of parallel 3°30′ W from 1 October to 31 March.

3 For the purposes of this Regulation, ICES rectangles 41F7 and 42F7 are bounded by a line running due west from the west coast of Denmark along parallel 56°00′ N to longitude 7°00′ E, due north to latitude 57°00′ N and due east to the west coast of Denmark.

ICES rectangle 41E6 covers the inner waters of the Firth of Forth and is bounded by longitude 3°00′ W.

ICES rectangle 39E8 is bounded by a line running due east from the east coast of England along parallel 55°00′ N to longitude 1°00′ W, due north to latitude 55°30′ N and due west to the English coast.

Article 10

Trawling and purse seining for mackerel, sprat and herring shall be prohibited in the Skagerrak from Saturday midnight to Sunday midnight and in the Kattegat from Friday midnight to Sunday midnight.

Article 11

1 Fishing for salmon in NAFO sub-area I shall open on 25 August.

2 For salmon fishing in NAFO sub-area I, only nets with a minimum mesh size of 140 mm may be used, with a tolerance of ± 5 per cent; this means that every measured mesh of a net must be within the limits of 5 per cent of 140 mm.

Article 12

This Regulation shall enter into force on the day of its publication in the *Official Journal of the European Communities*.

This Regulation shall be binding in its entirety and directly applicable in all Member States.

Done at Brussels, 25 January 1983.

For the Council
The President
J. ERTL

Notes

1 See p. 262 in this book.
2 *OJEC* (1982) C 228, 1 September, 14.
3 *OJEC* (1982) L 138, 19 May, 1.
4 *OJEC* (1978) L 378, 30 December, 1.
5 *OJEC* (1981) L 69, 14 March, 1.
6 *OJEC* (1982) C 140, 3 June, 3.

Annex I

TAC by stock and by sector envisaged for 1982 - share available to the Community

Species	ICES division or NAFO sub-area or division	TAC 1982 (tonnes)	Share available to the Community for 1982
Cod	III (a) Skagerrak	20,000[1]	16,500
Cod	III (a) Kattegat	16,400	9,900
Cod	III (b), (c), (d) (EEC zone)	117,000	115,000
Cod	IV, II (a) (EEC zone)	255,000	244,100
Cod	VI, V (b) (EEC zone)	31,500	31,500
Cod	VII except VII (a), VIII (EEC zone)	15,700	15,700
Cod	VII (a)	15,000	15,000
Cod	XIV (EEC zone), V (a) (EEC zone), XII (EEC zone)	15,000	15,000
Cod	NAFO 1	62,000*	62,000*
Cod	NAFO 3 Ps	28,000	5,170
Haddock	III (a), III (b), (c), (d) (EEC zone)	10,400 +	9,100
Haddock	IV, II (a) (EEC zone)	180,000	150,100[2]
Haddock	VI, V (b) (EEC zone)	38,000 +	38,000
Haddock	VII, VIII (EEC zone)	4,500 +	4,500
Saithe	II (a) (EEC zone), III (a), IV, III (b), (c), (d) (EEC zone)	128,000	67,940
Saithe	VI, V (b) (EEC zone)	26,000 +	26,000
Saithe	VII, VIII (EEC zone)	7,820 +	7,820
Whiting	III (a) Skagerrak	4,650 +	3,850
Whiting	III (a) Kattegat	17,500 +	15,800
Whiting	III (b), (c), (d) (EEC zone)	2,600 +	2,600
Whiting	IV, II (a) (EEC zone)	170,000	130,800[3]
Whiting	VI, V (b) (EEC zone)	16,400	16,400
Whiting	VII (a)	18,170	18,170
Whiting	VII except VII (a)	20,500 +	20,500
Plaice	III (a) Skagerrak	10,000 +	9,400
Plaice	III (a) Kattegat	7,000 +	6,300
Plaice	IV, II (a) (EEC zone)	140,000	130,000

Species	ICES division or NAFO sub-area or division	TAC 1982 (tonnes)	Share available to the Community for 1982
Plaice	VI, V (b) (EEC zone)	1,810 +	1,810
Plaice	VII (a)	4,500	4,500
Plaice	VII (b), (c)	200 +	200
Plaice	VII (d), (e)	5,500 +	5,500
Plaice	VII (f), (g)	1,450	1,450
Plaice	VIII (EEC zone)	250 +	250
American plaice	NAFO 3 Ps	5,000	550
Witch	NAFO 3 Ps	3,000	410
Sole	III (a), III (b), (c), (d) (EEC zone)	600 +	600
Sole	IV, II (a) (EEC zone)	21,000	21,000
Sole	VI, V (b) (EEC zone)	50 +	50
Sole	VII (a)	1,600	1,600
Sole	VII (b), (c)	60 +	60
Sole	VII (d)	2,600 +	2,600
Sole	VII (e)	1,700 +	1,700
Sole	VII (f), (g)	1,600	1,600
Sole	VIII (EEC zone)	3,100 +	3,100
Mackerel	III (a), IV, II (a) (EEC zone), III (b), (c), (d) (EEC zone)	25,000	0
Mackerel	VI, V (b) (EEC zone), VII, VIII (EEC zone)	401,000	375,000
Sprat	III (a)	77,000 +	48,000
Sprat	III (b), (c), (d) (EEC zone)	3,400 +	3,400
Sprat	IV, II (a) (EEC zone)	400,000 +	325,000
Horse mackerel	IV, VI, VII, VIII (EEC zone)	250,000 +	244,000
Hake	III (a), III (b), (c), (d) (EEC zone)	1,300 +	1,300
Hake	IV, II (a) (EEC zone)	2,750 +	2,750
Hake	VI, VII, VIII (EEC zone), V (b) (EEC zone)	35,750	26,250
Anchovies	VIII	32,000 +	3,000
Norway pout	III (a), IV (EEC zone), II (a) (EEC zone)	371,000 +	321,000
Blue whiting	IV (EEC zone) VI, VII, XII (EEC zone), XIV (EEC zone)	580,000 +	415,000

Species	ICES division or NAFO sub-area or division	TAC 1982 (tonnes)	Share available to the Community for 1982
Sand-eel	XIV (EEC zone), V (a) (EEC zone)	0	0[4]
Sand-eel	NAFO 1	0	0[4]
Redfish	V (EEC zone), XIV (EEC zone)	43,500	43,000
Redfish	NAFO 1	10,000	9,500
Redfish	NAFO 3Ps	18,000	2,000
Greenland halibut	V (EEC zone), XIV (EEC zone)	3,950	3,200
Greenland halibut	NAFO 1	20,000	7,250[5]
Halibut	XIV (EEC zone)	220 +	220
Halibut	NAFO 1	1,000 +	1,000
Shrimp	XIV (EEC zone), V (EEC zone)	5,500 +	3,050
Shrimp	NAFO 1	30,000	28,650
Shrimp	French Guyana	[6]	[6]
Herring	III (a)	60,000	25,400
Herring	III (b), (c), (d) (EEC zone)	34,900	33,900
Herring	IV (a), II (a) (EEC zone)	0	0
Herring	IV (b)	0	0
Herring	IV (c) (Blackwater stock excepted), VII (d)	72,000	68,000[7]
Herring	IV (c) (Blackwater stock)[8]	0[**]	0[**][9]
Herring	VI (a) (North)[10], VI (b), V (b) (EEC zone)	80,000	66,200
Herring	VI (a) (South)[11], VII (b,) (c)	11,000	11,000
Herring	VI (a), (Clyde stock)[12]	2,500	2,500
Herring	VII (a)[13] (Mourne stock)[14]	600	600
Herring	VII (a)[13] (Manx stock)[15]	3,200	3,200
Herring	VII (e)	500 +	500
Herring	VII (f)	0	0
Herring	VII (g) to (k)[16]	8,100	8,100[17]
Catfish	NAFO 1	6,000	6,000
Capelin	II (b)	0	0
Capelin	XIV (EEC zone), V (EEC zone)	10,000	0
Salmon	III (b), (c), (d) (EEC zone)	920	920
Salmon	NAFO 1: west of 44°W	–	1,253

Notes

1 Excluding 1600 tonnes attributed to the Norwegian coastal zone.
2 Excluding estimated 5600 tonnes of industrial by-catch.
3 Excluding estimated 22,180 tonnes of industrial by-catch.
4 Except for certain catch possibilities for experimental purposes.
5 12,000 tonnes not allocated.
6 See Regulation (EEC) No. 1177/82.
7 For the period 1 October 1982 to 28 February 1983.
8 Maritime region of the Thames estuary between Felixstowe and North Foreland within six miles from the UK baselines.
9 TAC and quota are for the period 1 October 1982 to 31 March 1983.
10 Reference is to the herring stock in ICES division VI (a), north of 56°N and in that part of VI (a) which is situated east of 7°W and north of 55°N, excluding the Clyde as defined in note[12].
11 Reference is to the herring stock in ICES division VI (a), south of 56°N and west of 7°W.
12 Maritime area situated to the north east of a line drawn between the Mull of Kintyre and Corsewall Point.
13 ICES division VII (a) is reduced by the zone added to the Celtic Sea bounded:
   - to the north by latitude 52°30′ N,
   - to the south by latitude 52°00′ N,
   - to the west by the coast of Ireland,
   - to the east by the coast of the United Kingdom.
14 Reference is to the herring stock within 12 miles of the east coast of Ireland and of Northern Ireland between 53°00′ N and 55°00′ N.
15 Reference is to the herring stock in the Irish Sea (ICES division VII (a)) excluding the zone referred to in note[14].
16 Increased by zone bounded:
   - to the north by latitude 52°30′ N,
   - to the south by latitude 52°00′ N,
   - to the west by the coast of Ireland,
   - to the east by the coast of the United Kingdom.
17 From 1 October 1982 to 31 March 1983.
+ Precautionary TAC.
* *Ad hoc* solution for 1982.
** Subject to revision following scientific re-assessment.

Annex II (extract illustrating geographical allocation of national quotas)

| | Stock | | | |
Species	Geographical regions	ICES/NAFO division	Member State	1982 quota (tonnes)
Cod	Skagerrak	III (a)	Belgium	50[3]
			Denmark	15,950[4]
			Federal Republic of Germany	400[3]
			Greece	
			France	
			Ireland	
			Italy	
			Luxembourg	
			Netherlands	100[3]
			United Kingdom	
			Available for Member States	
			EEC total	16,500
Cod	Kattegat	III (a)	Belgium	
			Denmark	9,700[2]
			Federal Republic of Germany	200[3]
			Greece	
			France	
			Ireland	
			Italy	
			Luxembourg	
			Netherlands	
			United Kingdom	
			Available for Member States	
			EEC total	9,900
Cod	Baltic Sea	III (b), (c), (d) (EEC zone)	Belgium	
			Denmark	90,000˙
			Federal Republic of Germany	25,000˙

Species	Stock Geographical regions	ICES/NAFO division	Member State	1982 quota (tonnes)
			Greece	
			France	
			Ireland	
			Italy	
			Luxembourg	
			Netherlands	
			United Kingdom	
			Available for Member States	
			EEC total	115,000
Cod	North Sea, Norwegian Sea	IV II (a) (EEC zone)	Belgium	8,700
			Denmark	50,000
			Federal Republic of Germany	31,700
			Greece	
			France	10,750
			Ireland	
			Italy	
			Luxembourg	
			Netherlands	28,250
			United Kingdom	114,700
			Available for Member States	
			EEC total	244,100
Cod	West Scotland Rockall, South Faroe	VI V (b) (EEC zone)	Belgium	100
			Denmark	
			Federal Republic of Germany	930
			Greece	
			France	10,000
			Ireland	3,900
			Italy	
			Luxembourg	
			Netherlands	

| Species | Stock | | Member State | 1982 quota |
	Geographical regions	ICES/NAFO division		(tonnes)
			United Kingdom Available for Member States	16,570
			EEC total	31,500
Cod	Bristol Channel, West and South Ireland, English Channel, Bay of Biscay	VII (except VII (a)) VIII (EEC zone)	Belgium Denmark Federal Republic of Germany Greece France Ireland Italy Luxembourg Netherlands United Kingdom Available for Member States	700 12,000 1,600 100 1,300
			EEC total	15,700
Cod	Irish Sea	VII (a)	Belgium Denmark Federal Republic of Germany Greece France Ireland Italy Luxembourg Netherlands United Kingdom Available for Member States	400 1,100 7,000 100 6,400
			EEC total	15,000
Cod	East Greenland,	XIV (EEC zone)	Belgium Denmark	3,500[4]

Species	Stock			
	Geographical regions	ICES/NAFO division	Member State	1982 quota (tonnes)
	Iceland, North of Azores	V (a) (EEC zone) XII (EEC zone)	Federal Republic of Germany	10,000
			Greece	
			France	
			Ireland	
			Italy	
			Luxembourg	
			Netherlands	
			United Kingdom	1,500
			Available for Member States	
			EEC total	15,000
Cod	West Greenland	NAFO 1	Belgium	
			Denmark	
			Federal Republic of Germany	
			Greece	
			France	
			Ireland	
			Italy	
			Luxembourg	
			Netherlands	
			United Kingdom	
			Available for Member States	62,000**
			EEC total	62,000**
Cod	St Pierre and Miquelon	NAFO 3Ps	Belgium	
			Denmark	
			Federal Republic of Germany	
			Greece	
			France	5,170
			Ireland	
			Italy	
			Luxembourg	

Species	Stock Geographical regions	Stock ICES/NAFO division	Member State	1982 quota (tonnes)
			Netherlands	
			United Kingdom	
			Available for Member States	
			EEC total	5,170
Haddock	Skagerrak and Kattegat, Baltic Sea	III (a) III (b), (c), (d) (EEC zone)	Belgium	50[6]
			Denmark	8,500[5]
			Federal Republic of Germany	540[6]
			Greece	
			France	
			Ireland	
			Italy	
			Luxembourg	
			Netherlands	10[6]
			United Kingdom	
			Available for Member States	
			EEC total	9,100
Haddock	North Sea, Norwegian Sea	IV II (a) (EEC zone)	Belgium	1,600
			Denmark	11,000
			Federal Republic of Germany	7,000
			Greece	
			France	12,200
			Ireland	
			Italy	
			Luxembourg	
			Netherlands	1,200
			United Kingdom	117,100
			Available for Member States	
			EEC total	150,100[7]

Notes

1   No fishing for this quota may take place within four miles of the baselines of the Kingdom of Norway and the Kingdom of Sweden.

2   No fishing for this quota may take place within three miles of the baselines of the Kingdom of Sweden.

3   No fishing for this quota may take place, in the Skagerrak, within 12 miles of the baselines of the Kingdom of Norway and of the Kingdom of Sweden respectively and, in the Kattegat, within 12 miles of the Kingdom of Sweden.

4   Catch possibilities reserved exclusively for the coastal fishermen of Greenland.

5   No fishing for this quota may take place, in the Skagerrak, within four miles of the baselines of the Kingdom of Norway and of the Kingdom of Sweden respectively and, in the Kattegat, within three miles of the baselines of the Kingdom of Sweden.

6   No fishing for this quota may take place, in the Skagerrak, within 12 miles of the baselines of the Kingdom of Norway and of the Kingdom of Sweden respectively and, in the Kattegat, within 12 miles of the baselines of the Kingdom of Sweden.

7   Excludes estimated industrial by-catch.

*   Voluntary *ad hoc* transfer in 1982 of 5000 tonnes from Germany to Denmark.

**   No allocation for Member States. *Ad hoc* solution for 1982.

References

Agra Europe (1981) *EEC Fisheries: Problems and Prospects for a Common Policy*, Special Report No. 11, Agra Europe Ltd, London.

Alexander, L. M. (1966) *Offshore Geography of Northwestern Europe*, London, Murray.

Alvarez (Judge) (1951) 'Anglo-Norwegian Fisheries Case', Judgement of 18 December, ICJ Report 146.

Boos, D. (1979) 'EEC Common Fisheries Policy', paper presented at conference on 'Fishing in European Waters', London, 13 December.

Bourgeois, J. H. C. (1979) 'EEC Fisheries Cases before the Court of Justice of the European Communities', report presented at conference on 'Fishing in European Waters', London, 13 December.

Braybrooke, D. and Lindblom, C. E. (1963) *A Strategy of Decision*, New York, Free Press.

British United Trawlers Ltd (1976) 'Proposals for a UK Fisheries Policy', Hull.

Calman, M. (1983) *The Times*, 4 January.

COI (Central Office of Information) (1976) *Britain and the European Community*, pamphlet 137, London, HMSO.

Christensen, J. M. (1977) 'Industrial fisheries', in *Fisheries of the European Community*, Edinburgh, White Fish Authority.

Christy, F. and Scott, A. D. (1965) *The Commonwealth of Ocean Fisheries*, Baltimore, Johns Hopkins Press.

Churchill, R., Simmonds, K. R. and Welch, J. (eds) (1973) *New Directions in the Law of the Sea*, London, British Institute of International and Comparative Law.

Commission (Commission of the European Communities) (1966) COM (66) 250 final 22 June.

(1968a) *Spokesman's Group*, relating to Question Ecrité No. 335/67 de M. Baas à la Commission de la CEE.

(1968b) *Volume et degre de l'emploi dans la pêche maritime,* Informations internes sur l'agriculture, 32.

(1968c) Proposition de reglement ..., *JOCE (Journal Officiel des Communauté Européennes),* C91, 13 September, 1–19.

(1970a) SEC (70) 1690 (COREPER) 11 May; SEC (70) 2442 (COREPER) 23 June.

(1970b) COM (70) 605 29 May.

(1970c) SEC (70) 2022 28 May.

(1970d) SEC (70) 1063 13 May.

(1970e) SEC (70) 3733 27 October.

(1970f) SEC (70) 2243 8 June; JUR/1788/70 19 June.

(1975a) SEC (75) 4503 final 22 December, especially 9–10.

(1975b) SEC (75) 4503 final 22 December, Table III.

(1976a) COM (76) 500 final 23 September, especially 1–23.

(1976b) COM (76) 59 final 24 February, especially 9.

(1976c) Proposal, *OJEC (Official Journal of the European Communities* – the English language version of *JOCE),* 19, C6, 10 January, 2–10.

(1977a) COM (77) 164 final 12 May.

(1977b) SI/77/1038 8 December.

(1977c) COM (77) 524 final 17 October.

(1977d) COM (77) 635 final 28 November.

(1978a) 'Community Fisheries Policy', Spokesman's Group, Information Memo, January.

(1978b) COM (78) 5 final 16 January.

(1978c) COM (78) 39 final 30 January.

(1979a) *Impact regional de la politique de la pêche de la CEE: Bretagne,* Informations internes sur la pêche, 1.

(1979b) *12th Annual Report,* Brussels.

(1980a) COM (80) 338 final 12 June.

(1980b) COM (80) 420 final 18 July.

(1980c) COM (80) 787 final 2 December.

(1980d) COM (80) 484 final 23 July.

(1980e) COM (80) 452 final 16 July.

(1980f) *The Regional Impact of EEC Fisheries Policy: Jutland,* Internal information on fisheries, 5.

(1980g) COM (80) 575 final 1 October.

(1981a) Declaration of 27 July, *OJEC,* 24, C224, 3 September.

(1981b) COM (81) 77 final 18 March.

(1981c) COM (81) 104 final 6 March.
(1981d) COM (81) 435 final 24 July.
(1981e) SEC (81) 105 21 January.
(1982a) Communication, *OJEC*, 25, C22, 29 January, 2.
(1982b) Proposal, *OJEC*, 25, C228, 1 October, 1–52.
(1982c) COM (82) 340 final 18 June.
Commons, House of (1963–4) *Parliamentary Debates*, vol. 676, cols 715–7.
Coull, J. R. (1972) *The Fisheries of Europe: An Economic Geography*, London, Bell.
Council (Council of the European Communities)
(1968) S/756/F/68 (CSA 228) 6 August; S/904/F68 (CSA 257) 22 October.
(1969a) S/3179/69 (CSA 43) 20 February.
(1969b) S/265/69 (CSA 64) 12 March.
(1970a) S/46/70 (CSA 10) 22 January.
(1970b) R/956/70 (AGRI 294) 13 May.
(1970c) R/1184/70 (AGRI 365) 4 June.
(1970d) S/432/70 (CSA 91) 25 May.
(1970e) R/1176/70 (AGRI 357) 4 June.
(1970f) R/1410/70 (AGRI 449) 26 June.
(1970g) S/42/70 (CSA 8) 28 January.
(1970h) R/1240/70 (AGRI 375) 12 June.
(1970i) R/906/70 (AGRI 273) 4 May.
(1970j) Regulation (EEC) 2141/70 of 20 October 1970 laying down a common structural policy for the fishing industry, *OJEC*, 14, L236, 27 October, 1.
(1970k) Regulation (EEC) 2142/70 of 20 October 1970 on the common organization of the market in fishery products, *OJEC*, 14, L236, 27 October, 5.
(1970l) R/2129/70 (AGRI 691) 20 October.
(1970m) R/840/70 (AGRI 252) 24 April.
(1976) S/353/76 (AGRI 17) 24 February.
(1977) Regulation (EEC) 350/77 of 18 February, *OJEC*, 20, L48, 19 February, 28.
(1978) Regulation (EEC) 1852/78 of 25 July, *OJEC*, 21, L211, 1 September, 30–3.
(1979a) Decision of 9 April, *OJEC*, 22, L93, 12 April, 40.
(1979b) Decision of 29 October, *OJEC*, 22, L277, 6 November, 10.
(1979c) Decision of 3 December, *OJEC*, 22, L312, 1 December, 31.

(1980a) Regulation (EEC) 2527/80 of 30 September, *OJEC*, 23, L258, 1 October, 1.

(1980b) Regulation (EEC) 753/80 of 26 March, *OJEC*, 23, L84, 28 March, 33.

(1980c) Declaration of 30 May, *OJEC*, 23, C158, 27 June, 20.

(1981a) Regulation (EEC) 3796/81 of 29 December 1981 on the common organization of the market in fishery products; Regulation (EEC) 3797/81 of 29 December 1981 providing for Community tariff quotas on certain fishery products; Regulation (EEC) 3798/81 of 29 December 1981 providing for Community tariff quotas on herrings: *OJEC*, 24, L379, 31 December, 1–51.

(1981b) Regulation (EEC) 2992/81 of 19 October, *OJEC*, 24, L299, 20 October, 24.

(1983a) Regulation (EEC) 170/83 of 25 January establishing a Community system for the conservation and management of fishery resources, *OJEC*, 26, L24, 27 January, 1–13.

(1983b) Regulation (EEC) 172/83 of 25 January fixing for certain fish stocks and groups of fish stocks occurring in the Community's fishing zone, total allowable catches for 1982, the share of these catches available to the Community, the allocation of that share between the member states and the conditions under which the total allowable catches may be fished, *OJEC*, 26, L24, 27 January, 30–67.

(1983c) Regulation (EEC) 171/83 of 25 January laying down certain technical measures for the conservation of fishery resources, *OJEC*, 26, L24, 27 January, 14-29 (see Articles 17-21).

(1983d) Regulations (EEC) 173/83 to 181/83 of 25 January, *OJEC*, 26, L24, 27 January, 68–108.

(1983e) Resolution of 25 January, *OJEC*, 26, C28, 3 February, 1.

E *(Europe* (Agence Internationale d'Information pour la Presse, Brussels); daily bulletins on Community activities)

(1964) 1909 5 August, 2; 1975 5 November, 4; 1986 18 November, 2.

(1969) 472 16 December, 6.

(1970a) 573 21 May, 8; 576 26 May, 5.

(1970b) 586 9 June.

(1970c) 602 1 January, 5; 606 7 July, 7; 655 30 September, 5; 668 19 October, 4; 670 21 October, 8.

(1971a) 846 9 July.

(1971b) 887 22 September.

(1971c) 918 8 November; 920 10 November.

(1971d) 933 30 November.

(1971e) 937 6 December.

(1971f) 942 13 December.

(1972a) 961 13 January.

(1972b) 956 6 January.

(1972c) 960 12 January.

(1972d) 963 15 January.

(1972e) 964 17–18 January.

Economist, The
  (1978a) 24 June.
  (1978b) 4 February, 55–6.
  (1978c) 21 July, 60.
  (1981) 10 January, 41.

ECOSOC (Economic and Social Committee of the European
  Communities)
  (1967) Avis, *JOCE*, 58, 29 March, 893–900.
  (1982) *Agricultural Aspects of Spain's Entry into the EC*, Opinion,
  Brussels, February, 46.

Engholm, B. (1961) 'Fishery conservation in the Atlantic Ocean', in
  G. Borgstrom and A. J. Heighway (eds) *Atlantic Ocean Fisheries*,
  London, Fishing News Books Ltd.

Eurofish Report (a fortnightly review of fishery affairs produced by Agra
  Europe Ltd, London)
  (1977a) 14 February.
  (1977b) 30 November.
  (1977c) 14 July.
  (1977d) 14 December.
  (1978a) 19 January.
  (1978b) 1 March.
  (1978c) 6 December.
  (1978d) 2 August.
  (1980) 5 March.
  (1981) 4 February.
  (1982) 10 February.
  (1983a) 26 January.
  (1983b) 24 February.

European Parliament
  (1968a) Resolution, *JOCE*, C10, 14 February, 58.

(1968b) Rapport, *JOCE*, Document 133, 30 September, 35–7.
(1968c) Rapport, *JOCE*, Document 174, 15 January, 9.
(1968d) Debats, *JOCE*, 98, 25 January, 219; 107, 24 October, 9.
(1978) Report, Working Documents 1978–9, Document 206/78, 4 July, 10.
Eurostat (various editions) *Fisheries*, Brussels, Statistical Office of the European Communities.
FAO (Food and Agriculture Organization (of the UN)) (1960–80) *Yearbook of Fishery Statistics*, various editions, Rome, FAO.
Final Act of the European Fisheries Conference (1964) *European Fisheries Convention*, London, HMSO, Cmnd 2355.
Financial Times, The
(1978) 30 September.
(1982) 2 December.
Fleischer, C. A. (1965) *Norway's Policy on Fisheries 1958-64*, London, British Institute of International and Comparative Law, Special Publication No. 6.
Gallagher, E. (1977) 'The Community's Common Fisheries Policy', in *Fisheries of the European Community*, Edinburgh, White Fish Authority.
Guardian, The (1982) 1 November.
Gueben, P. and Keller-Noellet, M. (1971) 'Aspects juridiques de la politique de la CEE en matière de pêche', *Revue du Marché Commun*, 144.
Hamley, E.
(1971) 'Fishing fears', *Bulletin No. 5 Common Market Safeguards Campaign*, August 1971, 2.
(1972) 'Is the EEC agreement really unfair to our fishermen?', *Fish Trades Gazette*, 12 February, 5–6
Hansard
(1971) 15 December, col. 728.
(1976a) 20 October, col. 1459.
(1976b) 6 May, col. 1484.
(1978) 19 January, cols 676, 677; 1 February, col. 471.
Heskin, A. (1977) 'A profile of the Irish fishing industry', *Fisheries of the European Community*, Edinburgh, White Fish Authority.
ICES (International Council for Exploration of the Sea)
(1965–81) *Bulletin Statistique des Pêches Maritimes*, annual editions, Charlottenlund.

(1970) *Report of the Working Group on the Atlanto-Scandinavian Herring*, Co-operative Research Report, Series A, 17, Charlottenlund.

(1971a) *Report of the North Sea Herring Assessment Working Group*, Co-operative Research Report, Series A, 26, Charlottenlund.

(1971b) *Report on the State of Herring Stocks Around Ireland and the North West of Scotland*, Co-operative Research Report, Series A, 21, Charlottenlund.

(1974) *Survey of Fish Resources in the North East Atlantic*, Co-operative Research Project 37, Charlottenlund.

(1979) *Report of the ad hoc Working Group on the Norway Pout Box Problems*, C. M. Papers and Reports, G:2, Charlottenlund.

Int. doc. (Internal document of the European Commission)

(1970) UK Delegation Statement, 1 June.

(1971a) Norwegian Government Declaration, 8 June.

(1971b) Norwegian Statement at EEC Ministerial Meeting, 9 November; Statement of Norwegian Delegation, 8 December.

(1971c) UK Declaration, 8 November.

(1971d) UK Declaration, 12 July.

(1971e) UK Notes to Commission, 11 December, 16 December, 6 January.

(1971f) Irish Declaration at EEC Ministerial Meeting, 7 June.

(1971g) Irish Declaration, 29 November.

(1971h) Confidential Danish Notes, 11 December; Danish Declaration at EEC Ministerial Meeting, 4 November.

(1971i) Community Delegation Note about Enlargement, 16 June.

(1971j) UK Delegation Declaration, 9 November.

(1971k) UK Proposal, 11 December.

Johnson, D. H. N. (1958) 'The Anglo-Norwegian fisheries case', *International and Comparative Law Quarterly*, 1, 145–80.

Johnston, D. M. (1965) *The International Law of Fisheries: A Framework for Policy-Oriented Inquiries*, New Haven and London, Yale University Press.

Judgement (Judgement of the European Court of Justice)

(1976) Cases 3, 4 and 6/76, 14 July, *OJEC*, 19, C248, 21 October, 4.

(1979) Case 141/78, 4 October, *OJEC*, 22, C280, 9 November, 5.

(1980) Case 32/79, 10 July, *OJEC*, 23, C199, 5 August, 6.

Laing, A. (1971–2) 'The Common Fisheries Policy of the Six', *Fish Industry Review*, 1, 9–10.

Mackay, G. (1981) 'The UK fishing industry and EEC policy', *The Three Banks Review*, 132, December, 59–60.

Mackintosh, J. P. (1972) *The Impact of EEC Policies on British Fishing and Agriculture*, London, European Movement Booklet, 6–8.

Martens, R. (1977) 'The Belgian fishing industry in the common market', in *Fisheries of the European Community*, Edinburgh, White Fish Authority.

Michielson, K. (1971) 'La pêche belge a pu s'adapter sans trop de difficultés à la politique commune', *La Pêche Maritime*, 1125, December, 963.

Millward, R. (1964) *Scandinavian Lands*, London, Macmillan.

Mitchell, A. (1977) *The Guardian*, 12 December.

Mocklinghoff, G. (1971) 'Pour l'industrie allemande de la pêche, la concurrence oblige à une vigilance constante et reste le moteur du progrès', *La Pêche Maritime*, 1125, December, 984.

Monde, Le (1972) 21 January.

Munch, F. (1973) 'Federal Republic of Germany', in R. Churchill, K. R. Simmonds and J. Welch (eds) *New Directions in the Law of the Sea*, London, British Institute of International and Comparative Law.

NEAFC (North East Atlantic Fisheries Commission)
(1963) *Convention of 1959*, Cmnd 2190, London, HMSO.
(1964) *Report of the Second Meeting*, London, NEAFC.
(1969) *Report of the Seventh Meeting*, London, NEAFC.
(1970) *Report of the Eighth Meeting*, London, NEAFC.
(1971) *Report of the Ninth Meeting*, Annex E, London, NEAFC.

Norgaard, J. (1971) 'L'adhesion du Danemark à la CEE depend plus de la balance economique et de la politique générale que de considerations strictement relatives à la politique de la pêche', *La Pêche Maritime*, 1125, December, 990.

Noel, E. (1979) *Working Together: the Institutions of the European Community*, Brussels, Commission of the European Communities.

OECD (Organization for Economic Co-operation and Development)
(1969-82) *Review of Fisheries in OECD Member Countries*, annual editions, Paris, OECD.
(1970) *Fishery Policies and Economics, 1957-66*, Paris, OECD.

O'Kelly, B. (1971) 'L'adhesion de l'Irlande au Marché Commun presente à la fois des avantages et des inconvenients', *La Pêche Maritime*, 1125, December, 993.

Opsahl, T. (1972) 'Le "non" norvegien', *Revue du Marché Commun*,

15, November, 716.

Regnier, J. (1977) 'The real meaning of Community', in *Fisheries of the European Community*, Edinburgh, White Fish Authority.

SI (Statutory Instrument (UK))
  (1977a) SI 290 Herring (Celtic Sea) (Prohibition of Fishing) Order.
  (1977b) SI 291 The Herring (Specified North Sea Waters) (Prohibition of Fishing) Order.
  (1977c) SI 200 The Norway Pout (Prohibition of Fishing) Order.
  (1977d) SI 440 The Fishing-Nets (North East Atlantic) Order.

Sibthorp, M. M. (ed.) (1975) *The North Sea: Challenge and Opportunity*, London, Europa Publications.

Simonnet, M. (1967) 'L'intégration européenne des pêcheries communautaires: la politique commune des pêches', *Revue du Marché Commun*, 101, 245.

Smit, W. (1977) 'The Netherlands sea fisheries', in *Fisheries of the European Community*, Edinburgh, White Fish Authority.

Steel, D. and Buchanan, N. (1977) 'Meaningful effort limitation: the British case', in *Fisheries of the European Community*, Edinburgh, White Fish Authority.

Thibaudau, R. (1971) 'Les pêches françaises dans la communaute économique européenne', *La Pêche Maritime*, 1125, December, 970, 971.

Tienstra, Th. J. (1971) 'La pêche néerlandaise et la politique des pêches de la CCE', *La Pêche Maritime*, 1125, December, 977–8.

Times, The
  (1976) 21 October.
  (1981) 6 March.
  (1982) 28 October.
  (1983) 26 January.

Treaties Establishing the European Communities (1973) 'Act concerning the Conditions of Accession and Adjustments to the Treaties' (Articles 100–3), in *Treaties Establishing the European Communities*, Luxembourg, EC, 959–62.

UN (United Nations)
  (1957) *Laws and Regulations on the Regime of the Territorial Sea*, UN Legislative Series, 695.
  (1958) *Resolution VI, Special Situation Related to Coastal Fisheries*, UN Conference on the Law of the Sea, UN Document A/CONF.

UNCLOS (United Nations Conference on the Law of the Sea) (1958–64) I, Geneva, 1958; II, Geneva 1960; III Caracas, 1964 (and subsequent sessions in New York and Geneva).

US Department of State (1975) *Limits in the Seas: National Claims to Maritime Jurisdictions*, Washington, DC, Office of the Geographer, December.

Wood, I. C. (1978) 'Towards a Common Fisheries Policy: a British viewpoint', *Eurofish Report*, 7 June.

White Fish Authority

(1977) *Fisheries of the European Community*, Edinburgh, White Fish Authority.

(1978) *The Sea Fisheries of the Community in the Context of Enlargement*, FERU (Fishery Economics Research Unit), Occasional Papers Series, 2, Edinburgh, White Fish Authority.

(1979) *Greek Fisheries and Accession to the European Community*, FERU, Occasional Papers Series, 2, Edinburgh, White Fish Authority.

(Various) *Annual Reports and Accounts*, Edinburgh, White Fish Authority.

Select bibliography

Anderson, L. G. (1977) *The Economics of Fisheries Management*, Baltimore, Johns Hopkins Press.

Barston, R. P. and Birnie, P. (eds) (1980) *The Maritime Dimension*, London, Allen & Unwin.

Bell, F. W. (1978) *Food from the Sea: The Economics and Politics of Ocean Fisheries*, Boulder, Colorado, Westview Press.

Coull, J. R., Goodland, J. H. and Sheves, G. T. (1979) 'Fisheries in the Shetland Area: A Study in Conservation and Development', Department of Geography, University of Aberdeen, mimeo paper.

Cox, K. R. (1979) *Location and Public Problems: A Political Geography of the Contemporary World*, Oxford, Blackwell.

Daltrop, A. (1982) *Politics and the European Community*, London, Longman.

Gulland, J. A. (1974) *The Management of Marine Fisheries*, Bristol, Scientechnica.

Hannesson, R. (1978) *Economics of Fisheries*, Bergen, Universitetsforlaget.

Henig, S. (1980) *Power and Decision in Europe*, London, Europotential Press.

Holland, S. (1980) *Uncommon Market*, London, Macmillan.

Johnston, D. M. (ed.) (1976) *Marine Policy and the Coastal Community*, London, Croom Helm.

Kirby, A. (1983) *The Politics of Location*, London, Methuen.

Lodge, J. (ed.) (1983) *Institutions and Policies of the European Community*, London, Frances Pinter.

Lords, House of (1980) *EEC Fisheries Policy*, Select Committee on European Communities, 67th Report, London.

Mason, C. M. (ed.) (1979) *The Effective Management of Resources: The International Politics of the North Sea*, London, Frances Pinter.

Muir, R. and Paddison, R. (1981) *Politics, Geography and Behaviour*, London, Methuen.

Parker, G. (1979) *The Countries of Community Europe: A Geographical Survey of Contemporary Issues*, London, Macmillan.

Rosenthal, G. G. (1975) *The Men Behind the Decisions: Cases in European Policy-Making*, Lexington, Mass., D. C. Heath.

Talbot, R. B. (1977) *The European Community's Regional Fund: A Study in the Politics of Redistribution*, Oxford, Pergamon.

Underdal, A. (1980) *The Politics of International Fisheries Management: The Case of the Northeast Atlantic*, Oslo, Universitetsforlaget.

Usher, J. (1981) *European Community Law and National Law: The Irreversible Transfer?*, London, Allen & Unwin.

Wallace, H., Wallace, W. and Webb, C. (1977) *Policy-making in the European Communities*, Chichester, Wiley.

White Fish Authority (1977) *Fisheries of the European Community*, Edinburgh, White Fish Authority.

Index

access: to fishing grounds, 21, 83–4; negotiations and agreement, (1982/3), 223–31, 244; open, 4; preferential, 185–7, 223–30; restricted, 164, 169–76, 188, 226–9, 251–2

'acquis communautaire', 94, 95, 103, 108, 114, 120, 121, 128, 164

Agreements as to the Transitional Rights, 76

Anglo-Icelandic Fisheries Case, 71–2

Anglo-Norwegian Fisheries Case, 70–1

aquaculture, 215, 218, 245

Atlantic: major fishing zones, 18–19; North East, 17–23, 58, 143–5; North West, 17, 20, 144–5

baselines, establishment of, 69, 70, 75–6

Belgium: coastal waters, fishing rights in, 274; effect of 200-mile limits on, 147, 148; fish catches, 24, 25, 31, 144, 197, quotas, 173, 197, 233–4, 236, 238; fish imports/exports, 29, 30, 86; fishing industry, 26, 27, 28–9, 167; structural aid, 245; and establishment of CFP in Community of Six, 99–101, 103; and EC enlargement negotiations, 120–1; and new CFP (1983), 246, 247

Bratteli, Mr, 111, 126–7, 139

Breton fishing rights round UK, 224, 225

British Trawlers' Federation, 51, 112

British United Trawlers Ltd, 160, 166, 170

Buchan, N., 240

by-catches, 5, 183, 184, 235, 283–5; of whitefish, 184, 187, 205–8

Canada, fishing rights accord, 213, 253, 257

CAP, 85–6, 94, 220

'Cap Caval' case, 184, 185, 208, 209

catches: fish (*see also under individual countries, and* quotas, catch, allocation of); EC, 17–20, 22–3, 143–7; total allowable, *see* TACs

CCT, 85, 86–8

CFP: establishment of, in Community of Six, 85–107; in EC enlargement negotiations, 108–41, text of fisheries agreement (1971), 129–31; proposals for a revised (1976), 149–57, 250; Hague Resolutions, 157–61; proposals for a modified (1978), 187–203; negotiations towards a reformed (1980s), 204, 210–42; agreement on a new (1983), 242, 244–7, 250–7, extracts of basic legislation, 262–97

cod, 58, 62, 64, 145–6, 195; equivalent, 233–5, 236, 238; quotas, 232–4, 236, 238, 292–5

Cod Wars, 51, 62, 72, 143, 160, 170

Commission, *see* European Commission

conservation of fish stocks, 6–7; enforcement, 7, 82, 187, 253, 255; European regimes for, 78–84; role in initial formulation of CFP, 92–3, 100–1, 105–7; in EC enlargement negotiations, 120, 121, 126, 131, 140; in CFP modification proposals

(1976), 152–3; in Hague
Resolutions, 158; in UK/Irish
conflict with continental states, 168,
174–5; autonomous UK measures
(1977), 182–5, 201, 205–8; in CFP
modification proposals (1978), 187;
agreements on (1980), 209–10; in
new CFP (1983), 252–3, 262–9
control, fisheries, 4–5, 7, 187, 253, 255
COREPER, 13–14
Council of Ministers, *see* European
Council of Ministers

Denmark: coastal waters, fishing rights
in, 275–6; fish catches, 24, 25, 41–3,
60, 144, 210–11; fish trade, 28, 29,
30; fishing industry, 24–5, 26, 27,
41–4, 217; fishing limits, 21, 69,
72–3, 130, 132–3, effect of 200-mile,
147, 148; industrial fishing, 42–3,
176–7, 182–3, 205–9, 238, 239;
quotas, 173, 197, 233–4, 236, 238;
structural aid, 245; and European
Fisheries Convention, 77; and CFP
in EC enlargement negotiations,
117–18, 120–1, 124–5, 126, 128,
130, 131–2; and CFP modification
proposals (1978), 190, 197; and
negotiations towards reformed CFP
(1980s), 213, 230–1, 237–43; and
new CFP (1983), 247
'dependence' on fishing, 6, 21, 24–8,
167, 173, 193
Directorate-General for Fisheries, 157
'dominant preference', UK demand for,
185–7, 200

EAGGF, 90, 96, 100, 101, 105, 111,
115; financing of POs, 89, 104,
213–14; structural aid, 100, 156,
158, 215–16, 245
ECOSOC, 9, 15, 93
EEZs, 200-mile/median line, 142–9,
150, 157–8, 159–61, 164–5, 171,
172–3
elections, national, and CFP
negotiations, 201–2
Elleman-Jensen, U., 241

equal access: exceptions to, 91, 97,
103, *see also* special exception zones;
in formulation of CFP in
Community of Six, 90–3, 94–7,
99–103; in EC enlargement
negotiations, 108–19, 120, 121,
122–6, 134–6; in CP modification
proposals (1976), 149–50; in
UK/Irish conflict with continental
states, 164–5, 169–70
Ertl, Josef, 203
European Commission, 7–12, 14; and
conservation, 168–9, 174, 210–11;
and EEZs, 143–5; Pout Box issue,
205–8; proposals for CFP in
Community of Six, 85–6, 87–102,
106–7; in EC enlargement
negotiations, 118, 120–1, 125, 129;
proposals for revised CFP (1976),
149–57, 215, 226; and UK
autonomous measures (1977), 182–4;
proposals for CFP revision (1978),
187–203, 226; and negotiations
towards reformed CFP (1980s),
216–19; quota/access negotiations
(1982), 226–30, 231–2, 235–7, 241;
and new CFP (1983), 251, 252–3
European Community (EC), viii, 7–8;
aid, *see* structural aid, Community
enlargement negotiations, 108–41;
institutions of, 7–16
European Council of Ministers, 7, 8–
10, 12–14, 93, 253, 256; majority
voting in, 12–13, 203, 239; and
formulation of CFP in Community
of Six, 87, 89, 91, 93, 98, 105–7; in
EC enlargement negotiations, 120–3,
125–6, 128; and CFP modification
proposals (1976), 149, 155, 157; and
stalemate in CFP revision (1979),
200; Declaration on formulation of
CFP (May 1980), 220–2, 231
European Court of Justice, 7, 8, 9,
15–16, 204–5; 'Cap Caval' case,
184, 208; Kramer case, 159; Irish
case, 181; Pout Box case, 184, 208
European Fisheries Convention, 74–8,
135, 136, 165, 229, 259

European Parliament, 7, 9, 14–15, 93, 187
excess capacity, of Community fleets, 156, 188, 216–18
exploratory fishing, 218, 245
external EC fisheries policy, 151–2, 159, 253–4

Faroes: dependence on fishing, 26, 45, 117; fishing industry, 24–5, 26, 27, 45, 46; fishing limits, 69, 72–3, 117, 130; fish trade, 28, 29, 30; and European Fisheries Convention, 76–7; and EC enlargement negotiations, 117–18, 120–1, 123, 124–5
fisheries control, 4–5, 7, 187, 253, 255
fishery management, 2–7, 152–3, 252
fishing limits, national, 6; 200-mile/ median line, see EEZs; pre-CFP, 68–78; in formulation of CFP in Community of Six, 91, 94; in EC enlargement negotiations, 120–1, 122–3, 125–6, 129–33, 136; in CFP modification proposals (1976), 150–1; in Hague Resolutions, 157–8; in UK/Irish conflict with continental states, 169–76; in new CFP (1983), 251–2; see also under individual countries, and special exception zones
fishing plans, 187, 188–9, 229
fishing rights: in Community, see access to fishing grounds, fishing limits, 'historic rights'; loss of, in third-country waters, 145–7, 160, 187, 193–6, 231, 232, 233, 234
fishing, spatial pattern of, 20–1
fishing zones, national, see fishing limits, special exception zones
Fleischer, Dr C.A., 77
'framework agreements', 151–2, 158, 253–4
France: and the CCT, 86–8; coastal waters, fishing rights in, 278; 'empty chair' policy, 13; fish catches, 20, 24, 25, 34, 144, 224, quotas, 173, 197, 233–4, 236, 238; fish imports/ exports, 29, 30, 86–7; fishing

industry, 26, 27, 29, 32–5; fishing limits, 130, 132, effect of 200-mile, 147, 148; and historic rights round UK, 165–6, 176, 224–6, 228, 246; losses in third-country waters, 32, 195; structural aid, 95–6, 99, 103–4, 245; and establishment of CFP in Community of Six, 86–9, 94–7, 99–107; and EC enlargement negotiations, 119, 120–1, 125, 129, 130, 132; and negotiations towards reformed CFP (1980s), 217, 224–6, 228, 248; and new CFP (1983), 246

Genscher, H.D., 241
Greece, 20, 215, 247; fish imports/ exports, 29, 30; fishing industry, 25, 26, 27, 56
Greenland: dependence on fishing, 26, 117, 158; fish catches, 44, 144, quotas, 232, 234; fishing industry, 26, 44; fishing limits, 73, 76–7, 117, 130, effect of 200-mile, 147; structural aid, 215–16, 245; and EC enlargement negotiations, 117–18, 120–1, 123, 124–5, 129, 130; and CFP modification proposals (1978), 188, 189, 193
guide prices, 89, 104
Gundelach, F., 198, 205

haddock, 66, 189, 195; in Pout Box, 182, 183, 205, 207–9; quotas, 232–5, 236, 238, 296
'Hague Regions' 189, 193, 226, 232, 233, 234, 235
Hague Resolutions, 157–9, 181, 182–3, 193, 220
Heath, Edward, 74, 126–7
herring, 58–63, 195, 255, 284–6; catch quotas, 211, 236; conservation, 80, 82–3, 182, 187, 189, 201, 210–11; overfishing of, 58–63, 82–3
Hillery, P., 134
'historic' (or 'special') rights 70, 75–6, 129–30, 135–6, 150, 151, 252; in British coastal zone, 76, 165–6, 176, 224, 226, 228–9, 259

historical catch performance, 190–3, 231

Iceland: dependence on fishing, 25–6; fishing industry, 24, 25–6, 27; fishing limits, 69, 71–2, 76–7, 143, *see also* Cod Wars; fish trade, 28
ICES, 78–9, 81, 82–3, 189, 207; and herring overfishing, 60, 61, 62, 82–3
ICNAF, 155, 157, 189, 191
import controls on fishery products, 86–8, 105, 211
industrial fishing, 62, 236; by Denmark, 42–3, 176–7, 182–3, 205–9, 238, 239; by Norway, 106, 177
inspectorate, Community, 253, 256
International Conference on Overfishing, 79–80
International Court of Justice, 70, 76
Ireland: autonomous 'conservation' measures (1977), 181–2; coastal waters, fishing rights in, 273; dependence on fishing , 173, 193; fish catches, 24, 25, 45, 47, 48, 144, quotas, 173, 193, 196–7, 232, 233–4, 236, 238; fish imports/exports, 29, 30; fishing industry, 26, 27, 45, 47, 115–16, 158, 172, 199; fishing limits, 73, 76, 116, 130, 132–3, 180, dispute over, with continental states, 164–79, effect of 200-mile, 147, 148; structural aid, 215–16, 245; and CFP in EC enlargement negotiations, 115–17, 120–1, 125, 126, 128, 130, 131–2, 134; and CFP modification proposals (1978), 188, 193, 196–7, 198–9; and new CFP (1983), 247
Irish Fishermen's Organization, 47, 172
Italy: effect of 200-mile limits, 147, 149; fish catches, 17, 24, 40, 144, 197, quotas, 197; fish imports/exports, 29, 30; fishing industry, 25, 26, 27, 38, 40–1; structural aid, 103–4, 215–16, 245, 247; and establishment of CFP in Community of Six, 98, 99–101, 103–4, 105; and

EC enlargement negotiations 120–1; and new CFP (1983), 247

joint-venture fishing operations, 218, 245, 248

Kirk, Kent, 242, 255
Kramer case, 159

Laing, A., 112–13, 114
laying-up premiums, 216–17
Lenihan, B., 186, 198
licensing system, Community, 154–5, 230, 252, 266–7
Luxembourg, 86, 103
'Luxembourg Compromise', 13, 239, 240

mackerel, 51, 63; quotas, 232, 234, 236, 238, 243
Management Committee for Fishery Resources, 252, 268–9; *see also* Management Committee for Sea Fisheries, 153
market organization: in formulation of CFP in Community of Six, 89, 96, 98–9, 100, 101, 104–5; in EC enlargement negotiations, 111–12, 120, 121, 123, 126, 131; reformed (1981–2), 211–14, 254
maximum economic yield (MEY), 3–4
maximum sustainable yield (MSY), 2–5
mesh-size regulations, 5–6, 79, 183, 187, 209–10
Mitchell, Austin, 170, 178
Mitterand, F., 202

NEAFC, 81–3, 84, 155, 157, 174, 184, 190–1, 257
nephrops, 184, 201, 209
Netherlands: coastal waters, fishing rights in, 279; effect of 200-mile limits, 147, 148; fish catches, 24, 25, 37, 39, 144, 197, quotas, 173, 197, 233–4, 236, 238; fish imports/exports, 28, 29, 30, 86; fishing industry, 26, 27, 37–9, 167; structural aid, 245; and establishment

of CFP in Community of Six, 88, 98, 99–107; and EC enlargement negotiations, 120–1; and new CFP (1983), 246, 247

non-discrimination, national, principle of, 91, 97, 120, 121, 164, 165, 188, 251–2; violations of, 109, 181

North Britain, 154, 158, 189, 232; dependence on fishing, 193, 246, 251

North East Atlantic: fishery resources of, 17–23, 143–5; overfishing in, 58

North East Atlantic Fisheries Commission, see NEAFC

North East Atlantic Fisheries Convention, 80–2

North Sea Fisheries Convention, 69, 73–4, 78

North West Atlantic, fishery resources of, 17, 20, 144–5

Norway: 'dependence' of inshore fishing communities, 54, 69, 70; fish imports/exports, 29, 30; fishing industry, 24–5, 26, 27–8, 51, 54–5, 60, 106; fishing limits, 69–71, 76–7, 109, 143; and EC enlargement negotiations, 17, 108–12, 120–1, 123, 124, 126, 134–5, 136–40; refuses to join Community, 139–40; quota/access negotiations (1982), 241–2; and new CFP (1983), 256

'Norway Pout Box', 182–3, 184, 185, 201, 202, 205–9

O'Kelly, Brendan, 177

Orkneys: as special exception zone, 123, 130; Shetland/Orkney 'Box', 226, 227, 229–30, 240, 241, 243, 252

ownership of fish resources, 174–6

overfishing, 2–5, 6, 58–66, 238, 239; of herring, 58–63, 82–3; International Conference on, 79–80

plaice, 65, 195; quotas, 232–5, 236, 238

POs, see Producers' Organizations

Portugal, 56; fish imports/exports, 29, 30; fishing industry, 24, 25, 26, 27, 57–8

price support system, 89, 104–5, 112, 211, 213

Producers' Organizations (POs), 156, 213–14; 'extension of discipline' for, 111, 123; in CFP in Community of Six, 89, 96, 97–8, 99, 100, 101, 104–5

quotas, catch, allocation of, 153–4, 162–4, 169, 173, 183–97; Commission's procedure for, 189–92; negotiations/agreement (1982/3), 231–43, 251, 265–6, 282–3, 292–7

redfish, 195; quotas, 232–5, 236, 238

reference allocation, 237, 243, 251

reference periods, 190, 231

reference price system, 105, 212–13

relative stability, concept of, 237, 251, 252, 254

'right of establishment', 94, 99, 109–10, 114, 118, 120, 175

Rippon, Geoffrey, 114, 124, 128, 134

Scientific and Technical Committee for Fisheries, 153, 210, 251, 252, 268–9

Scotland, 25, 28, 50, 51, 53; as special exception zone, 128, 130, 132

scrapping grants, 216–17

Shetland, 123, 130, 280; /Orkney 'Box', 226, 227, 229–30, 240, 241, 243, 252

Silkin, J., 199, 200, 201, 203, 204

Simonnet, R., 89

Spain: entry into Community, 247–9, 256; fish imports/exports, 29, 30; fishing industry, 24, 25, 26, 27, 56–7, 248

special exception zones, 117, 118, 120, 121, 122–3, 124–6, 130–3, 150–1, 251–2

structural aid: Community, 95–6, 97, 99, 100–1, 103–4, 156, 187–8, 215–17, 244, 245; national, 104, 219–20, 254

structural policy, 214–15; in

formulation of CFP in Community of Six, 89–90, 92, 97, 99, 100, 101, 103–4; in CFP modification proposals (1976), 155–6, 215; in CFP modification proposals (1978), 187–8, 215; in negotiations/agreement on reformed CFP (1983), 216–20, 254
Sweden, 25, 69

TACs, 152–3, 162–3, 189–90, 196–7, 235, 251, 281–91
third-country agreements, 151–2, 158, 188, 253–4
third-country waters, fishing rights in, 161; loss of, 145–7, 160, 187, 193–6, 231, 232, 233, 234
trade in fishery products: European, 28–9, 30; external Community, 96, 100–1, 105, 120, 152; within EC, 86–9, 92, 96, 104–5, 217, see also market organization
Treaty of Accession, 129, 150, 161, 165, 229; signing of, 139, 141
Treaty of Rome, 8, 10; non-discrimination principle, 97, 165; provisions for a fisheries policy, 85–6, 92; 'right of establishment' provisions, 94, 109, 118, 175

UNCLOS (1958, 1960), 74; III, 142–3, 151, 157, 160
United Kingdom: autonomous conservation measures, 182–5, 201, 205–8; coastal zone, fishing rights in, 223–30, 259–61, 270–2; demand for 'dominant preference', 185–7, 223–30; fish catches, 24, 25, 47, 49, 51, 52–3, 144, 166, 195–7, quotas, 173, 196–7, 231–4, 236, 237–8; fish imports/exports, 29, 30; fishing industry, 26, 27, 47, 49–51, distant-water, 49–51, 74, 112–13, 160, 170, 172, 177, excess capacity of fleet, 216, inshore, 74, 112–13, 114–15, 177; fishing limits, 112–13, 114–15, 130–3, 180, 185–6, 199–200, 223–30

(see also Anglo-Icelandic Fisheries Case, Anglo-Norwegian Fisheries Case, European Fisheries Convention), conflict over, with continental states, 164–79, 200-mile, 146–9, 160–1; losses in non-Community waters, 146–7, 190, 193–6, 246; structural aid, 244, 245; and CFP in EC enlargement negotiations, 112–15, 120–1, 123–4, 126–9, 130–4; and CFP modification proposals (1978), 193–7, 199–200, 223, 231; and negotiations towards reformed CFP (1980s), 212–13, 216, 217, 220, 221; quota/access negotiations (1982), 223–31, 232–4, 240–1, 248; and new CFP (1983), 246

vessel licensing, 154–5, 229–30, 252, 266–7

Walker, P., 240
West Germany: coastal waters, fishing rights in, 277; effect of 200-mile limits, 147, 148, 161; fish catches, 24, 25, 35, 36, 144, quotas, 173, 197, 233–4, 236, 238; fish imports/exports, 29, 30, 86–7; fishing industry, 26, 27, 35–7; and rights and losses in third-country waters, 176, 194, 195–6, 213; structural aid, 245; and establishment of CFP in Community of Six, 95, 96–8, 99–107; and EC enlargement negotiations, 120–1; and CFP modification proposals (1978), 193–4, 195–6, 197; and negotiations towards reformed CFP (1980s), 213, 217, 232; and new CFP (1983), 246, 247
whiting, 195; blue 195; in Pout Box, 182, 183, 205, 207–9; quotas, 232–5, 236, 238
withdrawal prices, 89, 104, 105, 123, 213–14